U. S. Strategy in
the Indian Ocean

Monoranjan Bezboruah

The Praeger Special Studies program—
utilizing the most modern and efficient book
production techniques and a selective
worldwide distribution network—makes
available to the academic, government, and
business communities significant, timely
research in U.S. and international economic, social, and political development.

U. S. Strategy in the Indian Ocean

The International Response

PRAEGER SPECIAL STUDIES IN INTERNATIONAL POLITICS AND GOVERNMENT

Praeger Publishers   New York   London

Library of Congress Cataloging in Publication Data

Bezboruah, Monoranjan, 1946–
   U.S. strategy in the Indian Ocean.

   (Praeger special studies in international
politics and government)
   Originally presented as the author's thesis,
University of Mississippi.
   Bibliography: p.
   Includes index.
   1. Indian Ocean region--Politics and government.
2. United States--Foreign relations--Indian Ocean
region. 3. Indian Ocean region--Foreign relations--
United States. I. Title.
DS335.B49   1977   327'.09182'4   77-2786
ISBN 0-03-021811-X

PRAEGER SPECIAL STUDIES
200 Park Avenue, New York, N.Y., 10017, U.S.A.

Published in the United States of America in 1977
by Praeger Publishers,
A Division of Holt, Rinehart and Winston, CBS, Inc.

789   038   987654321

Printed in the United States of America

To

Srijuta Triloottama Bezboruah, my mother,

whose serenity continues to inspire me.

I wish to acknowledge with gratitude the valuable help and assistance of the following persons and institutions during the preparation of this study.

Professor Goberdhan Bhagat, of the University of Mississippi, gave me advice and encouragement which helped me from the outset.

The interviewees, Mr. Stuart Barber, Admiral (Ret.) Arleigh Burke, Admiral (Ret.) John C. McCain, Rear Admiral (Ret.) Gene La Rocque, Mr. George T. Churchill, Ambassador T. N. Kaul, Dr. Earl C. Ravenal, Mr. Vorley M. Rexroad, Commander Gary G. Silk, and Dr. Michael H. Van Dusen, granted me the privilege of a first-hand account of factors and forces that have actively contributed to the subject under study.

The Library of Congress gave me the study facility that proved so useful during my research and writing.

The Department of Defense, the Department of State, the Naval War College (Newport, Rhode Island), and the Air War College (Montgomery, Alabama) allowed me the privilege of using their library resources at different stages of my research.

Finally, my various friends in Washington, D.C., particularly, Dr. A. S. Borpujari, Dr. J. G. Borpujari, Dr. Keith Eiler, MACE, Carol, and Laalit gave me their words of support and encouragement throughout the endeavor.

I would like to add that the views expressed are my own, and I am responsible for any mistake and omission.

CONTENTS

LIST OF TABLES AND MAPS

This book is a study of the strategy of the United States in the Indian Ocean during the years 1968 to 1976 and of the developments that have influenced it. The following are the basic questions that have influenced it. The following are the basic questions that the study seeks to answer. First, what is the current U.S. strategy in the Indian Ocean? Second, how has this strategy evolved? Third, what are the current trends and prospects of policy?

In the discussion of this strategy, a number of allied subjects are also considered, including the interest and policies of the Soviet Union as they relate to the Indian Ocean and particularly the manner in which the United States should respond to Soviet activity in the area; the interests, policies, and responses of the lesser powers, namely, the People's Republic of China, Japan, France, and the United Kingdom, which also have considerable Indian Ocean involvements; and the concerns, the apprehensions, and the resultant perspectives of the littoral countries themselves toward developments in the ocean. Without such an historic-analytic consideration of related factors, no geopolitical analysis of the U.S. strategy in the Indian Ocean would be meaningful.

Although the United States long has had casual association with the Indian Ocean, the period of its significant strategic concern in that area began in 1968. That year marked a landmark in the annals of the ocean. The British Labour government announced the decision to withdraw from east of Suez, paving the way for the so-called power vacuum in the region; units of the Soviet navy entered the ocean to begin the course of its regular presence in those waters; the U.S. Joint Chiefs of Staff recommended the establishment of a joint U.S.-U.K. military facility in the Indian Ocean island of Diego Garcia, which, through a period of convolutions, has at last become what it originally was intended to be; finally, from the vantage point of the littoral countries, 1968 was the year when the "rivalries and machinations" of the big powers intruded into this vital ocean and ended an era of "relative predictability and order."[1]

The Indian Ocean is now a primary focus on international politics and strategy. Its geopolitical prominence makes it a pivotal factor in the global balance of power. Indeed, it frequently is called the "ocean of the future," while the Atlantic and the Pacific are thought of as "oceans of the past."[2] The importance of the ocean lies not only in its strategic location and in its vital sea-lanes but also in the possibility that it affords for control of the landmasses that surround it

xv

and of its ingresses and egresses. Its waters also wash lands that are rich in raw material resources—especially oil, the vital lifeblood of modern economies.

U.S. strategy in the Indian Ocean, a prominent defense and foreign policy issue both home and abroad, is seen as a primary determinant of world events in the decades ahead. The Indian Ocean raises important questions for U.S. foreign and defense policy. These include the real nature and objectives of the Soviet presence; the repercussions of implementing the expansion project on Diego Garcia; the Nixon doctrine as it affects U.S. strategy in that part of Asia; the costs and constraints of U.S. naval buildups in terms of an escalating arms race; the politicodiplomatic costs of an Indian Ocean buildup in the face of pronounced littoral country reservations; and the formulation of the U.S. Indian Ocean strategy in the aftermath of the Vietnam experience.

In spite of its importance, no significant inquiry yet has been made of U.S. strategy in the Indian Ocean, although several congressional hearings have been held on the general subject of developments in that area. The Senate, for example, has debated several times the issue of the expansion of the Diego Garcia base. However, the inherent limitations of such congressional proceedings preclude the possibility of an in-depth scholarly study. Various aspects of recent developments in the Indian Ocean have attracted scholarly attention, but an integrated study of all the issues involved has still not appeared. Thus, this study aims to be both timely and useful.

Congressional hearings, debates, committee reports, treaties, and other official documents are the primary sources for this study. Personal interviews with individuals who had been and still are associated with the subject are utilized as appropriate. General studies of the subject, including articles in journals, periodicals, and newspapers and publications and papers of specialized agencies, have provided important information and insight.

The study begins, in Chapter 1, with a brief examination of background factors, including a discussion of the geopolitical prominence of the Indian Ocean in historic perspective. Insight into this factor is seen as essential to an understanding of current developments and of the interplay between realism and idealism in the dynamics of modern international politics. A discussion of one of the central developments in the Indian Ocean area in the post-World War II era—the decline of the British presence and the United Kingdom's 1968 decision to withdraw from what once was known as the British lake—is incorporated in Chapter 2 as part of the background. An appreciation of the forces and factors that set the stage for that withdrawal and of the processes by which it was accomplished is essential to an understanding of the contemporary situation.

The international response to U.S. strategy is discussed in Part III. The discussion begins, in Chapter 7, with a study of the Soviet response and is followed by a brief review in Chapter 8 of the responses of other world powers, especially the People's Republic of China, Japan, and Western Europe (the United Kingdom and France). A general consideration of the littoral countries' perspectives on U.S. strategy—and particularly of the attitude of the area's four most important powers, South Africa, Iran, India, and Australia—is provided in Chapter 9. An understanding of all of these factors is considered essential to the evaluation of U.S. strategy itself.

Finally, Part IV advances an evaluation and certain tentative policy conclusions (Chapter 10) and sets forth conclusions concerning current U.S. strategy in the Indian Ocean area (Chapter 11).

NOTES

1. Marcus F. Franda, "The Indian Ocean: A Delhi Perspective," Fieldstaff Reports 195 no. 1, Asia, American Universities Field Staff, 1975, p. 1.

2. Alvin J. Cottrell, "Indian Ocean of Tomorrow," Navy Magazine, March 1971, p. 10.

The Indian Ocean

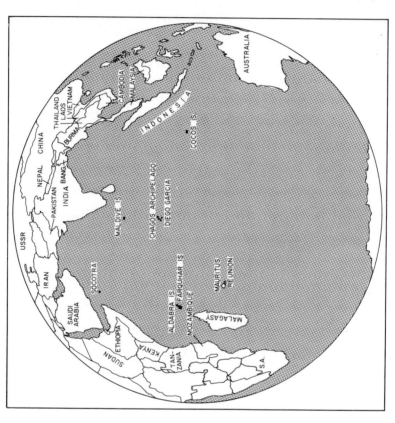

Source: U.S., Department of the Army, Defense Mapping Agency Topographic Center, South Asia, A Bibliographic Survey (Washington, D.C.: Government Printing Office, 1973).

1

THE INDIAN OCEAN: GEOPOLITICAL PROMINENCE IN HISTORIC PERSPECTIVE

Whoever controls the Indian Ocean dominates Asia.
This Ocean is the key to the Seven Seas. In the 21st
century the destiny of the world will be decided on
its waters.

> Alfred Mahan, cited in
> Guido Gerosa, "Will the
> Indian Ocean become a
> Soviet Pond?" Atlas 19
> (November 1970): 20.

The Indian Ocean,[1] covering only about 20 percent of the
world's ocean areas, has consistently occupied a position of preeminence unrivaled by the Pacific or the Atlantic. The ocean
figured prominently not only in the lives of people in the littoral
countries but also of the people of distant lands. The geopolitical
prominence of the ocean of the pre-Gaman era was intimately
connected with the fabulous riches and spices of the Indies.[2] The
spice trade with the East, "one of the great motivating factors of
history and one which yielded the largest profits to merchants as
commodities in universal demand,"[3] could only be conducted across
the Indian Ocean, making the waters so much more important. The
importance of spices in times past is probably surpassed only by
the present-day prominence of oil. The importance of the ocean in
providing access to the ports of India can be gauged from the fact
that Gama's arrival at Calicut was labeled as "the realisation of a
200 year old dream."[4] In an age when pepper was "ranked with
precious stones," the importance of the ocean providing access to
the spices could well be understood. The Indian Ocean remained the

hub of seafaring for long centuries. [5] In fact, the art of sailing itself may have originated in these waters. [6]

The geopolitical prominence of the Indies naturally made the Indian Ocean central to the strategic configurations of various peoples of the pre-Gaman epoch. Not only the peoples who lived on the shores (the Egyptians, the Indians, the East Africans, and the Arabs) but also the Phoenicians, Greeks, and Romans in the West and the Chinese in the East sought access to the ocean in their efforts to expand influence and secure gains in the area. The ocean came to see incessant maritime activity from antiquity on, and in due course became the primary focus of European strategic and geopolitical considerations both during and after the Crusades. [7]

Toward the end of the seventeenth century, the Indian Ocean, already a focal point of Western rivalry, showed a clearer picture of the rival countries' concentration. Portuguese power, drastically reduced, came to a center in Goa and Timor; the Dutch remained impressive with their hold over Sri Lanka (Ceylon), Indonesia, Malacca, and the Indian posts of Nagapatam and Cochin; the British were concentrating on northern India and were building up an extensive trading organization; and the French were staking their claims to a few islands of the western sea and to relatively minor posts on the southern shores of India.

The extension of European rivalry for prominence came to link the Indian Ocean with developments in Europe, especially in and around the Atlantic. The predominance that the British had acquired over the Atlantic at the Battle of Trafalgar (1805) soon ensured their control over the Cape of Good Hope route to the Indian Ocean. The Napoleonic wars finally helped complete the structure of the British naval empire. Extensive areas were taken from the French and the Dutch, some of which later were returned by the Treaty of Paris (1814). [8]

All areas considered essential in the Indian Ocean, however, were retained. Thus, the Cape of Good Hope was retained for its strategic value, as was Ceylon, with its harbor Trincomalee that overlooked both the Malabar and the Cormandel coasts of India and was regarded as important for India's security. [9] Malacca, guarding the strategic gateway to the Indian Ocean, and the most coveted trade channel in the eastern sea, was acquired from the Dutch in exchange for posts in Sumatra, which Great Britain had conquered during the Napoleonic wars. The strategic importance of Singapore was duly noted, and the island was taken from the sultan of Johore. Burma and Malay were also added to the British Empire. [10] With British ascendancy indisputable, the gulf had already become a British mare clausum. [11] In the aftermath of the Treaty of Vienna (1815), Britain emerged as the predominant power in the Indian Ocean area. Indeed,

within the huge quadrilateral that extended roughly
from the Cape to the Red Sea, eastward to the Malay
peninsula, across the Indoneasian archipelago to the
northern shores of Australia, and thence back to the
Cape, no jealous rival could threaten British hegemony.[12]

The Indian Ocean truly become a British lake and Great Britain the
"colossus of the world."[13]

The opening of the Suez Canal in 1869 brought Europe even
nearer to the Indian Ocean. The effect of the French-built canal,
however, was to strengthen the British hold on these waters. Great
Britain's acquisition of authority over Egypt and the annexation of
Cyprus, coupled with its unquestionable supremacy in the Mediterranean route to India, turning it into a "private subway for Britain,"[14]
with control over Gibraltar, Malta, Port Said, and Aden, British
authority over the new route could not be challenged. Suez became
an exclusive British waterway, in fact, the strongest link in the chain
that bound India to Britain.[15]

In the decades immediately preceding World War I, the Indian
Ocean area saw renewed vying for territorial gains and influence
among the European powers. France established itself in the Affars
and the Issas (Somalian Dijibouti) overlooking the British stronghold
of Aden (1888). France also took the Malagasy Republic (Madagascar)
under its exclusive control (1895). The possession of Madagascar,
with its natural harbor, Diego Suarez, overlooking the strategic
Mozambique Channel, made France once again a potential Indian
Ocean power.

Germany entered into the Indian Ocean fray very late, but
was successful in establishing itself on the coastline of East Africa
by bringing Tanzania (Tanganyika) and Heligoland under control (1890s).
Barred from the Atlantic and the Red Sea routes to the Indian Ocean,
which were securely under British control, Germany tried to reach
the waters through a direct overland route. The Berlin-to-Baghdad
Railway was thus planned to ensure Germany a solid presence in the
vicinity of the ocean. The railway, indeed a great conception, was
an attempt by Germany to outflank strategically British sea predominance.

Italy entered the region by occupying Somalia (1880s). It also
planned a naval base in Massawa, Eritria (Ethiopia), and aimed for
a political role in Yemen. The Italian plan was to secure a strong
presence in the Red Sea area for a future land empire on the east
coast.[16]

The European interests in the Indian Ocean area, especially
around the Red Sea, naturally generated considerable apprehension
on the part of the British authorities. The Berlin-to-Baghdad Rail-

way was viewed with utmost concern as the manifestation of a strategy to Germanize Mesopotamia and possibly blackmail British interests. [17] However, British possessions in the area were not materially affected, and Great Britain continued to sail the waters of the Indian Ocean as the absolute power.

World War I effectively ended Germany's presence and its possessions in the Indian Ocean region. The Turkish presence in the Middle East was also considerably reduced with the defeat of the Ottoman Empire. Great Britain considerably gained from World War I, although French and Italian activities in the area intensified somewhat in the years thereafter. France developed the Diego Suarez base for possible command of the Indian Ocean. [18] Mussolini worked for the Italian land empire in the Red Sea area. [19] However, World War II came too early and the Italian dream of supremacy in the Red Sea region did not materialize.

The Washington Naval Conference (1922) ended Great Britain's exclusive maritime supremacy by according the United States naval parity. However, Great Britain's prominence in the ocean continued—with London expressing apprehensions at the emerging naval might of Japan.

The Indian Ocean did not become a major operational theater in World War II, but it figured boldly in the strategic calculations of both the Axis and the Allied powers. The predominant thrust came from Japan in the area of the Bay of Bengal. In a swift and effective campaign, Japan captured Singapore, the bastion of British maritime strength in the eastern sea in 1942. [20] The hold over Singapore enabled Japan to control the passages between the Indian Ocean and the Pacific via the Straits of Malacca. [21] One by one, Indonesia, Burma, the Andamans and Nicobar islands, and Hong Kong came under Japanese control (January-March 1942). Ceylon and its major naval base in Trincomalee were heavily bombed, and the island's fate hung in the balance (April 1942). The British fleet based in Trincomalee survived the Japanese onslaught only by leaving the Ceylonese coasts for the East African shores just in time. [22] The supremacy of the eastern sea, for 150 years a part of the British lake, thus passed into the hands of the Japanese. [23]

The post-World War II period saw extensive changes in the Indian Ocean area. The Pax Britannica itself had expired during the war, and the United Kingdom reconciled itself to a lesser role that it could afford to maintain. The European colonial edifice in the Indian Ocean area crumbled quickly. Led by such countries as India, the ex-colonies gained independence and started their "tryst with destiny."* The Indian Ocean area quickly assumed an enhanced

---

*With the independence of Mozambique, Timor (in the process of being incorporated into Indonesia), and the proposed independence

geopolitical prominence in international affairs. Today, there are more than 40 independent countries around the littoral and in the immediate hinterland of the Indian Ocean. More than one quarter of the world's population lives there. The Indian Ocean states provide a substantial number of members in the United Nations. The area and the people share several common or intertwined political and security problems that have the potential of affecting the entire human community.

In spite of a common heritage as former European colonies, as well as regional ties, the countries of the Afro-Asian Ocean are not a homogenous community. While Australia, New Zealand, and South Africa are white, developed, Western societies, almost all the other littoral and hinterland societies are Afro-Asian and are at different levels of political, social, and economic development.[24] The area includes varied geography, cultures, religions, and political systems and lacks any trace of economic and social cohesion. The apparent lack of solidarity or a sense of community of interests is admitted even in the official Sri Lankan (Ceylonese) memorandum before the United Nations: "Although it forms a geographical and historical entity, there are few cooperative links between countries in the region, and these are either bilateral or subregional."[25]

In fact, some of the most bitter divisions among nations and people are to be found in this region.[26] The lack of common religious, political, and ethnic traditions, coupled with competing local interests, makes the area potentially vulnerable to disruption both from within and without.[27] As the area's geopolitical prominence increasingly attracts external influences, the area's countries find themselves subject to greater physical and economic handicaps. President Sukarno of Indonesia touched on this issue as early as 1955 at the Bandung Conference.[28] However, in spite of the early awareness of some of the leaders of the region of such handicaps, attempts to gain strength through unity or even through a modicum of joint efforts have never been successful. Instead, bitter rivalries, armed clashes, and irrendentism among the littoral countries seem to have increased in both intensity and frequency.

Economic progress, which was looked upon as a panacea for many politicosocial problems by some of the countries in the area, has not produced the expected changes. The failure of the rate of economic progress to keep pace with the spiraling population and the unfulfilled expectations raise the specter not only of a Malthusian apocalypse but also of widespread internal trouble and increasing destabilization in the years ahead. To complicate the situation, the gap between the developing countries of the region and the devel-

---

of the French territory of the Afars and the Issas, and the Seychelles, very few areas are still under foreign rule.

oped Western world, with but a few exceptions, is said to be constantly widening. Prior to the energy crisis of 1973, that gap was said to have reached an appalling 3,000 percent. An expert aptly described this divergence as a "time bomb for humanity as a whole."[29] Except for the few oil-exporting countries, the postenergy crisis years have brought only adverse effects to the Indian Ocean littoral and immediate hinterland countries.[30]

The geopolitical prominence of the Indian Ocean area is often summarized in a concept akin to Sir John H. Mackinder's "heartland theory."[31] It could indeed be said that among the major powers, the nations that can influence the peripheral countries here would have predominant political power in the world.[32] The Indian Ocean is the major artery for the littoral countries. Inasmuch as good overland routes are scarce, primarily because of the geographic peculiarities of the region, the ocean still offers the best access to the lands around it.[33] This exclusive dependence on the ocean naturally leaves the littoral countries potentially vulnerable to any external power that can acquire a dominant control over the Indian Ocean sea-lanes.

The European imperial powers developed colonial trade with home countries, "as spokes to a hub," with little interest in developing intraregional maritime relationships. They left the spokes, so to speak, unconnected with each other, much less to another wheel.[34] The spokes have not yet been interconnected, and the area still remains primarily dependent on ocean waters for external trade. Primary products still flow largely to the outside world, for the nondeveloped littoral and immediate hinterland states offer only limited markets.[35] The Indian Ocean sea routes thus remain extremely important for the littoral and the hinterland areas.

In recent years, these ocean routes have gained added importance for a different reason—food. With over one quarter of the world's population, the area produces only one sixth of the world's cereals.[36] Though the potential for increased food production in the area is very great, both the lack of a real "political commitment to agriculture" and unpredictable changes in climate are expected to heighten the area's food shortages in the near future.[37] The vulnerability of certain littoral countries to the "food weapon" will essentially increase as the shortages become acute. Increases in the costs of oil and fertilizers, and the impact of these costs on the balance of payments, further aggravate the food situation for most of the area countries. With increased dependence on imported food-grains (primarily from the United States, Canada, Australia, and, to a lesser extent, Argentina), the sea routes may very well become the lifeline for some of the Indian Ocean littoral countries.

The strategic raw materials of the Indian Ocean area are transported to the importing countries via oceanic routes. The primacy of the Indian Ocean routes for some of these key raw materials, especially of oil from the Persian Gulf and the Arabian coasts, as shown in Table 1.1, cannot be overemphasized. The truth of the matter is that, for a country like Japan, the Persian Gulf routes that carry a constant stream of tankers, 40 miles apart, are its major source of survival. [38]

The control of Indian Ocean sea-lanes would thus give a major power a perfect tool for influencing not only the littoral states but many industrialized countries of Western Europe and Japan as well. And control of the lanes, though a remote possibility at best, can be achieved. The geopolitical features of the Indian Ocean itself make it susceptible to control at five main points:

> The Cape of Good Hope, at the southern tip of Africa, Bab-el-Mandeb Strait at the southern end of the Red Sea, the Strait of Hormuz at the southern end of the Persian Gulf, the Straits of Malacca between Malaysia and Indonesia and the Sundra Strait between Java and Sumatra. The first of these overlooks the shipping routes around Africa, the second guards the southern end of the Suez Canal, the third stands sentinal over the oil flow by sea from the Persian Gulf and the Arabian Peninsula and the fourth and fifth control sea borne traffic into the Indian Ocean from the Western Pacific Ocean. [39]

TABLE 1.1

Percent of Total Supply of Crude Oil and Selected Metals
Carried over the Indian Ocean to
Some Major Western Countries, 1968

Countries	Supplies					
	Oil	Iron Ore	Copper	Lead	Zinc	Bauxite
United States	1.7	—	—	—	—	—
Japan	99.97	52.1	41.6	20.4	12.4	97.1
United Kingdom	60.8	0.9	40.9	30.9	54.2	5.4
France	44.0	0.6	32.7	11.2	0.2	7.0
West Germany	31.6	4.4	—	2.4	0.2	20.2

Source: Yuan-li Wu, Raw Material Supply in a Multipolar World (New York: National Strategy Information Center, 1973).

The distinct possibility of closure of the straits and channels into and adjoining the Indian Ocean also heightens the potential danger. The narrow sea passages can be blocked, either by the littorals or by an external power, with considerable ease. The strait of Bab-el-Mandeb, for example, was blockaded by the Arab littoral countries during the October 1973 Arab-Israeli War. Of particular importance is the possibility of a closure of the Straits of Malacca, which could prove extremely costly to a nation like Japan. The narrow straits and channels face increasing threats of domination, in the light of the facts that territorial water limits have been recently extended to 12 miles and that some of the area countries, particularly Indonesia, are advocating the concept of "archipelago," which will make almost all the straits around them territorial waters. [40]

The geopolitical prominence of the ocean has also increased, generally with emphasis on the defensive-offensive possibilities of the deep seafloor. In fact, it has been said that "The nation that first learns to live under the seas will control them, and the nation that controls the seas will control the world."[41] To cite one example, the ninety east ridge of the Bay of Bengal, one of the straightest undersea mountain ranges on earth (3,000 miles long and up to 13,000 feet high), provides an ideal place for strategic nuclear devices. It is widely expected that both missile systems and anti-ballistic missile systems to counter multiple warhead missiles will eventually be deployed on the seabed. [42]

The Indian Ocean's proximity to at least two major powers, the Soviet Union and the People's Republic of China, enhances its importance as an area of strategic interest and military deployments for the United States. This possibility of strategic deployment naturally increases Moscow's concern for a counterpresence in efforts to neutralize or at least to make such deployment costly. With the regular basing of the Poseidon and Polaris, the ocean has already come into the strategic orbits of the two superpowers. [43] In fact, the growing geopolitical prominence of the Indian Ocean area leads many observers to believe that global strategy, in general, and the strategic interests of the major powers, in particular, will soon focus on this third largest body of water. [44]

NOTES

1. For the accepted definition of the Indian Ocean and for certain physical features, see United Nations, Document (A/Ac. 159/1, Annex IV), 1974, p. 1; Samuel W. Matthews, "Science Explores the Monsoon Sea," National Geographic 132 (October 1967): 554.

2. Vasco de Gama's arrival at Calicut is considered the dividing line between the pre-Gaman and the post-Gaman period of the history of the Indian Ocean by Auguste Touissant in his History of the Indian Ocean (Chicago: University of Chicago Press, 1966), pp. 5-6.

3. K. M. Panikkar, Asia and Western Dominance (London: Allen & Unwin, 1959), p. 22.

4. Ibid., p. 21.

5. M. Cary and E. H. Warmington, The Ancient Explorers (London: Penguin Books, 1963), p. 74.

6. Ibid. See also K. M. Panikkar, India and the Indian Ocean (London: Allen & Unwin, 1945), p. 22.

7. For a detailed account of the Portuguese, Dutch, and English rivalry for prominence in and around the Indian Ocean, see R. S. Whiteway, The Rise of Portuguese Power in India 1497-1550 (Westminster: Archbald Constable, 1899); Arnold T. Wilson, The Persian Gulf (London: Allen & Unwin, 1954); K. M. Panikkar, Malabar and the Portuguese (Bombay: D. B. Taraporevala Sons, 1929); K. M. Panikkar, Malabar and the Dutch (Bombay: D. B. Taraporevala Sons, 1931); Saul Rose, Britain and South East Asia (Baltimore: John Hopkins University Press, 1962); J. S. Furnivall, Netherland's India. A Study of Plural Economy (Cambridge: University Press, 1967); Gerald Sanford Graham, Great Britain in the Indian Ocean, a Study of Maritime Enterprise 1810-1850 (Oxford: Clarendon Press, 1967); Ravinder Kumar, India and the Persian Gulf Region 1858-1907: A Study in British Imperial Policy (Bombay: Asia Publishing House, 1965).

8. Graham, op. cit., pp. 24-57.

9. Graham, op. cit., p. 17.

10. Auguste Toussaint, "Shifting Power Balances in the Indian Ocean," in The Indian Ocean: Its Political, Economic, and Military Importance, ed. Alvin J. Cottrell and R. M. Burrell (New York: Praeger, 1972), p. 9.

11. John Barret Kelly, Britain and the Persian Gulf 1795-1880 (Oxford: Clarendon Press, 1968), p. viii.

12. Graham, op. cit., p. 1.

13. Panikkar, Asia and Western Dominance, op. cit., p. 94.

14. Panikkar, India and the Indian Ocean, op. cit., p. 72.

15. Ibid.

16. Ibid., p. 74.

17. Kumar, op. cit., p. 183.

18. Panikkar, India and the Indian Ocean, op. cit., p. 77.

19. Ibid.

20. Ibid., p. 78. Singapore was meant to be the "Gibraltar of the East."

21. Whiteway, op. cit., p. 398.

22. Alan Villiers, The Indian Ocean (London: Museum Press, 1952), p. 228.

23. Panikkar, India and the Indian Ocean, op. cit., p. 81.

24. See World Bank Atlas: Population, Per Capita Product and Growth Rates (Washington, D.C.: World Bank, 1974), for population, area, gross national product, and density of the littoral and hinterland countries.

25. Srimavo Bandaranaike, "Ceylon's Memorandum of the Indian Ocean Security" (Presented at the Singapore Conference of Commonwealth Heads of States, January 1971).

26. Anthony Harrigan, "The Afro-Asian World," U.S. Naval Institute Proceedings 90 (May 1964): 47.

27. T. B. Millar, "Geopolitics and Military/Strategic Potential," in Cottrell and Burrell, eds., op. cit., p. 64.

28. See Indonesian Ministry of Foreign Affairs, First Asian-African Conference (Djakarta: Ministry of Foreign Affairs, 1955).

29. W. A. C. Adie, Oil, Politics, and Seapower. The Indian Ocean Vortex (New York: Crane, Russak, 1975), p. 5.

30. Ibid.

31. K. P. Misra, "Afro-Asian Ocean," Seminar 146 (October 1971): 5.

32. Ibid. Alvin Cottrell writes, ". . . from geographic position, from the number of riparian states bordering it, from the conflicts among these states, from the degree to which they are dependent upon it, and from the importance of the ocean in terms of value of its own interior and world sea lanes . . . the Indian Ocean is too strategic for the world." "Indian Ocean of Tomorrow," Sea Power 14 (March 1971): 11.

33. Harrigan, op. cit., p. 50.

34. T. B. Millar, "Control of the Indian Ocean," Survival 9 (October 1971): 5.

35. Cottrell and Burrell, op. cit., p. 16.

36. Ibid., p. xix.

37. New York Times, March 17, 1975, p. 13.

38. William Graves, "Iran Desert Miracle," National Geographic 147, January 1975, p. 35.

39. Alaister G. L. Hutchinson, The Strategic Significance of the Indian Ocean (Alabama: Air War College, 1972), p. 2.

40. U.S., Congress, Senate, Subcommittee on Oceans and International Environment, Committee on Foreign Relations, U.S. Oceans Policy Hearings, 93d Cong., 1st sess., S. R. 82, 1973, p. 55. The archipelago concept provides that "an archipelago state may draw straight baselines connecting the outermost points of its outermost islands and measure its territorial sea from those base-

lines. An archipelago state is defined as one whose component islands and other natural features form an intrinsic geographical, economic and political entity which have or may have been historically regarded as such. The waters within the baselines would be owned by the State and subject to its sovereignty. "

41. Arvid Pardo, "Who Will Control the Seabed?" Foreign Affairs 46 (October 1968): 129.

42. Ibid.

43. Bandaranaike, op. cit.

44. Anthony Harrigan, "Security Interests in the Persian Gulf and Western Indian Ocean, " Congressional Record, v. 121, 1st sess., July 28, 1975, p. S13969.

BRITISH WITHDRAWAL FROM EAST OF SUEZ AND THE PROJECTED VACUUM

When India has gone and the great Colonies have gone,
do you suppose that we can stop there? Your ports
and coaling stations, your fortresses and dockyards,
your Crown Colonies and protectorates will go too.
For either they will be unnecessary as to the toll-
gates and barbicans of an empire that has vanished,
or they will be taken by an enemy more powerful than
yourselves.

> Lord Curzon, "The True
> Imperialism, " The Nine-
> teenth Century and After,
> vol. 18 (January 1908),
> p. 157.

British influence and position eroded considerably during
World War II. The myth of the invincible British Empire disap-
peared before the advancing Japanese army. The gigantic "system
of bluff" that was carefully built up during the preceding years stood
exposed as the defenses in the Indian Ocean area collapsed.[1] After
the dismal defeats in Southeast Asia and a poor show even in the
subcontinent, a British return to the early colonial setup seemed
inconceivable.[2] Moreover, the forces of nationalism were too
strong to allow for a return to the colonial system of the past.
Great Britain itself accepted the realities of the situation, while it
sought to preserve its economic interests, as the erstwhile colonies
were gaining independence.[3]

The independence of India—the keystone of defense in the
region—naturally called for a total reappraisal of the British position
east of Suez. With the basis of Great Britain's imperial power gone,

the validity and the objectives of its presence in the area became problematic. [4] A reevaluation, however, of the east of Suez policies somehow did not take place, and British presence remained without change, even though the primary reason for its existence was gone.

In spite of growing financial pressures, and even though a declining international power, Great Britain maintained its grandiose world role. London's close link with the various regions of the world—Africa, Asia, Europe—was seen as unique, justifying its continued global posture. Thus, Ernest Bevin, the foreign secretary, told the House of Commons in May 1947 that Great Britain would continue to play its historic part "as one of the Powers most vital to the peace of the world. . . ."[5]

Even earlier, a 1946 White Paper had pointed out specifically that, to ensure the hard-fought victory in World War II, a British presence in various parts of the world was to be continued. Its rationale assumed that a withdrawal would be tantamount to the abandonment of the responsibilities Great Britain continued to bear as a result of its efforts in the war. [6] It was an assumption based on what Sir Oliver Franks, one-time ambassador to the United States, described as "a habit and furniture" of the British mind, rather than the result of careful reflection. [7]

Economic interests also influenced the postwar British policy of a continued military presence in the Indian Ocean region. Pragmatic Labour leaders realized that Great Britain's economic life was closely linked with its interests in the East. In fact, as the Labour insider Richard Crossman revealed, Labour leader Ernest Bevin constantly reminded the Parliamentary party that Great Britain had to hold the east of Suez area at any cost for purely economic reasons. Bevin believed that a withdrawal from the Indian Ocean would adversely affect the standard of living of the British workers. London was determined to keep the Middle East and the Persian Gulf area as its privy. Thus, while it put the chief burden of saving Europe on the United States, Great Britain took extra care to see that the United States played at most a secondary role in the East. [8]

The British perception of contemporary world events, and specifically the threat of Communist expansion, came to add extra significance to its presence east of Suez. The need to check Communist expansion as evidenced in the Malay insurrection (1948-50) and the Korean War (1950-53) made the continued British presence in Singapore and Malaya mandatory. [9] A strong presence in and around the area of the oil-rich Persian Gulf, likewise, was seen as imperative. [10] To consolidate its defense requirements for the area, Great Britain entered into the Baghdad Pact (1954). [11] Its participation in the pact was seen as adding to London's voice and influence throughout the Middle East.

In the Far East, Communist China was viewed as the primary
threat. British leaders agreed with Washington that a Communist
advance in the area would threaten the global balance, and so Great
Britain contributed positively toward the creation in 1954 of the
Southeast Asia Treaty Organization (SEATO). Although, SEATO
ultimately took the shape that the United States wanted, Great Britain
initially tried to establish a wider security arrangement, incorpor-
ating almost all the countries of the area, particularly the Commonwealth countries.[12] London believed that such broad-based participation was essential for any successful alliance system.[13]

Great Britain also formulated a new strategic policy for its
role east of Suez, in which the alliances served as a complement.
London devised two ways to continue its overseas role at a lesser
cost in men and materiel. First, a central strategic reserve force
was created that was to be stationed in Great Britain but that could
move fast to the theater of conflict in time of need. Second, a relatively self-contained naval task force came into being to show the
flag and deal with smaller contingencies.[14] In spite of this strategic
reserve force, however, the British overseas army remained gar-
risoned, with bases spread throughout the East.[15]

The Suez operation of 1956 was the watershed in British strategy.[16] The Russian threat of bombing over London; effective Egyptian resistance, more important, the threat that America might
force the devaluation of the pound; and finally the threat that India
might quit the Commonwealth ultimately led to a dismal end of the
Suez fiasco.[17] The debacle made London realize that success of any
military or political action on its part would depend squarely on
Washington's reaction. American blessing, if not active participation,
became a precondition for any such success.[18] Suez thus necessitated a total reappraisal of British Near Eastern and Far Eastern
defense policy since

> The failure at Suez was perhaps the most crucial national
> setback in modern British history. It was the sequel to a
> record of unrivaled success. It was a reversal so funda-
> mental and far-reaching that it toppled Britain from the
> ranks of the premier nations of the world. In political and
> military terms it undermined bases of British prestige
> and policy that dated from World War II. . . . After Suez,
> . . . Britain could no longer be regarded as a world power;
> she could scarcely be viewed as a major regional power.[19]

That British strategy built around the chain of fixed bases
could no longer be relied on was made evident as soon as Afro-Asian
host countries refused to make them available in times of crisis.

The Defence White Paper of 1957 reflected such rethinking, and characterized itself as "the biggest change in military policy ever made in normal times."[20] To provide a highly mobile, self-contained, and effective combat armed force with amphibious capability that would no longer depend on fixed bases, the Defence Paper put emphasis on sea power, and brought the Royal Navy to the forefront in the east of Suez role.[21] Thus, the role of the Royal Navy was bolstered in such a way that the latter came to be viewed as the sustainer of the Pax Britannica. It was considered that, so long as the navy was able to provide an adequate visibility in the east of Suez area, the Pax Britannica would still continue on the high seas.[22]

   The post-Suez British strategic apparatus proved its worth during the Kuwaiti operation of 1961. An Iraqi attempt to subjugate Kuwait was seen as a threat to Western interests in general and to British interests in particular. Great Britain secured almost half its oil from Kuwait. The British economic investment in Kuwait was also substantial. London's view of the importance of Kuwait, as revealed by Dwight Eisenhower in his The White House Years, was:

> Macmillan felt that Kuwait was really the key to the overall Middle East oil production problem. . . . By itself it could produce oil enough for all Western Europe for years to come. The problem then would become that of retaining access to Kuwait and an adequate flow of oil therefrom. One of the requirements for success in this would be to achieve better relationships with the surrounding nations, most importantly Saudi Arabia.[23]

Confronted by an Iraqi claim to the territory of Kuwait, Great Britain launched a smooth and quick operation and effectively stalled any Iraqi advance. Confidence in the strategic mobile force doctrine soared after the operation, and the secretary of state for war declared that the British army was prepared for intervention east of Suez if British or allied interests necessitated such a move.[24] The Kuwaiti operation, the first instance of the deployment of British troops quickly and effectively over long ranges, though a prime example of the effectiveness of the concept of mobile force doctrine, also demonstrated the need for support bases in the area.[25]

   The 1962 White Paper heralded an increasing emphasis on Great Britain's role east of Suez. In fact, Great Britain clearly acknowledged east of Suez as strategically more important than Europe, for, as Europe was becoming increasingly more stable, signs of mounting instability and turmoil appeared in Africa and Asia.[26] This White Paper laid down the nation's defense policy for the next five years, and listed the following basic objectives for Britain's defense:

> to maintain the security of United Kingdom; to carry
> out the obligations for the protection of the British
> territories overseas and those to whom Britain owes
> a special duty by treaty or otherwise, and; to make
> contribution to the defence of the free world, and
> prevent war, etc., under collective security treaties
> or on individual treaty obligations. [27]

In order to fulfill the objectives, mobility in sea and air was
emphasized. Maritime, naval, and air mobility was seen as the
way out for the undependable overseas bases or for any withdrawal
from the same. As the paper said,

> We may suffer restrictions on our freedom to use some
> territories for military purposes, and we must accord-
> ingly adapt our strategy. We must insure against
> the possible loss of fixed installations overseas by
> keeping men and heavy equipment afloat. [28]

The Kuwaiti success with amphibious forces evidently encouraged
defense strategists, and thus only improvements in the basic strategy through new additions were suggested.

Thus, although British strategy in general and east of Suez in
particular came to emphasize maritime strategy for increased flexibility and mobility, the existing forces in Arabia, the Persian Gulf,
and Southeast Asia retained their role as local representatives of
British commitments and credibility. [29] In the overall British plan
to concentrate the forces in three main bases, Aden and Singapore
joined ranks with Great Britain. *

The British strategic emphasis seemed to be proven accurate
by events following the adoption of the White Paper. A spillover
from the Laotian civil war between the Pathet Lao and the Royal
Laotian Army threatened the security of Thailand, and as a signa-
tory of SEATO, Great Britain responded promptly to a Thai request
for troops and equipment. In the process of responding to the direct
Thai request, London enlarged its obligations under SEATO into
collective as well as individual ones. British Prime Minister Harold
Macmillan made it very clear that a SEATO ally could make an
effective request for military support on its own, without going
through the collective organization, which any formal group action
would demand. [30]

---

*The idea was to avoid the dispersal of the forces into small
pockets and to concentrate in the three bases from which troops
would fan out into areas of action by air as well as by sea.

In 1962, soon after the British troops returned to their base in Singapore, London was obliged to come to New Delhi's aid against an attack from China. The assumed British obligation to defend its Commonwealth partners was apparent from the way London responded to New Delhi's request. In fact, Macmillan assured the House of Commons that whatever the Indians "ask us to do to help them, we will do."[31]

Elsewhere, Great Britain used a quick Kuwaiti type of intervention in Brunei in the latter part of the same year. Troops sent from Singapore effectively shut out a local rebellion, proving once again the effectiveness of the flexible, mobile commando concept.[32]

The 1963 White Paper maintained the accepted tone in reiterating the importance of the British overseas role, particularly east of Suez. Although the need for reorientation of British interests in NATO was advocated by many Labour members, Whitehall remained convinced of the efficacy of an eastern presence. The events of 1962 had convinced the British government that the price of a continued presence outside Europe, although soaring, was manageable from the point of view of London's interests and obligations.

The events of 1963 and those in January 1964, however, proved the contention that British commitments were indeed not only costly but also overextended. British forces saw action in different parts of the Indian Ocean and found itself unduly taxed in logistics and resources. The Indonesian confrontation against the newly created Malayan Federation, the violent oppositions on the part of various sections of the Adenese people, the British-inspired Adenese accession to the South Arabian Federation, a coup in Zanzibar and the resultant rippling effect in neighboring East African ex-colonies leading to requests for British intervention—all of these heavily strained the British presence in the area.

However, the request for British aid and protection from the governments of former colonies generated across-party-lines support for the need for the east of Suez presence. Even the lukewarm Labourites of earlier days came to extol the British role outside Europe. Denis Healey, a prominent Labourite, believed that prevention of anarchy and war in parts of Asia, the Middle East, and Africa would be the primary job of Great Britain in the years ahead.[33] Harold Wilson, the most important Labour leader, recommended a British reduction in its commitments in Europe to facilitate a continued Afro-Asian presence, for "1,000 troops deployed East of Suez is a bigger contribution to peace than 1,000 in Germany."[34] Wilson continued his emphasis on an east of Suez presence and even promised, before entering 10 Downing Street, that the British peacekeeping role, "which will, over the next generation, be the main contribution of this country to world affairs . . . will mean contribution of this country East of Suez."[35]

When Labour came to power in October 1964, it quickly became apparent that the overextended British role outside Europe could not be continued without increased expenditures under the heading of defense. Even more acute was the manpower strain, and it was evident that "if the number of tasks entrusted to the armed forces could not be reduced, the number of men to fulfill them had to be increased."[36] In spite of the difficulties, Wilson opposed any reduction in the eastern role and hyperbolized that "our Frontiers are on the Himalayas."[37]

The growing pinch of an extended British world role, however, as the cost of domestic concerns, slowly but surely swelled the ranks of the opposition against a British presence east of Suez. Wilson, nonetheless, asserted the new Labour government's view on the British peacekeeping role clearly and emphatically. In the course of the foreign affairs debate, the prime minister promised to review the defense expenditures but insisted that Great Britain could not afford to relinquish its world role—a role, which, "for shorthand purposes, is sometimes called our 'east of Suez' role. . . ."[38]

The 1965 White Paper on Defence reflected Labour's thinking, and, while cutting expenditures, the Defence White Paper did not advocate any cut in commitments. The paper admitted the overstretched and, in some ways, dangerously underequipped, state of British defense forces, and blamed the Conservatives for their failure to make any "real attempt to match political commitments to military resources, still less to relate the resources made available for defence to the economic circumstances of the nation."[39] Referring, however, to the volatility and significance of the area, the White Paper observed that it would be "politically irresponsible and economically wasteful" for London to withdraw from east of Suez.[40]

Wilson tried to emphasize the international character of Great Britain's east of Suez presence and hoped that other Western countries would come forward to share the burden.[41] In the absence of any positive sign of such sharing, Great Britain tried to reduce the spiraling defense expenditures through cuts in its military presence in Europe and through a greater emphasis on cost effectiveness of weapons. The continuance of the world role, however, kept defense costs high, prompting a leading newspaper to lament that London had not tried to "strike the balance between Britain's resources and Britain's responsibilities."[42]

The Labour leaders' insistence on a continued overseas role, especially in the East, was also influenced by their perception of Anglo-American relations. The continued British presence in the area was seen as an essential requirement of these relations. Wilson insisted that what impressed Washington was not Great Britain's military strength but its ability to mount peacekeeping operations that no one else could mount. [43] Indeed, Washington regarded a British presence in the East as very important for the non-Communist world. In fact, it offered to share part of the cost for Great Britain's presence in the Indian Ocean as early as the Kennedy administration. [44] Actually, Washington had tried much earlier to foster the doctrine of interdependence for defense purposes. In their Declaration of Common Purpose, issued on October 25, 1957, Eisenhower and Macmillan emphasized the need for interdependence among the "countries of the free world," and called for sharing of resources and tasks for defense purposes. [45]

The growing opposition from British public leaders against the continued peacekeeping role east of Suez was noted with great concern in the United States. Apparently, as an offer of financial help, and also to carve out a place for itself, the United States proposed the idea of joint staging posts in the Indian Ocean. The idea of staging posts was, of course, first offered by the Royal Air Force to overcome the overflight difficulties experienced during the Suez crisis. The strategy was to use a chain of small islands as staging posts for refueling and other necessities. Free from the complexities of fixed bases that were located in the independent countries, the chain of staging posts assured for the RAF an "all red" air route to the region (see Map 2.1)

The details of the U.S. decision to participate in the east of Suez presence are still not known precisely, as much of that discussion has been kept secret at the request of the British government. [46] But an Anglo-American search for suitable base sites in the Indian Ocean started much before Labour came to power. Wilson, emphasizing the importance of a continued British presence east of Suez, gladly welcomed the American offer of joint participation. A new British Indian Ocean Territory (BIOT) was created to ensure the availability of strategically located "real estates" for future joint military uses. BIOT consisted of the Chagos Archipelago, including the Diego Garcia atoll, and the three islands of Deschorres, Farquahar, and Aldabra, which were detached from the colonies of Mauritius and Seychelles, respectively. After the announcement of the creation of BIOT in the House of Commons on November 10, 1965, British officials visited Washington to discuss "the nuts and bolts of Anglo-American defence coordination east of Suez." [47] Washington commended the British decision to continue its east of Suez role as an indication of London's appreciation of the "universal nature of the defense responsibilities," and expressed the hope that other members of the Western alliance would make like contributions. [48]

Discussing the increasing Anglo-American defense and peacekeeping prospects in the Indian Ocean area, the Sunday Times sug-

MAP 2.1

Great Britain's "Red Hot Line": The Island Staging Posts Scheme

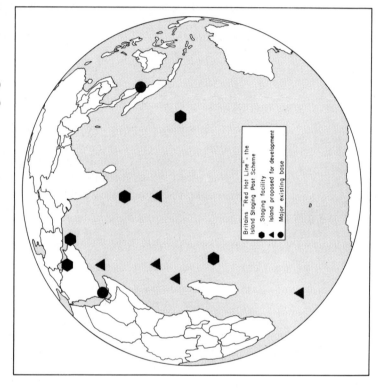

Source: U.S. Department of the Army, Defense Mapping Agency Topographic Center, South Asia, A Biblio–graphic Survey (Washington D.C.: Government Printing Office, 1973).

gested a long-term plan "in the direction of an eventual peripheral
strategy; something along the lines, for example, of a British base
in northwest Australia and an American base in Okinawa. . . ."[49]
The editorial also expressed the hope that Great Britain's role as a
world power and its experience with the area could provide constructive influence on U.S. policy toward the region.[50]

In spite of the aid, assistance, and pressure from Washington,
as well as Labour's desire to maintain the role, opposition to the
continued presence east of Suez grew in great proportion. When
certain Indian Ocean littoral countries expressed concern about
this growing domestic opposition, the Labour government sought to
reaffirm its commitments to the east of Suez presence in no uncer-
tain terms. Denis Healey, the defence secretary, asserted in a
speech in Canberra that Britain had "no intention of ratting on any
of [its] commitments," and that it intended to remain in a military
sense a world power.[51]

The government, however, could not ignore the opposition
and the economic necessities calling for a reduction in its overseas
presence. The Defence Review of the following year (1966) made
an effort to reach a compromise between politicomilitary needs and
economic necessities by announcing that, while "a major capability
outside Europe" would be maintained, Great Britain would withdraw
from the base at Aden as soon as South Arabia became independent
in 1968.[52] Although the Tory manifesto ridiculed the withdrawal
announcement as a "breach of obligations" and promised to fulfill
the treaty obligations in the area if elected to power, the Labour
government went ahead with its decision to get rid of the Aden base
as an economic necessity.[53]

The White Paper reiterated the past election (October 1964)
Labour pledge to relax the strain imposed on the economy by the
defense program it had inherited. The government warned against
the high expenditure in defense (7 percent gross national product) as
extremely costly for the British economy, when capital for modernization of plants and for implementing the total production output for
export was increasingly needed. It therefore promised to bring down
defense costs to 6 percent of the gross national product by 1969-70.[54]

The 1966 White Paper further acknowledged the importance of
overseas obligations, but also took note of the dangers of a militarized foreign policy. It emphasized that Great Britain would not
enter into major operations east of Suez except in cooperation with
allies, who would provide London with the facilities that might be
required for such operations.[55] London also announced that "there
would be no attempt to maintain defence facilities in an independent
country against its wishes."[56] According to Defence Secretary
Denis Healey, the review would be concerned specifically with the

years from 1970 to 1980 and, to a lesser extent, with those from
1980 to 1990, thus signifying the British intention to remain a world
military power.[57] A continued presence east of Suez was seen as
actively contributing to world peace.[58]

While Prime Minister Wilson talked of a British role in Africa
and possible protection to India against China's newly acquired
nuclear threat, the new foreign secretary chided the proponents of
a lesser British peacekeeping role in his first speech. George
Brown, who replaced Michael Stewart as the foreign secretary, told
the Labour Party Conference at Brighton in October 1966 that Great
Britain could not dissociate itself from a part of the world "in which
the greatest danger to peace now lies."[59] The mood of the party
was, however, quite different and a resolution on the issue was
passed against the government. It demanded, with a great majority
backing, that a decisive reduction be made in the military commitments east of Suez by 1969-70 in order to end the excessive strain
on the armed forces and overdependence on American support and
to bring the defense budget well below the proposed £1,750 million.[60]

The apparent inability of Great Britain to act alone in its
peacekeeping role indeed compromised its presence in Asia and
Africa. Wilson's admission that Great Britain was no longer in a
position to "wage a war as a separate national undertaking" automatically neutralized its east of Suez role in the eyes of the rank
and file Labour members. This admission of Great Britain's limitation also raised questions about the excessive cost for the degree
of its effectiveness as a continued presence east of Suez. Indeed,
members of the Labour party came to question the very efficacy of
a British presence in the area as an appendage for the United States.
Some members even openly questioned as to whether a continued
British presence in the area might not be resented by the Asians.[61]

Although the debate continued, the interests and the determination of the government to continue business as usual were evident
from the Defence estimates of 1966-67. These provided £235 million for operations east of Suez (excluding Hong Kong) as compared
to £100 million for Europe and £66 million for the Mediterranean.
In service personnel, the Far East and the Middle East accounted
for 80,900 people, as compared to 64,800 for Western Europe and
22,200 for the Mediterranean and the Near East.[62]

Economic factors, especially the deteriorating balance of payments situation, came to play an increasing role in the east of Suez
debate. The main purpose of the Defence Review of 1967 was indeed
recorded as to "bring defence expenditure into balance with the
nation's resources."[63] To cut the cost of defense in foreign exchange
and to reduce the admittedly overextended character of British (overseas) commitments to a manageable size, the Defence White Paper

sought to reduce overseas land forces and bases. [64] To maintain a
credible balance east of Suez with maximum cost effectiveness, the
paper emphasized a new maritime strategy. In the event of a vacuum created by the reduction of the land forces and the bases, an
amphibious force, to be backed by necessary air support and coverage from the island staging posts, was suggested as an ideal substitute. Instead of the costly aircraft carriers, new command ships
with vertical short takeoff and landing ships were emphasized.

The Defence White Paper of 1967 reflected for the first time
the changing priorities of the British government toward the East.
The announcement of the impending withdrawal from Aden clearly
signaled the trend of things to come. The government clearly
admitted the need for such a reduction; in fact, Labour leadership
asserted that its differences with the rank and file on the matter
centered only around the question of the pace of the withdrawal. [65]

In a review of the policies relating to defense and overseas
commitments, it was agreed that Great Britain should reduce its
troop level in the Far East to one half by 1970-71 and withdraw
altogether from the area soon afterward. [66] The Supplementary
Statement on Defence Policy of July 1967 finalized the decision.
Deployment plans and commitments were to be regeared for an
early withdrawal. Consequently, British troop levels in Singapore
were reduced from the usual figure to one half, 40,000 service and
civilian personnel combined, a figure barely sufficient for a naval,
amphibious, and air strategic presence. [67] The Labour government
declared that, its east of Suez policy being finally set, there would
be no further defense reviews.

The financial crisis of autumn of the same year, however,
forced the Labour government to reduce drastically national budget
estimates for 1968-69. The pound sterling itself was devalued in
November. In an effort to cut more money from defense, the government finally announced the decision to withdraw entirely from
east of Suez by 1970-71. The Statement on Defence Estimates of
1968 elaborated the House of Commons announcement of January 16,
1968, and promised to have a supplementary statement covering
the implications of the withdrawal by the middle of the year. The
Defence Estimates Statement specifically said that the future
defense efforts of Great Britain would center around Europe and the
North Atlantic rather than east of Suez. [68] The government categorically stated its desire to withdraw its forces completely from east
of Suez by the end of 1971. [69] The statement also expressed the fact
that the final decision of withdrawal was preceded by some discussions with some of the area countries that were to be affected by the
withdrawal. [70] The Defence Estimates also expressed the Labour
government's desire to work out some additional understanding in

connection with the Anglo-Malaysian Agreement to cover the post-1971 period. Membership in CENTO (Central Treaty Organization) and SEATO was to be continued. The reduction in deployments east of Suez for the coming months was spelled out in detail to prevent further overextension.

The main aim of the Labour government was stated to be the balancing of military tasks and resources.[71] The Supplementary Statement on Defence Policy, which appeared on July 11, 1968, finally shifted British strategic emphasis to Europe. With the shift, the Labour government concluded one chapter and opened another.

The announcement of a firm timetable for withdrawal from east of Suez ended an era and generated widespread criticism both within the country and abroad. The Economist reflected the general trend of criticism and warned that it is a decision

> to retire, except in Europe, to the role of a spectator.
> For half a dozen years in the 1970s, which many people
> in southern Asia think will be decisive for that region,
> Britain will possess no means of influencing the course
> of events except verbal persuasion and such weight as
> its trading position gives it. If this is what being a good
> European means, Mr. Wilson and Mr. Jenkins are very
> good Europeans indeed.[72]

The Conservative party was outraged, as it believed that a continued British presence east of Suez was essential to protect Great Britain's trade and commercial interests, which were considerable by any accounting.[73] Labour's insistence on withdrawing from the area, despite offers of burden sharing or financial contribution from some of the local governments on the Persian Gulf, was branded as both immoral and foolhardy. The sudden reversal of Labour's longstanding desire to maintain Great Britain's presence in the East was even branded as a "crowning exhibition of weakness" in an area where it was badly needed to maintain the considerable British economic and financial interests.[74]

The initial clamor against Labour's decision to withdraw from the East, however, soon lost its edge in the face of greater economic realities. Even the Conservative leaders came around to agree with the fact that Great Britain could no longer provide an imperial presence outside Europe. Alec Douglas Hume, the leading Conservative member and the shadow foreign minister, noted that:

> No sensible person would argue that Britain can deploy
> power even on the scale that we used in past years. But
> Conservatives argue that a comparatively modest mili-

tary presence if it is to position with the consent of
friends and allies can secure political results out of all
proportion to its size. [75]

With an across-the-party line acceptance of the economic realities,
and the consequent necessity to end the British imperial legacy outside Europe, the Defence Policy of 1969 successfully heralded a new
era. It reiterated "that political and economic realities reinforce
defence arguments for concentrating Britain's military role in
Europe."[76]

The speed and the extent of the proposed withdrawal were
viewed throughout the world as too large and hasty. Some friendly
countries even felt "fobbed off."[77] The United States and some of
the affected countries of the area did not hide their feelings of displeasure at London's decision. The security planners in Washington regarded a continued British presence in the area as pivotal
for Western interest. Washington's anxiety was that the sudden
withdrawal of Great Britain came at a time when the United States
itself was preoccupied with Vietnam and domestic dissensions over
its world peacekeeping role. The New York Times reflected Washington's feelings in a lead editorial that deplored the British withdrawal as creating a dangerous power vacuum over a vast and
volatile area that the West would find difficult to fill. [78] The projected power vacuum soon appeared as catastrophic in the light of
an imminent Soviet entry into the Indian Ocean.

NOTES

1. Henry Vincent Hodson, Twentieth Century Empire (London:
Faber & Faber, 1948), p. 49.

2. Christopher M. Woodhouse, British Foreign Policy Since
the Second World War (New York: Praeger, 1960), p. 180.

3. Ibid.

4. Robert Scott, Major Theatre of Conflict: British Policy in
East Asia (London: Alliance Trade Study, 1968), p. 1.

5. Great Britain, Parliamentary Debates, Commons, 5th
series, vol. 437, May 16, 1947, Column 1965.

6. Great Britain, Ministry of Defence, Statement Relating to
Defence, Cmd. 6743, 1946, pp. 2-3.

7. Britain and the Tide of World Affairs," Listener, 52/1314,
Nov 11, 1954, p. 788.

8. Richard H. S. Crossman, "Western Defence in the 1960's,"
Journal of the Royal United Service Institution, August 1961, p. 328.
ANZUS (Australia, New Zealand, and the United States, 1952) did

make Great Britain secondary for Australia's and New Zealand's defense purposes, and London accepted the intrusion of the United States since it did not affect its vital presence in the region immediately east of Suez.

9. Scott, op. cit., p. 2.

10. William Luce, "Britain's Withdrawal from the Middle East and the Persian Gulf," Survival 8 (January 1966): 24.

11. Great Britian, Parliamentary Debates, Commons, 5th series, vol. 539, April 4, 1955, Column 897.

12. Christopher Mayhew, Britain's Role Tomorrow (London: Hutchinson, 1967), pp. 29-30.

13. Ibid., pp. 29-30.

14. William P. Snyder, The Politics of British Defence Policy, 1945-1962 (Columbus: Ohio State University Press, 1964), p. 11.

15. Phillip Darby, British Defence Policy East of Suez 1947-1968 (London: Oxford University Press, 1973), p. 76.

16. Richard N. Rosecrance, Defense of the Realm: British Strategy in the Nuclear Epoch (New York: Columbia University Press, 1968), p. 233; DeWitt C. Armstrong, "The British Re-Value Their Strategic Bases," Journal of the Royal United Services Institution, November 1969, p. 423.

17. Rosecrance, op. cit., p. 13.

18. Donald D. Maclean, British Foreign Policy Since Suez 1956-1968 (London: Hodder & Stoughton, 1970), p. 178.

19. Rosecrance, op. cit., p. 233. For an account of the lessons of Suez see, Anthony Nutting, No End of a Lesson: The Story of Suez (London: Constable, 1967).

20. "Tarbrook, Britain's Future Strategic Reserve," Brassey's Annual, 1958, p. 71.

21. Snyder, op. cit., p. 15; Armstrong, op. cit., pp. 429-30.

22. Great Britain, Parliamentary Debates, House of Lords, 5th series, vol. 214, March 10, 1959, Column 858.

23. Dwight D. Eisenhower, The White House Years (New York: Doubleday, 1963-65), p. 123.

24. Great Britain, Parliamentary Debates, Commons, 5th series, vol. 655, March 8, 1962, Column 618.

25. Anthony Verrier, Journal of the Royal United Services Institution (November 1961): 485.

26. Great Britain, Parliamentary Debates, House of Lords, 5th series, vol. 238, March 21, 1962, Column 579.

27. Statement of Defence 1962, The Next Five Years, Cmnd. 1639, cited in Brassey's Annual, 1962, p. 275.

28. Ibid.

29. Brian B. Schofield, British Sea Power: Naval Policy in the Twentieth Century (London: B. T. Batsford, 1967), p. 217.

30. Great Britain, Parliamentary Debates, Commons, 5th series, vol. 659, May 17, 1962, Columns 1534-35.

31. Macmillan also met President John Kennedy in the Bahamas and asked the United States to help India against China. The United States did come to India's aid. For details, see Harold Macmillan, At the End of The Day: 1961-1963 (New York: Harper & Row, 1973), ch. 8, pp. 221-35, and Appendix 4, pp. 553-55.

32. For details, see J. L. Moulton, "Brush-Fire Operation—Brunei, December 1962," Brassey's Annual, 1963, pp. 77-84.

33. Great Britain, Parliamentary Debates, Commons, 5th series, vol. 690, February 26, 1964, Columns 469-70.

34. Ibid., vol. 687, January 16, 1964, Columns 449-50.

35. Ibid., vol. 696, June 17, 1964, Columns 1396-412.

36. The Times (London), June 2, 1964, p. 13.

37. Maclean, op. cit., p. 234.

38. Great Britain, Parliamentary Debates, Commons, 5th series, vol. 704, December 16, 1964, Columns 423-24.

39. Great Britain, Ministry of Defence, Statement on Defence Estimates 1965, Cmnd. 2592, 1965, opening paragraph.

40. Ibid., paragraph 20.

41. Ibid., paragraph 21.

42. The Observer (London), August 15, 1965, p. 6.

43. Great Britain, Parliamentary Debates, Commons, 5th series, vol. 704, December 16, 1964, Columns 425-26.

44. Anthony Verrier, An Army for the Sixties. A Study in National Policy, Contracts and Obligation (London: Secker & Warburg, 1966), p. 112.

45. Maclean, op. cit., p. 40.

46. U.S., General Accounting Office, Financial and Legal Aspects of the Agreement on the Availability of Certain Indian Ocean Islands for Defense Purposes, Report of the Comptroller General of the United States, B-184915, 1976, p. 7.

47. The Times (London), January 26, 1966, p. 9.

48. Harlan Cleveland, quoted in The Times (London), January 28, 1966, p. 11.

49. The Times (London), March 14, 1965, p. 11.

50. Ibid.

51. Statement to the National Press Club, reported in The Times (London), February 3, 1966.

52. Great Britain, Ministry of Defence, Statement on Defence Estimates 1966, Part 1: The Defence Review, Cmnd. 2901, 1966, paragraph 23.

53. Ibid., paragraph 1.

54. Ibid., paragraph 2.

55. Ibid., paragraph 19.

56. Ibid.

57. Mayhew, op. cit., p. 19.

58. Great Britain, Cmnd. 2901, op. cit., paragraph 16.

59. Morgan Giles, "The Case for a British Presence East of Suez," Brassey's Annual, 1967, p. 44.

60. Ibid.

61. Christopher Mayhew, a leading Labour leader and a cabinet member wrote: "I once had an argument about our East of Suez role with Ho Chi Minh. It was in Hanoi in 1954. I remember him saying: 'Suppose we Vietnamese—together perhaps with the Indians—proposed ourselves for a peace-keeping role in Europe. What would you Europeans think?' " Mayhew, op. cit., p. 25.

62. Great Britain, Ministry of Defence, Statement on the Defence Estimates 1966, Part 2: Defence Estimates 1966-67, Cmnd. 2902, 1966.

63. Great Britain, Ministry of Defence, Statement on the Defence Estimates 1967, Cmnd. 3203, 1967.

64. Ibid.

65. Great Britain, Parliamentary Debates, Commons, 5th series, vol. 742, February 28, 1967, Column 395.

66. Darby, op. cit., p. 317.

67. J. L. Moulton, "British Defence Policy 1968," Brassey's Annual, 1968, p. 1.

68. Great Britain, Ministry of Defence, Statement on the Defence Estimates 1968, Cmnd. 3540, 1968, paragraph 3 (a).

69. Ibid.

70. Ibid.

71. Ibid., paragraph 2.

72. "The Washing of Hands," The Economist (London) 226, no. 6491 (January 20, 1968): 17.

73. C. N. Barclay, "Britain's Role in Southeast Asia," Military Review 49, no. 6 (June 1969): 74.

74. D. C. Watt, "The Decision to Withdraw from the Gulf," Political Quarterly, July–September 1968, p. 310.

75. Great Britain, Parliamentary Debates, Commons, 5th series, vol. 757, no. 45, January 24, 1968, Column 426

76. Great Britain, Ministry of Defence, Statement on Defence Estimates, Cmnd. 3927, 1969, opening paragraph.

77. "The Washing of Hands," op. cit., p. 18.

78. New York Times, January 12, 1968, p. 26. See also editorial in New York Times, January 17, 1968, p. 46.

U.S. STRATEGY IN
THE INDIAN OCEAN

3

U.S. PRESENCE IN THE INDIAN OCEAN: A NEW CONCERN, A NEW URGENCY

The focus of military confrontation by the mid-1970's is likely to be the Indian Ocean world. Thus if U.S. interests are to be protected, it is essential that American defense planning be geared to the specific challenges likely to emerge in the Indian Ocean area.

> Anthony Harrigan,
> "America's Deteriorating
> Defense Posture," Modern
> Age 15, no. 2 (Spring
> 1971): 160.

The Indian Ocean, until recently a subject of peripheral security interest, has today acquired a prominent place in current U.S. strategic planning. The extension of superpower rivalry in the aftermath of the Soviet entry has transformed the smallest of the three oceans into an area of strategic importance equal to that of the Atlantic and the Pacific.

Although the increasing U.S. concern about the area is a recent phenomenon, U.S. interest in the waters begins much earlier. By the late eighteenth century, New England traders and whalers regularly visited the Indian Ocean.[1] During World War II, the United States moved into the ocean in a larger way. Partly to meet the advancing Japanese and partly to secure the sea-lanes for the lend-lease weapons for the Soviet Union, the United States developed substantial strength in the ocean. However, as the war ended, the United States retreated into the Atlantic and the Pacific and left the Indian Ocean to the British. Although the United States left the

waters as a British responsibility, it kept a modicum of presence
in the area. Thus, Kagnew Base, in Asmara, Ethiopia, which the
United States leased from Great Britain in 1943, was retained. The
Middle East Forces (MIDEASTFOR), stationed in Bahrain, was also
retained. [2]

Great Britain, although reduced in power and strength in
Europe, viewed the Indian Ocean area as its own, and maintained
itself as the primary Western presence in the region. Thus, while
London invited the United States to take over the responsibility of
preserving Western Europe, it took extra care to be the only formidable Western presence in the Indian Ocean.

The overwhelming concern of the United States, as the principal actor in the post-World War II international scene, was to
contain the Communist expansion in Europe. The Indian Ocean area
then did not become a major theater of the cold war, although there
was a semblance of the East-West struggle there. France and
England still had extensive colonial possessions in the area, and
their presence, especially that of England, provided a sense of
security for the United States.

The Korean War pushed back the U.S. defense perimeter,
and U.S. strategic concerns extended to include a great part of
Asia. John Foster Dulles, the enigmatic United States Secretary of
State (1953-59), did extend his alliance system to incorporate some
of the littoral countries, but the U.S. presence was still limited.
Washington entered the South East Asia Treaty Organization (SEATO),
in 1954, to check the southward expansion of the Chinese, which, in
the notion of a monolithic communism, appeared to be an agent of
Moscow. Washington also created ANZUS (Australia, New Zealand,
and the United States) to ensure protection of the two European
nations (Australia and New Zealand) in the region. Additionally,
the United States encouraged the formation of the Central Treaty
Organization (CENTO), where it participated as an observer. [3]

In all these arrangements, Washington sought, and secured,
major participation by London. The United States looked upon
London for a continued major presence in the region, a presence
that seemed to have gained legitimacy and wide acceptance in the
course of the past two centuries. Even the nonaligned bloc of Indian
Ocean littoral countries (those that refused to join any military
alliance) accepted the British presence as a matter of historic fact.
Thus, Washington continued to depend primarily on the British and,
to a lesser extent, on the French for the protection of its rather
nominal interest in the Indian Ocean region. The U.S. presence
in the area remained limited, with the Bahrain-based MIDEASTFOR
providing a symbolic flag-showing profile. With the ocean still

remaining, for all practical purposes, a British lake, the United States could comfortably continue to have strategic outlooks centered in the Atlantic and Pacific oceans.

It was probably the Suez crisis which more than anything else epitomized the changing Afro-Asian ocean scene, that finally persuaded Washington to look at the Indian Ocean region anew. The Suez crisis toppled Great Britain into a second-rank power. And the failure of London in its military action following the Egyptian nationalization of the Suez Canal, July 26, 1956, cast grave doubts on the future effectiveness of any British-led peacekeeping role in the area. [4] Emerging Afro-Asian nationalism, which was manifested prominently in the denial of various base facilities and overflight privileges to the British by the littoral countries, brought home the fact that the extensive paraphernalia for logistics support might not be automatically available in the event of any U.K.-U.S. peacekeeping role in the future. [5] The growing evidence of the diminishing British potency, as well as the near-total end of the French hold over the region with the end of its formal colonial rule over Madagascar in 1958, prompted some U.S. defense planners to foresee a possible power vacuum in the region.

The defense planners of the United States clearly saw the inability of Great Britain to continue its presence east of Suez indefinitely, as a shrinking British Empire found overseas presence and commitments to be overtaxing. While Washington tried to persuade London against a precipitous withdrawal, strategic planners were actively laying out contingency plans for a continued Western presence in the event of a British withdrawal. The Labour Government's announcement (January 1968) of the British withdrawal, nonetheless, came as a surprise. Washington considered the decision as rather hasty and inopportune. What surprised the United States more, however, was the Soviet entry into the ocean. A modicum of Soviet presence in the strategic Indian Ocean was, of course, expected. But the particular timing, the extent, and the nature of the Soviet entry caught the United States unaware. The impressive Soviet entry into the region (March 1968) in the wake of the British decision to withdraw from the area was seen as part of a calculated Russian move to fill the vacuum created by the withdrawal. These historic events laid the groundwork for contemporary analysis of the strategic role of the Indian Ocean.

U.S. PERCEPTION OF RUSSIAN INVOLVEMENT IN THE INDIAN OCEAN

The United States views any lessening of the Western presence in the Indian Ocean area as dangerous, particularly in the light of

increased Soviet activities. Western disinterest in the region might
lead to the loss of the area by default. With what are perceived as
overwhelming Western interests in the area, Moscow's buildup and
activities can be allowed to go unmatched only at tremendous cost.
As a superpower with global interests and responsibilities, the
United States consequently feels it has a role to play in any effort
to fill the vacuum that might have been created by the British withdrawal.

The entire gamut of the Soviet offensive—military, political,
economic, and diplomatic—is viewed as a danger, and is seen as
necessitating an accompanying Western buildup to counter the
Russians. The U.S. presence in the ocean is seen as "tangible
evidence" of the Western interests in the area, as well as an
expression of its determination to prevent the Soviet Union from
becoming predominant in the region. Such a presence is also seen
as essential to ensure that Western interests will be kept in mind in
the "regional political equation." A naval presence acts as the
suggestive arm of diplomacy, and as retired Admiral Elmo Zumwalt
once said, such a naval presence could also be effective as a "gesture of friendship, note of assurance, implication of threat, glimpse
of power. . . ."[6] The absence of such a deterring presence would
lead to the exclusion of the West by default. Henry Kissinger, former
Secretary of State, is quoted as saying that "perception of clear defi-
ciencies in U.S. military capabilities would cause us to lose political and diplomatic influence to the Soviets by default."[7]

In the U.S. view, Soviet naval expansion in the Indian Ocean
signifies the global reach of its navy, and is often seen as an indication of a general effort of the USSR to expand its political influence.
The historic record of Russian conduct is cited in this context. It
is said that Lord Palmerston observed as far back as May 1853 that
"Russian policy tends to impose its will on indifferent and weak
Governments while it withdraws in the face of active resistance,
waiting for the opportunity to come back."[8] A Soviet prominence
in the ocean is also seen as a possible inducement for the Soviet
leaders to take additional risks in the pursuit of targets of opportunity.

A major U.S. and Western European interest is the oil and
sea routes, and Soviet preeminence in the Indian Ocean is seen as
threatening. Although the Soviet need for Persian Gulf oil and
Moscow's import of natural gas from Iran are indications of possible
Russian interests in the overall stability of the gulf region, a stronghold over the area could be used by Moscow to the detriment of the
Western nations. The possibility of a Soviet-inspired disruption of
the oil flow through sabotage in the oil fields and in the refineries
increases if Moscow acquires greater control over the region.[9]

Continued access to the Persian Gulf oil is vital to U.S. interests, and continuing flow of oil to its allies and to its forces both at home and abroad is intrinsically of strategic interest to the United States. [10] While Moscow is nearly self-sufficient in energy requirements, both Washington and its allies in Western Europe and Japan have to depend on oil from the Persian Gulf area. This dependence is nearly total in the case of Japan (85 percent) and Western Europe (75 percent). [11] Therefore, U.S. interest in the Persian Gulf oil is crucial; and NATO's capability is, to a great extent, dependent on a secure oil supply from that region as well. [12]

In spite of Project Independence, U.S. oil imports are expected to rise considerably in the years ahead. As Table 3.1 indicates, the United States will import as much as 50 percent of its oil requirements by the year 1980, a large amount (about 20 percent) of which is bound to come from the Persian Gulf region of the Indian Ocean. Because 60 percent of the world's oil reserves are located in the gulf region, the unique importance of the Persian Gulf will continue. In spite of impressive finds elsewhere, a steady discovery of additional reserves has kept the gulf resources almost at the same percentage. [13] A continued U.S. presence in the area becomes essential for securing its vital interests, "which are spelled out in one short three-letter word, a very short word, o-i-l, oil."[14]

TABLE 3.1

Total U.S. Oil Supply
(million barrels per day)

Source	1960	1976	1980	1990
Domestic (conventional)	8.2	10.3	10.0	11.8
Domestic (synthetic)				
Oil shale	—	—	—	0.5
Coal	—	—	—	0.2
Imports	1.8	8.0	10.5	12.2
Total	10.0	18.3	20.5	24.7*

*Over the forecast period, U.S. oil demand will grow much more rapidly than domestic oil supply. Consequently, the United States will require increasing quantities of imports to fill the gap between domestic supply and demand. Oil imports are forecast to increase from 44 percent of total oil supply in 1976 to about 50 percent of supply by 1980 and then maintaining about this share through 1990.

Source: Energy Outlook 1976-1990, Exxon Company, Public Affairs Department, Houston; 1975, p. 16.

A U.S. presence in the Indian Ocean is seen as a deterrent against any disruption of the vital sea-lanes. The sea is still the greatest highway. It is also the cheapest and the most used route for trade and commerce. The importance of the sea routes has been duly noted in the context of sea power. An ability to secure an even, uninterrupted flow of trade and commerce becomes the sine qua non of an effective sea power.

According to Alfred T. Mahan, the ultimate purpose of the mastery of the sea signifies the monopolization of the sea-lanes for one's exclusive use and the consequent deprivation of the same to one's adversary. The essence of sea power, even today, is seen as the capability to dominate sea-lanes so as to secure the free passage of one's ships and the denial of the free passage to the opponent.[15] Indeed, the command of the sea in its classic sense came to mean "quite simply the power to use the sea and to deny its use to an enemy."[16] Thus, the aim of a sea power is to deprive the use of the sea-lanes to its adversary, as such closure would hold at bay a nation's commerce, trade, and ultimately even its very sustenance.[17]

The possibility of Soviet domination in the Indian Ocean has been widely talked of. The main Soviet naval mission is seen as an interdiction of U.S. efforts to use the sea-lanes for the support and logistics purposes of its allies. The Soviet emphasis on submarines and antiship missiles is taken as clear evidence of the desire to control the sea-lanes. A powerful presence and buildup in the Indian Ocean could enable the Soviet navy to disrupt seaborne commerce, and the petroleum flow, so vital to the West. Such a crippling blow to the West appears plausible from the experiences of the "German submarine blockade in two world wars."[18]

The U.S. concern for the safety and the availability of the Indian Ocean sea-lanes is influenced by the importance of their availability to its allies, particularly the two most important but also most vulnerable allies—West Germany and Japan. Because of their economic might, any loss of either "could change the balance of industrial might against the West."[19] Thus the vital nature of the sea-lanes to Western Europe makes them vital to the United States itself, since Washington views its allies' security as an inalienable part of its own security.[20]

The dangers to the sea-lanes from the Soviet Indian Ocean presence, however, can be overestimated. In discussing the threat to the sea-lanes, one has to keep in mind that sea-lanes are an abstract concept. It is the passage of the ships that is actually at stake. Sea-lanes being "just lines on the chart," it is the voyages of the ships that must be ensured. The central concern ought to be the concrete ships rather than the abstract sea-lanes.[21]

The possibility of a Soviet attack on Westbound oil-laden tankers or even on cargo ships is possibly farfetched. The geographic peculiarities of the Indian Ocean enable an external power to shut off the ocean's ingresses and egresses, but neither the Soviet Union nor any other power has that capability today. In the case of oil, disruption of the flow can be caused by controlling the Strait of Hormuz or any other such choke point, as Admiral Zumwalt alleged. However, the consequences of such an act would themselves be a deterrent. Moreover, the strategically located Strait of Hormuz is, as the Central Intelligence Agency (CIA) admits, "too deep and wide to be blocked by sunken ships and too wide to be effectively controlled by coast artillery."[22]

In the projected disruption of the sea routes, the Soviet navy seems to be in no position to enforce such a control as yet in the Indian Ocean. By pure logistics, the Soviet navy does not have the wherewithal to deploy its submarines and other supporting ships in the Indian Ocean for prolonged sea warfare.[23] There seems to be little wisdom in any purported Moscow plan to disrupt oil tanker movements or any other ship movement at the Indian Ocean points of origin, when the same could be done more effectively in the Atlantic, the Pacific, or the Mediterranean. Soviet capability to do such mischief in the Indian Ocean waters will remain strictly limited so long as the Soviet navy cannot be assured of shore-based air protection.

Moreover, it is difficult to imagine that Moscow will seek to disrupt the ocean order when it itself benefits from it through its increasing maritime trade and commerce. Any Soviet attempt to disrupt Western commerce and shipping will make the Soviet naval units hostages, and its merchant marine, built with such care and determination, will be the first casualty. The Soviet naval presence itself is perhaps more accurately understood as "supplemental to political endeavours, and military and economic assistance programs in the region."[24]

Soviet leaders are definitely aware of the grave consequences of any attempt to disrupt the oil flow or allied shipping. And, as former Secretary of Defense James Schlesinger noted, the Soviet Union has "historically been a relatively prudent and sober power."[25] Moscow will remain sober and prudent in its attitude toward the oil and the sea-lanes of the area, as any deviation from such a course or an attempt at adventure would result in a Western response at the time, the extent, and the place of the West's own choosing. Even short of a nuclear exchange, Moscow will face various dangers, including the closure of the Baltic and the Black seas exits and the seizure of Eastern Bloc shipping outside its own waters, trade embargo and freezing of Soviet credit and assets abroad, and the rupture of diplomatic relations and the restraint of Soviet nationals abroad. [26]

A substantial part of the Western maritime capability is geared to fighting a submarine campaign in general war. Admiral John S. McCain, one of the early proponents of a permanent U.S. buildup in the Indian Ocean, asserted that in the face of any Soviet attempt to disrupt the sea-lanes, the United States would attack enemy submarines "at every available opportunity in all parts of oceans."[27] In the face of such declared U.S. intention and will for a ruthless response, Moscow will think hard before even attempting the seemingly impossible. The sea routes are of vital interest to the United States, and Moscow realizes it. Moscow also understands that because these routes are so vital, any attempt to tamper with them would invite appropriate military response.

Vital interest itself is defined as that interest against the infringement of which a country is prepared to take some kind of serious military action. [28] In the light of such consequences, a Soviet attempt to blackmail the West through interdiction of the vital Indian Ocean sea-lanes and the strategic oil flow does not appear to be a distinct possibility. The Soviet navy lacks the capability to interrupt vessels in the Indian Ocean, and the absence of a significant submarine buildup in the waters suggests that Moscow does not view the interruption of Western commerce, particularly oil shipments from the Persian Gulf, as one of its major objectives. [29]

The hyperbolic and exaggerated nature of the U.S. reaction to the Soviet entry into the Indian Ocean can be dangerous. Apart from the consequences of crying wolf, a portrayal of the Soviet navy with tentacles that are "going out like an octopus into the Indian Ocean" may be self-defeating. The U.S. naval reaction has two fallacies that are potentially capable of unbalancing American sea power in the region. [30] One fallacy relates to the alleged vacuum in the ocean that the Soviets are trying to fill. The idea of a vacuum ignores the fact that "the Indian Ocean is not a power locus such as the Atlantic but is basically a transit area."[31] Soviet gains from a presence in these waters need not cause a U.S. loss in the area. The "zero-sum game mentality of the Cold War warriors" does not take cognizance of the changed situation. [32] The second fallacy is the belief that navies exist only to fight navies—reminiscent of "such faded slogans as 'we want eight, and we won't wait.' "[33] The U.S. Navy's attempt to match the Soviet navy in the Indian Ocean, ship for ship, type for type, is also seen as rooted either in a parochial view of sea power or in a belief that congressional appropriations for the navy increase directly, if not geometrically, to Soviet tonnage. [34]

STRATEGIC REASONS

The Indian Ocean provides the United States with a strategic spot for deployment of sea-based missiles aimed at the Soviet Union. The geographic location of the waters, especially around the Red Sea, the Persian Gulf, and the Arabian Sea, provide some of the best locations for U.S. sea-based missile deployment as a deterrent against the Soviet Union.

In spite of their cost, the submarine-based undersea long-range missiles are prized because of their great survivability.[35] The stationing zone and the opaqueness of the ocean, which provides greater safety from anti-submarie warfare, have made submarine launched ballistic missiles the ideal weapons system of the future.[36] The U.S. Navy's decision to opt for a full-scale undersea long-range missile program was characterized as a momentous development in the field of strategic weapons for advantages of mobility and consequent lesser vulnerability. Since 1960, the Department of Defense has been inclined to favor the submarine launched missiles over the land-based ones, "no matter how hardened the latters' silo may be."[37]

U.S. interest in the defense potential of the ocean is also apparent from the fact that ocean engineering in the United States is still primarily defense oriented. Washington views the importance of oceanography as enormous and approaches it as "a necessary support element in all warfare areas."[38] A glance at the approximate U.S. government expenditures on ocean studies proves the point. For example, the United States spent in two selected years over $2.5 billion on the following lines:[39]

	1964	1970
Defense	$454 million	$1,000 million
Civil	$127	$ 300
Waste treatment	$335	$ 305

U.S. emphasis on the defense aspects of oceanography is, in fact, blamed as the reason for its lag in the other parts of the field, such as fishing or aquaculture.[40]

As land-based missiles become increasingly vulnerable, the undersea long-range missiles have become the key to U.S. strategic offense and defense. The U.S. Navy, as Admiral Zumwalt noted, has come to view its assignment as the strategic force as its primary responsibility.[41] U.S. superiority over the Soviet Union is already commanding insofar as naval prowess is concerned.[42]

Both schools of defense, the sufficiency school and the infinite deterrence school, have supported the idea of an increasingly sea-

based strategy.* The determination of U.S. strategic planners to
continue using the sea-based strategic potential was also evident
from the fact that additional constraints on the strategic use of the
seabed were opposed in relation to the Seabed Arms Control Treaty,
of which the United States is a high-contracting party. Although the
treaty forbids "the emplacement of nuclear weapons or other weapons
of mass destruction on or in the seabed beyond a 12 mile maritime
zone," submarines and other such vehicles that can navigate under-
neath the water, but above the seabed (without being in contact with
the seabed), are viewed by Washington as any other ship and thus
not subject to the prohibitions of the treaty. [43] The Joint Chiefs of
Staff openly warned that "any additional constraints on military use
of the seabeds beyond the prohibitions contained in the treaty" bear
a potential for "grave harm to the U.S. national security interests."[44] The tone of the seaward strategic move is often expressed
in the triplet:

> Keep deterrence out at sea
> Where the real-estate is free
> And it is far way from me. [45]

In the context of sea-based strategic deployments, the Indian
Ocean has come to be thought of as a grand location in U.S. strategic planning against Moscow and, to a lesser extent, against a
recalcitrant Peking.

ECONOMIC REASONS

U.S. economic interests in the Indian Ocean area are considerable and these interests are advanced as justification for a U.S.
buildup in the area. Admiral Zumwalt says that the Indian Ocean
region has "become a focal point of U.S. foreign and economic
policies and has a growing impact on our security."[46] Economic
interests play a pivotal role in shaping U.S. foreign policy and a
projection of American power and influence abroad is often "rooted
in economic necessity, in the needs of an expanding economy for
new markets and new resources unavailable at home."[47] Thus,
economic considerations transform the U.S. quest for a strategy
in the Indian Ocean from a purely military matter into a broad
policy concern.

---

*The sufficiency school is for adequate and sufficient deter-
rence, while the infinite deterrence school wants to acquire as much
as feasible.

U.S. economic interests in the Indian Ocean area center on the key resources and the transportation routes that are used to carry these resources to the West. The economic impact of the area on Western societies was amply proved by the short oil embargo following the Mideast War of 1973.

Apart from oil, U.S. dependence on foreign sources of other raw materials is projected to increase considerably in the coming decades. Various factors have contributed to the United States move from near self-sufficiency in natural resources to the present stage of increasing dependence on imports in vital areas. Comparatively lesser costs of the foreign resources, the increasing use of alloy-supporting minerals that the United States cannot procure from domestic sources, and the consumer orientation of its economy portend an era of increasing U.S. dependence on resources from abroad. [48]

As compared to the Soviet Union, which can satisfy its resource needs entirely on its own except for aluminum, flourine, and tungsten, the United States, as Table 3.2 shows, has to depend on external sources of supply for as many as 18 critical materials. [49] Many of these critical materials come from the Indian Ocean area, making Washington vulnerable to adverse developments in the region. A strong U.S. presence becomes essential to ward off maneuvers aimed at the availability of these supplies. [50]

Some U.S. strategists favor an augumented Indian Ocean presence primarily to ensure continued access to these strategic resources, particularly oil. U.S. military planning specialists are even cited as reckoning that by the end of the present decade "as the result of rivalry for Near East oil, the strategic interests of the United States and global strategy in general" will revolve around the Persian Gulf region of the Indian Ocean. [51]

U.S. companies have large investments in the Indian Ocean region that make a forceful U.S. presence in the waters seem opportune. By a conservative estimate, U.S. investment in the area is said to be well over $10,000 million. These investments earn profit and help positively in the U.S. balance of payments. The investments in oil alone earn billions in profits for the United States. [52] The U.S.-based multinationals have control over most of the transportation and sales of the oil resources of the area. Even if the production and refining of oil are nationalized, the control over these two stages of the "well-to-consumer" process will continue to ensure handsome earnings for these oil giants.

The Indian Ocean area, in general, has remained a billion-dollar-plus market for American products. The petrodollar boom with increased oil prices has made the oil-producing countries of the Persian Gulf and also Indonesia a seller's paradise. As these

TABLE 3.2

U.S. Import of Critical Materials

Mineral	Percent Imported
Manganese	100
Cobalt	98
Titanium	97
Chromium	91
Aluminum	88
Tantalum	88
Platinum group	86
Tin	86
Fluorine	86
Nickel	80
Tungsten	60
Germanium indium	60
Beryllium	50
Zirconium	50
Barium	40
Iron	23
Lead	21
Copper	18

Source: U.S., Department of Defense, Joint Chiefs of Staff, United States Military Posture for FY 1977, by General George Brown, USAF, 1976, p. 6.

oil-producing countries race toward modernity, the industrialized West, in general, and the United States, in particular, have found a rich market for their goods and services. The struggle for modernization has come to center on the desire of the newly rich countries for powerful defense forces. The area has become the most lucrative arms market of the decade. The potential arms market offers valuable opportunity to the recession-prone U.S. armament industries in the post-Vietnam era.

The extent of the market can be gauged by the fact that of the $10.8 billion government arms sales of 1974, over three fourths were accounted for by purchases of Iran, Saudi Arabia, and Kuwait. More than three fourths of the U.S. government arms sales for 1975 ($9.8 billion) also went to these countries. The percentage of the Persian Gulf buy in the overall U.S. arms sales is expected to

increase.[53] Additionally, both Saudi Arabia and Iran have entered
into long-term trade deals with the United States. Iran and the
United States, for example, have a $15 billion agreement for a five-
year period, which is expected to include billions of dollars of arms
delivery to the Irani forces.[54]

The United States has consistently advocated a continued Western presence in the Indian Ocean region, which provides nearly one
fourth of the entire UN membership and a third of the world's population. Myriad treaties, arms sales and aid agreements, executive
arrangements, and unspoken understandings have bound the United
States to many of the Indian Ocean littoral and hinterland countries.[55]
Of late, the United States has openly identified its interests with the
survival of the monarchical regimes of Iran and Saudi Arabia that
border the Persian Gulf region. Arrangements of common defense
require a visible presence and a credible posture in the area. With
the British withdrawal, a U.S. presence in the Indian Ocean has
acquired greater urgency as the symbol of continued Western interest in the security and safety of the nations in the region. Such a
visibility gains added importance when viewed in the context of the
U.S. effort to counter the damaging littoral countries' perception
of U.S. post-Vietnam withdrawal from the world at large and the
Afro-Asian region in particular. Recent U.S. attempts to check
Russian advances in black Africa, especially the personal involvement of Henry Kissinger to prevent another Russian Angola type of
success in Rhodesia, is seen as closely dependent on a potent U.S.
visibility in that part of the Indian Ocean.[56]

In short, the United States believes that neither its interests
nor those of its littoral friends and allies would be served by a
supposed U.S. inability to operate effectively in the waters.[57] The
United States believes that in an area as important as the Indian
Ocean, it is dangerous to let the Soviet Union acquire a capability
that would be substantially greater than its own.[58] Thus, to the
United States, its presence in the ocean becomes a matter of new
urgency.

NOTES

1. U.S., Congress, House, Subcommittee on the Near East
and South Asia, Committee on Foreign Affairs, Proposed Expansion
of U.S. Military Facilities in the Indian Ocean, testimony of Seymour
Weiss, 93d Cong., 2d sess., 1974, p. 22. The early American interests in the Indian Ocean are also evident from the seal of the town of
Salem, Massachusetts—Divitis Indiae usqua ad ultimum sinum (To the
farthest gulf for the wealth of India). Cited in G. Bhagat, Americans
In India 1784-1860 (New York: New York University Press, 1970).

2. MIDEASTFOR was created in 1949 and is based at Manama, Bahrein. When the sultanate of Bahrein became independent, the United States entered into the necessary agreement to retain its presence and related facilities. For details, see U.S., Department of State, "Development in Bahrein of the United States Middle East Force," Treaties and Other International Acts, Series 7263, December 1971.

3. For details of the nature of the U.S. participation and so forth, see U.S., Department of State, "Central Treaty Organization," International Organization Series, no. 1, 1970.

4. For accounts of the Suez crisis, see A. J. Barker, Suez: the Seven Day War (New York: Praeger, 1965); and Anthony Eden, Full Circle (Boston: Houghton Miffin, 1960).

5. For a discussion of the said refusal of base and overflight facilities, see Phillip Darby, British Defence Policy East of Suez 1947-1968 (London: Oxford University Press, 1973), pp. 57-133.

6. George P. Hunt, "Our Four-Star Military Mess," Life (June 18, 1971), p. 63.

7. U.S., Congress, House, Armed Services Committee, Military Construction and Authorization 1975, 93d Cong., 2d sess., 1974, pp. 561-62.

8. Cited in Profiles G. A. Dem, "The Foreign Policy of the U.S.S.R. from Its Establishment as a State Until 1969," NATO's Fifteen Nations (October-November 1972): 24.

9. Frank Uhleg, Jr., "Speculating on Soviet Naval Strategy," Brassey's Annual, 1973, p. 123.

10. U.S., Congress, House, Committee on Foreign Affairs, The Indian Ocean: Political and Strategic Future, 92d Cong., 1st sess., 1971, p. 180.

11. U.S., Congress, Senate, Committee on Armed Services, Disapprove Construction Projects on the Island of Diego Garcia, testimony of James R. Schlesinger, 94th Cong., 1st sess., 1975, p. 26.

12. U.S., Department of the Navy, Office of Information, letter to Representative Donald M. Fraser, in U.S., Congress, House, The Indian Ocean, op. cit., p. 180; U.S., Congress, House, Proposed Expansion of U.S. Military Facilities in the Indian Ocean, Weiss testimony, op. cit., pp. 24-36.

13. Sir William Luce, "Britain's Withdrawal," Survival 11, no. 6 (June 1969): 189.

14. U.S., Congress, Senate, Committee on Armed Services, Selected Materials on Diego Garcia, Senator Stennis' remark, 94th Cong., 1st sess., 1976, p. 39.

15. See also John Philips Cranwell, The Destiny of Sea Power, and Its Influence on Land Power and Air Power (New York: Norton, 1941), pp. 20-25.

16. Ibid., p. 100.

17. Julian S. Corbett, Some Principles of Maritime Strategy (New York: Longmans, Green, 1911), p. 89.

18. J. L. Moulton, British Maritime Strategy in the 1970's (London: Royal United Services Institution, 1969), p. 63.

19. J. K. Holloway, "The Post-Vietnam Navy: The Rhetoric and the Realities," U.S. Naval Institute Proceedings 98 no. 8/834 (August 1972): 52-59.

20. Simon Serfaty, "America and Europe in the 1970's: Integration or Disintegration?" ORBIS 17, no. 1 (Spring 1973): 98.

21. I. L. M. McGeoch, "Clausewitz, Mahan and Mackinder, Inc." Journal of the Royal United Services Institution (November 1961): 530.

22. U.S., Central Intelligence Agency, Atlas: Issues in the Middle East (Washington, D.C.: Government Printing Office, 1973), p. 39.

23. Nigel D. Brodeur, "Comparative Capabilities of Soviet and Western Weapon Systems," in Soviet Naval Policy: Objectives and Constraints, ed. Michael MccGwire, Ken Booth, and John McDonnell (New York: Praeger, 1975), p. 464.

24. U.S., Congress, House, The Indian Ocean, op. cit., testimony of Robert J. Pranger, deputy assistant secretary of defense (International Security Affairs) for Policy Plans and National Security Council Affairs, p. 172.

25. "The Indian Ocean," Defense Monitor, op. cit., p. 9.

26. Moulton, British Maritime Strategy in the 1970's, op. cit., p. 63.

27. Admiral John S. McCain, Jr., USN, "The Total Wet War," in U.S., Congress, House, Congressional Record, 89th Cong., 2d sess., May 4, 1966, 112, pt. 8: 9861-64.

28. Bernard Brodie, Strategy and National Interest (New York: National Strategy Information Center, 1971), p. 12.

29. U.S., Congress, Senate, Armed Services Committee, Military Construction Authorization FY 1975, testimony of William Colby, 93d Cong., 2d sess., 1974, p. 166. See also letter to Senator John Stennis, July 21, 1975, cited by Senator Gary Hart, Congressional Record, 94th Cong., 1st sess., July 28, 1975, 121:13953.

30. Holloway, "The Post-Vietnam Navy," op. cit., p. 58.

31. Ibid.

32. Ibid.

33. Ibid.

34. Ibid.

35. Robert McNamarra is quoted as saying that for $1,000 million over five years, he can place in operation 250 Minuteman solid fuel, land-based intercontinental ballistic missiles or five Polaris boats. L. W. Martin, The Sea in Modern Strategy (London: Chatto & Windus, 1967), p. 33.

36. Ibid. See also Kenneth J. Hogan and Jacob W. Kipp, "U.S. and USSR Naval Strategy," U.S. Naval Institute Proceedings 99, no. 11/849 (November 1973): 40.

37. W. T. Gunston, "Developments in Aircraft and Missiles," Brassey's Annual, 1972, p. 253.

38. Keith Critchlow, Oceans: Lifestream of Our Planet (London: George Phillip and Son, 1972), p. 116.

39. Ibid.

40. Ibid., p. 118.

41. Zumwalt on navy's four-part assignment: first, "Strategic Force, putting our missile clout underwater, away from the homeland. . . . "; Hunt, "Our Four-Star Military Mess," op. cit., p. 62.

42. Robert Herrick, "Soviet Naval Strategy," U.S. Naval Institute Proceedings 785 (July 1968): 149.

43. U.S., Congress, Senate, Committee on Foreign Relations, Seabed Arms Control Treaty, 93d Congress, 2d sess., 1974, p. 7.

44. Ibid., p. 10.

45. Ibid., p. 21.

46. U.S., Congress, Senate, Committee on Foreign Relations, Briefings on Diego Garcia and Patrol Frigate, Zumwalt testimony, 93d Cong., 2d sess., 1974, p. 7.

47. Richard Barnet, Roots of War (New York: Atheneium, 1972), p. 139.

48. U.S., Department of Defense, Joint Chiefs of Staff, United States Military Posture for FY 1977, by General George Brown, USAF, 1976, p. 5.

49. Ibid.

50. U.S., Congress, House, Committee on Armed Services, Full Committee Consideration of H.R. 12565, 93d Cong., 2d sess., March 18, 1974, p. 58.

51. Drew Middleton, cited in Krasnaya Zvezda (in Russian), February 13, 1974, p. 31, reported in Foreign Broadcast Information Service (FBIS), vol. 2, February 21, 1974.

52. U.S., Department of the Navy, Office of Information, letter to Representative Donald M. Fraser, in U.S., Congress, House, The Indian Ocean, op. cit., p. 180. The oil industry's capital investment in the Persian Gulf region is valued at approximately $3.5 billion. U.S., Congress, House, Proposed Expansion of U.S. Military Facilities in the Indian Ocean, Weiss testimony, op. cit., p. 24.

53. Washington Post, December 31, 1975, p. 2.

54. For a detailed account, see U.S., Congress, House, Committee on International Relations, The Persian Gulf, 1975: The Continuing Debate on Arms Sales, 94th Cong., 1st sess., 1975; see also "Anatomy of the Arms Trade," Newsweek, September 6, 1976, pp. 39-45.

55. The United States has formal treaty arrangements with Ethiopia, Saudi Arabia, Iran, Bahrain, Pakistan, Thailand, Australia, and New Zealand. For details, see U.S., Department of State, Office of the Legal Advisor, Treaties in Force, A List of Treaties and Other International Agreements of the United States in Force on January 1, 1975, Publication 8798, (1975).

56. U.S., Congress, Senate, Report on Indian Ocean Arms Limitations, State Department Letter to the Congress, released by Senator John Culver's office, April 21, 1976.

57. U.S. Congress, House, Proposed Expansion of U.S. Military Facilities in the Indian Ocean, Weiss testimony, op. cit., p. 27.

58. Ibid.

4

THE NIXON DOCTRINE AND
THE NEW ACCENT ON
THE NAVY

General overseas roll-backs + sharply reduced foreign commitments + declining usefulness of overseas bases + Nixon's (Guam) Doctrine" (Asians to
fight their own conventional wars) = return to oceanic
strategy.

R. D. Heinl, Jr.,
"American Defense Policy
and Strategy for the 1970's,"
Brassey's Annual, 1972,
p. 34.

In the post-Vietnam disenchantment with land-based involvement in Asia, the U.S. Department of Defense has come to look
toward the navy with increased expectation. The reemphasis on
the navy was also due to the outcome of the Vietnam experience.
Vietnam, it is said, convinced the U.S. defense planners that it
is better to fight potential Asian adversaries on the sea and in the
air, where they are visibly weaker, than on the land, where they
seem to be stronger.[1] In the changed atmosphere, the navy and
the marines have come to be viewed as the "most expedient forces
in the Pentagon because they ensure prompt and effective intervention abroad."[2] Intervention, of course, remains a major part
of foreign policy "as are diplomatic pressures, negotiations and
war."[3]

The seaward move in the Asian theater was also influenced
by the cost and consequences of the U.S. use of bases in certain
countries of the Indian Ocean periphery. Such base involvement
cost the United States not only in overt compensations and covert

underpriced military sales and supplies but also in political and
diplomatic terms by getting it entangled in local quarrels and disputes. [4] The naval presence in the international waters off the
territorial limits is seen as the best way to loom large on the Indian
Ocean scene. In fact, a carrier based on the high seas is the best
base for influencing the littoral countries' policies concerning U.S.
interests.

U.S. policy toward the Indian Ocean area, as stated under the
Nixon doctrine, augured a reorientation of U.S. involvements. Under
the Nixon doctrine, the security arrangements of the 1950s would be
recast to provide a more balanced Washington role, in the shape of
increased sharing of the burden and responsibility by allies for
their own protection and a "more equitable sharing of the material
and personal costs of security."[5] American involvement in the area
would continue on a lesser scale. The concept was to structure a
peace that required the "greater participation of other nations
but . . . also . . . the sustained participation of the U.S."[6] A
corollary of the Nixon doctrine was that U.S. foreign policy toward
a country would be governed more by that country's foreign policy
than by its domestic policy. The nonideological pragmatic approach
was clearly expressed by Richard Nixon when he said that "accommodation to the diversity of the world community is the keystone of
our current policy."[7]

This doctrine stipulated that, in some instances and theaters,
the United States would be militarily involved and in some instances
involvement would be much more unlikely. [8] In the Indian Ocean
area, it was the oil-rich Persian Gulf that specifically attracted
Washington's attention. The president believed that the gulf countries ought to take up the matter of security in the post-British
withdrawal, and encouraged Iran and Saudi Arabia, the two principal countries, to take up the leading roles in maintaining this
security. In the process of this encouragement, the United States
has become the leading partner in an ambitious military buildup
of the region. [9] MIDEASTFOR was maintained as a contributing
factor for the peace and stability for the region. [10]

The Nixon doctrine, in spite of its apparent objectives, did
not try to reduce U.S. leadership. The policy only emphasized
other countries' contributions to the task of security and the maintenance of peace. The United States remained involved in the Indian
Ocean, and emphasis was placed on a balanced American role in the
affairs of the region. As Nixon said in his 1973 message to Congress:

> The Nixon Doctrine recognizes that we cannot abandon
> friends, and must not transfer burdens too swiftly. We

must strike a balance between doing too much and thus
preventing self-reliance, and doing too little and thus
undermining self-confidence. [11]

The key was a balanced U.S. role that would continue to represent U.S. interests in the area but would also encourage the
friendly littoral countries to contribute to their own security. While
the United States would provide air and naval presence as a possible
deterrent, the allies would supply their own ground forces. The
U.S. Department of Defense considered the Indian Ocean buildup in
tune with the Nixon doctrine. [12] Admiral Elmo Zumwalt believed that
Diego Garcia would enable the United States to be away from populated bases in the littoral countries and help to reduce the U.S. profile in the area. [13]

The Pentagon's "grand ocean strategy" for the Asian scene
was also the result of geographic necessity. In the Indian Ocean
area, the United States could bring to bear conventional military
power in efforts to influence local events only through sea power.
In fact, it is sea power that has been able to perpetuate the myth
that the United States is also an Asian power. The possibility of
increased use of sea power in limited wars, "including limited wars
conducted almost entirely at sea," is seen as very strong for the
coming decades. [14] The strategic submarines deployed in the vast
water areas all over the globe have freed the U.S. carriers for such
limited warfare assignments. The United States thus will be on
much better grounds in its efforts to deal with small "brushfires,"
which it expects in great numbers in and around the Indian Ocean.
Although the carriers have become increasingly vulnerable to
missilery, and although some Soviet observers have already labeled
them as "floating mortuaries," the aircraft carriers still provide
the U.S. Navy with a flexibility for limited faraway engagements
that is unrivaled.

The new accent on the navy in the parlance of the United States'
Indian Ocean strategy suited Washington's purposes. With their
flexibility, mobility, and relative independence from their location
in international waters, the naval units seem to be uniquely suitable
for the viable presence that the United States desires to provide
in the area. [15] Sea power is ideally suited to execute a defense
policy of "graduate" deterrence.[16] While the land-based forces in
the area were confronted with the problems of overt resentment from
the host countries' populace (as evidenced in Thailand, Pakistan,
and Ethiopia), the naval presence in the Indian Ocean waters would
not raise the issue in great intensity because of its location in international waters; rather, it would assure the United States that its
will, interests, and calculations would be taken into account in local
configurations.

Concomitant with the Nixon doctrine and to the maintenance of a viable defense posture in the overall Indian Ocean region is an increased emphasis on the strategic mobility concept. The Diego Garcia atoll figured prominently in the navy's and the Department of Defense's "strategic island concept" plan of the late 1950s.[17] The expanded facility at the atoll was viewed as central for peacetime projection as well as wartime assignments of the U.S. Navy for the area.[18] Possible U.S. naval missions in the Indian Ocean are listed as the full range of deterrence, strategic nuclear capability, sea control, projection of power ashore, support of allies, and peacetime presence.[19] These missions could be expressed in broader classifications, as is usually done. The four categories—strategic nuclear deterrence, sea control, projection of national power, and naval presence—provide a large role for the navy in strategic planning.[20] The goal of the naval presence is defined as "the use of naval forces short of war to achieve political objectives."

Broadly, the naval presence acts both as a deterrent to actions that are adverse to U.S. interests and as an encouragement to developments that further U.S. interests.[21] The implications of deterrence through a naval presence in the Indian Ocean were also acknowledged by a Department of State official during the course of his testimony before the House Subcommittee on the Near East and South Asia. He observed that naval power will continue to contribute, "in a deterrent sense, not in an active involvement sense," to making it clear that a condition of stability is the right way to settle problems.[22]

In the strategy of the Nixon doctrine, where the United States would not play the role of world fireman but would supply the fire trucks and the hoses in the case of a fire, the naval presence will remind the littoral countries of U.S. determination to keep its commitments while the indigenous affected parties primarily provide the wherewithal from their own resources.[23] The Diego Garcia facility will allow the United States to "preposition" the necessary logistics supports for such contingencies. In the event of necessity, U.S. military units from the Atlantic and the Pacific will steam into the area and they can be backed logistically by a short hop from the strategically located facility at Diego Garcia. If sea power is fundamentally a matter of appropriate bases, productive and secure, Diego Garcia adds tremendously to the effectiveness and the adequacy of the United States in the region.[24] Although originally a facet of Kennedy's flexible response strategy, the fire-brigade concept—best described as garrisons in absentia—constituted a major part of the Nixon doctrine.[25]

The strategic location of Diego Garcia adds to its importance as a tangible constituent of the Nixon doctrine strategy. The importance of geographic position in the exercise of sea power is still acknowledged. In fact, sea power is still equated with the "product of fleet and position."[26] Since "fleet times position equals sea power," the proximity of Diego Garcia contributes significantly to the effectiveness of sea power in the region.[27] In the context of the Nixon doctrine's "island strategy," which sought to replace land bases with outlying anchorages (Japan in the north to Indonesia and Australia in the south), Diego Garcia constitutes a pivot of American naval power in the Indian Ocean.[28]

NOTES

1. C. N. Barclay, "Britain's Role in Southeast Asia," Military Review Digest 49, no. 6 (June 1969): 72.

2. Moscow in English to South Asia, 1600 GMT, October 31, 1974, reported in Foreign Broadcast Information Service (FBIS), vol. 3, November 1, 1974. The recent Brookings Institution study, Where Does the Marine Corps Go From Here?, by Martin Binkin and Jeffrey Record (Washington, D.C., 1976), however, states that in the post-Vietnam era a reappraisal of the amphibious warfare concept becomes essential in the light of "a changing international environment, which raises questions about the military and political viability of seaborne attacks on hostile beacheads" (p. vii).

3. Hans J. Morgenthau, "Imperialism and Intervention. . . ," in At Issue: Politics in the World Arena, ed. Steven L. Spigel, (New York: St. Martin's Press, 1973), p. 178; Richard J. Barnet, Intervention and Revolution. The United States in the Third World (New York: World, 1968), pp. 77-93.

4. U.S., Congress, House, Subcommittee on the Near East and South Asia, Committee on Foreign Affairs, Proposed Expansion of U.S. Military Facilities in the Indian Ocean, 93d Cong., 2d sess., letter by Stuart Barber, p. 175.

5. Richard Nixon, U.S. Foreign Policy for the 1970's. Shaping a Durable Peace, report to the Congress, May 3, 1973, p. 113.

6. U.S., Congressional Research Services, U.S. Foreign Policy for the 1970's. An Analysis of the President's 1973 Foreign Policy Report and Congressional Action, 1973, p. 131.

7. Ibid., p. xiii.

8. Nixon, op. cit., p. 14.

9. U.S., Congress, House, Committee on International Relations, The Persian Gulf: The Continuing Debate on Arms Sales, 94th Cong., 1st sess., 1975.

    10. See U.S., Department of State, "Deployment in Bahrain of the United States Middle East Force," Treaties and Other International Acts, Series 7263, 1972.
    11. Nixon, op. cit., p. 2.
    12. William Beecher, "U.S. Move in Indian Ocean Is Linked to Commitments," New York Times, January 8, 1972, p. 10.
    13. U.S., Congress, Senate, Committee on Appropriations, Second Supplemental Appropriations for FY 1974: Hearing on H.R. 14013, 93d Cong., 2d sess., p. 215.
    14. L. W. Martin, The Sea in Modern Strategy (London: Chatto and Windus, 1967), p. 14.
    15. U.S., Congress, Senate, Committee on Appropriations, Department of Defense Appropriations FY 1972, 92d Cong., 1st sess., 1972, pt. 3, Navy, p. 30. In Admiral Zumwalt's words, the Nixon doctrine implies "greater reliance on our mobile, controllable, and politically independent sea-based forces."
    16. John S. McCain, "The Total Wet War," Congressional Record, 89th Cong., 2d sess., May 4, 1966, 112, pt. 8:9863-64.
    17. U.S., Congress, Senate, Second Supplemental Appropriations FY 1974, op. cit., p. 2151.
    18. Ibid.
    19. U.S., Congress, House, Proposed Expansion of U.S. Military Facilities in the Indian Ocean, op. cit., p. 135.
    20. Stanfield Turner, "Missions of the U.S. Navy," Naval War College Review (March-April 1974): 14.
    21. Kenneth R. McGruther, USN, "The Role of Perception in Naval Diplomacy," Naval War College Review (September-October 1974): 3-12.
    22. U.S., Congress, House, Proposed Expansion of U.S. Military Facilities in the Indian Ocean, op. cit., testimony of Seymour Weiss, p. 44.
    23. Ibid.
    24. From Diego Garcia a task force will take two days to reach any part of the Indian Ocean, whereas the United States took six days to sail to the Bay of Bengal (during the 1971 India-Pakistan war) through the Straits of Malacca. The United States would have needed 15 days if the Straits of Malacca were unavailable because it would have had to take the route south of Australia—a strong reminder of the geopolitical prominence of Diego Garcia. See H. Labrousse, "Will the Indian Ocean Remain a Zone of Peace?" Defense Nationale (Paris), February 1976, pp. 43-67.
    25. Michael T. Klare, War Without End: American Planning for the Next Vietnam (New York: Knopf, 1972), p. 155.
    26. Edward Wegner, "Theory of Naval Strategy in the

Nuclear Age," U.S. Naval Institute Proceedings 98, no. 831 (May 1972): 193.

27. Interview with John S. McCain, Washington, D.C., March 1976.

28. For an account of Nixon's island strategy, see Alvin J. Cottrell and Walter F. Hahn, Indian Ocean Naval Limitations: Regional Issues and Global Implications (New York: Crane, Russak, 1976).

5

DIEGO GARCIA:
PIVOT OF
U.S. STRATEGY

Here [Diego Garcia] is where the U.S. should seek a
base if we mean to contest the Russian bid for supremacy. "As Malta is to the Mediterranean, Diego Garcia
is to the Indian Ocean—equidistant from all points."

> Admiral John McCain,
> USN (Ret.), reported in
> "Notebook," Proceedings
> 95, no. 5 (May 1969): 153.

U.S. strategy for the Indian Ocean—the long-term "plans of
action designed to secure long-term ends"—has come to center
around the tiny atoll of Diego Garcia. Noting the increasing importance of the waters, the United States proposed to expand the austere
communications facility into a full-fledged logistics base. Although
the increasing U.S. presence and concern for extensive logistics
paraphernalia in the Indian Ocean appear as recent phenomena, in
reality, the process of a U.S. search for Indian Ocean base and
shore facilities dates back to the early 1960s. At that time an off-
shore base study team from the Pentagon visited various Afro-Asian
countries to arrange for future use of base and allied facilities.
Particular interest was shown in the newly built British base in
Mombasa, Kenya. The Seychelles were also talked about in this
context. Diego Garcia, however, did not feature in the calculation,
since the aim of the Pentagon was to secure something already in
existence and at the least cost. Diego Garcia had nothing to offer—
at least not yet.

The off-shore base study team's attempt to nail down existing bases for future U.S. use without regard to the indigenous politics, however, appalled the civilian assistant director of the Long-Range Objectives Group of the Chief of Naval Operations (CNO), who also detected "a vacuum of realistic planning to meet possible future national and navy needs in the Indian Ocean."[1] Viewing the myriad dangers of shore-based facilities located among populous littoral countries, the group instead formulated a strategic island concept centering around the thesis that the United States should plan to secure access to certain strategically located islands in the ocean for possible future military use. Buoyed by the fact that there were so many such islands in the Indian Ocean, the group did not see any real difficulty in persuading Great Britain to enter into such an agreement.

The group's first proposal was very general; it just discussed the need and examined the problem as to what was available. It decided to have a piece of real estate that would be available for an anchorage and would have the potential for an airstrip. The aim was to secure a place for a minimal facility but not enough territory for a major base. The parallel was drawn to the Mariana Island in the Pacific, which during World War II was not a base but provided the potential for emergency use. Many islands were examined, and the Diego Garcia atoll was found to be the most suitable. Apart from its strategic location, the atoll, with its protected lagoon and the necessary ground for the airstrip, was found to be the most suitably endowed for the purpose. *

In 1960, the civilian assistant director initiated negotiations through Admiral Arleigh Burke to persuade London to detach the Diego Garcia atoll into an independent British Indian Ocean Territory (BIOT). BIOT was thus the brainchild of the U.S. Navy, which was designed to ensure the availability of the strategically located atoll even after Mauritius (the mother country) became independent. In Arleigh Burke, the navy found a strong advocate of the strategic island concept. Admiral Burke claims to have foreseen the British withdrawal from the Indian Ocean soon after World War II when London invited the U.S. Navy to take over the responsibility of policing the Mediterranean, which the United States did by creating

---

*This section is based on personal interviews with Stuart B. Barber, civilian assistant director, Long Range Objectives Group, CNO, (Ret.); Admiral Arleigh Burke, USN (Ret.); Admiral John McCain, USN (Ret.); and Dr. Earl C. Ravenal, director, Asian Division (Systems Analysis), Office of the Secretary of Defense (1967-69). Private interviews held in Washington, D.C., February-April 1976.

the Sixth Fleet. Admiral Burke "saw through" the debilitated British navy, and, in fact, advocated a U.S. Indian Ocean presence as early as 1949. While the first sea lord in England found the concept of BIOT beneficial and plausible, many in London did not want to see the U.S. Navy in the Indian Ocean and did not support the BIOT plan.

In the United States itself, the navy plan for Diego Garcia was opposed by the air force, which opposed the navy's projection of the need for such a secure airstrip as that of Diego Garcia. The air force thought very poorly of the island base concept and found it unnecessary in the light of the available British facilities that were accessible to it. The reestablishment of the staging post at Gan (Maldives) in early 1957, which was being surreptiously used also by the air force, made any additional facility at Diego Garcia appear unnecessary.

The 1962 Vietnam War, however, contributed positively to a change in the U.S. Air Force's view. The war brought the Indian Ocean squarely into Anglo-American strategic consideration. The airlift, in pursuance of the Kennedy-Macmillan decision to come to the aid of India, showed the air force the need for secure and accessible landing posts in and around the ocean. With the Middle East and the Persian Gulf countries' refusal to allow such over-flights, the airlift had to take a much longer route. The need for a chain of secure staging posts, which would provide a corridor connecting the Atlantic with the Indian Ocean and even the Pacific, was seen as essential for future peacekeeping and strategic requirements.

The Indo-Chinese dispute also heightened the navy's desire to be in the Indian Ocean. The U.S. Navy talked about an Indian Ocean Fleet (Eighth Fleet) for a permanent presence in the ocean.[2] Extensive speculations about a chain of naval bases were prominently aired in many quarters. The visit of General Maxwell Taylor to New Delhi and the first visit of a U.S. aircraft carrier to the waters (ostensibly for familiarization) raised the possibility that as part of a proposed nuclear umbrella the United States had decided to have a permanent presence in the Indian Ocean.[3] In the light of the effectiveness of the Seventh Fleet in containing Peking's moves toward Taiwan, it was normal for Washington to view an independent Indian Ocean fleet as the best means to provide a counterpresence against the Chinese southward expansion. The Kennedy administration, while expressing dissatisfaction at the British discussions relating to possible contraction of their east of Suez presence, focused attention on the future contingencies when the United States might not "be assured of the availability of allied support facilities" even in the event of need.[4]

The Indian Ocean came to attract wider attention in the strategic thinking of the United States in view of the prospective Polaris development. The ocean offered a privileged area for deployment against both Moscow and Peking. A need for communication facilities to facilitate submarine launched ballistic missile deployment became evident, which led to the establishment of the Omega communications station in the Northwest Cape of Australia. Diego Garcia came to acquire additional importance as the possible site for such a communications station, either as an additional unit or as a possible alternative to the communications station in Eritrea, Ethiopia. The Joint Chiefs of Staff came to support the Diego Garcia concept.

By 1964, the Indian Ocean decisively entered into America's calculations. Early that year, Washington actively formulated the idea of a series of joint Anglo-American staging posts in the ocean. Although the Indian Ocean area was still regarded primarily as a British peacekeeping responsibility, London itself welcomed the prospect of Washington's participation.[5] The U.S. Navy's plans for the Diego Garcia atoll, in fact, came to be seen as complementing the British bases in Aden and Singapore.[6] Such participation and cost sharing appeared helpful at a time when Great Britain was actively considering ways and means to reduce its defense expenditures. Accordingly, an Anglo-American team surveyed various Indian Ocean islands, such as the Cocos, the Seychelles, the Aldabra, and the Chagos Archipelago, which included Diego Garcia. The team's concern was to select a few strategically located islands to create a chain of island stepping-stones across the Indian Ocean that would replace dependence on problematic land bases.[7] It was hoped that when simmering Aden on the Red Sea was phased out as Great Britain's chief base west of Singapore, "the 'thin red line' of Anglo-American peackekeeping would almost certainly be anchored on one or two Indian Ocean island bases."[8]

The Department of Defense and the Department of State began examining the longer term strategic requirements of the United States in the Indian Ocean area at about the same time. The State Department came to favor an Indian Ocean presence as "a political stabilizer, all the more as it would help to keep Britain in the area."[9] Defense Secretary Robert McNamara, however, was skeptical about the U.S. Navy being present in yet another ocean. He decided, however, to support a token U.S. naval presence in the ocean as a possible encouragement to Great Britain to continue its visibility east of Suez.[10]

The U.S. Navy faced a tough competitor in the U.S. Air Force in relation to the Diego Garcia plan. The air force insisted on having its own staging post at Aldabra Island, which the navy thought would be cost prohibitive in the absence of a workable harbor. The Royal Air Force lent strength to the U.S. Air Force by supporting the staging post concept on Aldabra Island. The British accommodated both the services. Thus, when BIOT was finally created, it included both the Chagos Archipelago and Aldabra, along with two additional islands, Deschorres and Farquahar.

Aldabra and Farquahar were the bigger islands and were designated for the use of the U.S. Air Force, while Deschores was added to the list because the navy wanted the island as a possible site for additional anchorage and fuel storage. The three islands of Aldabra, Deschores, and Farquahar were taken from the Seychelles and the Chagos Archipelago from Mauritus, respectively.

Soon after Anthony Greenwood, the minister of state for colonies, announced the creation of BIOT on the floor of the House of Commons (November 10, 1965), the British government entered discussions with the United States about future uses of the colony. An executive agreement between the United States and the United Kingdom concerning the availability of BIOT for defense purposes was signed in London on December 30, 1966.[11] Ostensibly the agreement made the island sites available to the United States "without charge."[12] However, as is known today, the United States paid Great Britain at least $14 million as part of the detachment costs for the islands. In a classified note to the agreement of December 30, 1966, the United States agreed to "provide up to half of the total British detachments costs, but not to exceed $14 million.[13]

As of September 19, 1975, the stated British detachments costs were as shown in Table 5.1.

TABLE 5.1

Diego Garcia Detachment Costs (millions of dollars)

Description	Amount*
Compensation to Mauritius for loss of sovereignty	8.40
Copra plantation	3.75
Construction of commercial airfield in Mahe, Seychelles	17.36
Compensation to Mauritius for relocation of inhabitants	1.82
Total	31.36

*One pound sterling is taken as equal to $2.80, the rate of exchange used for the 1966 agreement.

Source: U.S. Government Accounting Office, Financial and Legal Aspects of the Agreement on the Availability of Certain Indian Ocean Islands for Defense Purposes, Report of the Comptroller General of the United States, B-184915, 1976, p. 1.

The United States paid its share of the detachment costs by waiving
$14 million out of the proposed amount to be accrued from the
British obligations to pay 5 percent research and development surcharges on procurements under the U.S.-U.K. Polaris sales agreement of April 6, 1963.[14] However, due to the Department of
Defense's desire to accomplish the detachment before Great Britain
announced its intention to withdraw from east of Suez, the United
States, in fact, loaned the stated amount ($14 million) from the
Polaris Trust Fund.[15] The waiver of surcharges would have meant
a much longer delay, as the amount hitherto accrued was still
lower than the stipulated $14 million.[16]

The payment and the financial arrangement for the detachment
cost sharing were made and executed without any congressional
approval because the Department of Defense believed that completion
of the arrangements through proper congressional channels would
have resulted in inordinate delay.[17] The method of financing thus
successfully masked the "real plans and costs" and amounted to
"clear circumvention of the congressional role."[18] However, in
the light of the available information, the General Accounting Office
did not believe that any legal irregularity took place in the course
of the transaction. As far back as November 12, 1965, a Defense
Memorandum for State's deputy legal adviser viewed the Polaris
offset technique payment for the important defense-related acquisition as "merely giving up of one right in exchange for another
right of equal or greater value."[19]

The British government took steps to "depopulate" the Chagos
Archipelago, which was viewed as essential by the U.S. planners.[20]
The concern for safety arising out of the U.S. experience in many
overseas bases also indicated, in advance, the nature of the U.S.
strategic plans for the Chagos Archipelago. It was clear that, from
the beginning, the U.S. plans for the Diego Garcia atoll centered
around something much more than just an austere communications
station. The military plans for Diego Garcia were firmly laid as
early as 1963; military construction funds were sought for fiscal
year 1964, which were not approved by the Congress because
"firm rights to the site were not available."[21]

The original naval plan for the Diego Garcia atoll sought to
provide "a little balancing time for the naval units" to be deployed
in the waters.[22] The navy proposed that the entrance channel to
Diego Garcia's lagoon be dredged to 40 feet so that oil tankers and
carriers could be berthed comfortably. Its plan also called for a
modest oil storage capability to accommodate three fleet oil loads.[23]
It envisaged an airstrip of 8,000 feet for patrol planes and transports,
as well as hangars and repair facilities, for about a squadron (12
planes). The plan did not envisage any permanent living quarters,
since with the Diego Garcia weather, it was thought that camping

out would be ideal. The plan was to have a minimum logistics
facility that would cater to usual repairs and would help in the
rotating of crews. Although plans for regular berthing of tenders
were not included, it was believed that in the event of permanent or
regular deployment of submarine launched ballistic missiles, the
facility would be able to provide the essential logistics supports.
There was also no plan for regular deployment of carriers, since
the Vietnam War was taking all of them.

The U.S. Air Force, however, maintained its opposition to
the naval plans centering exclusively around the Diego Garcia atoll
and therefore delayed their implementation. The air force wanted
to pursue its plan for a staging post at Aldabra, in spite of the
navy's belief that such construction would be too costly and time
consuming. It was the Royal Air Force's plan for a staging post on
Aldabra that finally convinced the U.S. Air Force to abandon its
plans. The RAF's plan for construction of the staging post on
Aldabra raised the ire of ecologists all over the world, and finally
the idea of building any staging post on that island was shelved. [24]
Also, London had to give up the RAF's plan for Aldabra for economic reasons, as the pound was being devalued in late 1967. [25]

Thus, the U.S. Air Force gave up its plan and lent support
to the navy's plan on Diego Garcia. However, the air force's
insistence on a facility of its own on Aldabra cost the navy two years
in forwarding its own revised plans for Diego Garcia. [26]

The Diego Garcia development project was offered as an Anglo-
American joint defense project. The United States welcomed the
British decision to participate in the project, even though the participation was largely ornamental, [27] because the British association
with the plan offered a legitimacy for the buildup in the ocean, long
known as a British lake. Apart from legitimacy, London's association also cushioned the possible charge that the United States was
moving into the area that Great Britain was preparing to leave after
a long period of colonial domination.

By the summer of 1967, a detailed proposal for a logistics
facility on Diego Garcia was presented by the armed services for
the approval of the secretary of the defense. The systems analysts
of the Asian Division, who were asked to analyze, evaluate, and make
a recommendation about the proposal, felt it to be cost prohibitive. [28]
The Joint Chiefs of Staff sought to justify the construction of a logistics
facility on Diego Garcia both as a necessary addition to the services'
flexibility to meet any potential contingency in the entire region and
as an alternate fueling station for the carrier task forces in transit
from Norfolk, Virginia, to Vietnam. [29]

The systems analysts did not share this evaluation and regarded
the construction as unnecessary. Such a logistics base was seen as
unnecessary in the belief that, in the event of any of the "two dozen

contingencies mentioned by the Joint Chiefs of Staff," the concerned nations of the area would make their ports and facilities available to the U.S. forces.[30] The distance of the atoll was also seen as an impediment to any U.S. effort to come to the aid of the nations in South Asia against China, a possibility that was strongly hinted at by the Joint Chiefs of Staff.

With the availability of the Persian Gulf facilities for refueling, the idea of Diego Garcia as a refueling station appeared to the analysts as superfluous as well as cost prohibitive, both in terms of sailing time and money.[31] Any U.S. presence in the region was also shown as unproductive against political instability and adverse developments that could possibly emerge in any of the friendly littoral countries of the region. In fact, it was successfully pointed out that an American buildup in the Indian Ocean would promote an arms race between the two superpowers in yet "another geographic area that had, up to this time, been spared that infliction."[32] The analysts also believed that in spite of the stated initial cost suggestion of $26 million, a facility at the atoll, once started, would ultimately cost well over $100 million.[33] The secretary of defense accordingly disapproved the Diego Garcia construction.

In the following year (1968), the U.S. Navy commissioned an Indian Ocean Base Study that recommended a carefully developed limited logistics facility for the Diego Garcia atoll.[34] The study, approved by the chief of naval operations, Admiral Thomas H. Moorer, emphasized the value of the limited development on the strategically located atoll as an effective alternative to unnecessary and problematic commitments to peripheral nations that the U.S. basing and support needs might require.[35] The base requirements were limited to three main factors: surveillance, low-profile presence, and capability for contingency operations by carriers, which were viewed as "politically non-alarming, militarily limited goals."[36] The ability to operate air patrols and minor surface forces out of the Diego Garcia facility would add to the U.S. Navy's flexibility in the region. The navy believed that the construction of the logistics facility at the strategically located atoll would also act as a signal of U.S. resolve not to "abandon the Indian Ocean to the status of a Soviet lake."[37] The need for a logistics facility for the area was seen as immediate, and the U.S. Navy asked the Department of Defense to take up the construction immediately because completion of the facility in that remote location would require at least two years.[38]

The year 1968 appeared propitious for the votaries of the Diego Garcia proposal. The British decision to withdraw from east of Suez was seen by Washington policy-makers as precipitating important developments affecting the balance of power of the region.

To aggravate the situation, the Soviet navy started regular deployment in the Indian Ocean, leading Washington to see the specter of Soviet domination in the area. Although Washington, after a careful review of the developments, decided against a full-fledged American presence in the ocean, it came to view the modest Diego Garcia expansion proposal favorably. The Joint Chiefs of Staff voiced a newer set of proposals when the 1967 plan to build the $26 million base was presented as

> a sort of option B, sandwiched between a minimum option—doing nothing—and a maximum option—the whole list of functions originally conceived by the Joint Chiefs of Staff: Oil storage, communications, air staging and operations, staging of ground forces, forward basing of submarines and other vessels—at a cost of $55 million.[39]

The rationale for the $26 million plan was offered as a long-felt necessity for an austere communications facility and a forward base for nuclear submarines deployed in the waters. In the light of the maximum option, the plan appeared modest and prudent.[40]

The analysts still found any buildup in the area as superfluous, especially, with the commissioning of the satellites, a land-based communications center in the middle of the Indian Ocean. Any augmented U.S. presence in the waters centering around the proposed facility at Diego Garcia was labeled as a political liability as well as a sure "stimulant" for a "competitive naval buildup" in the area.[41] Deployments from the Pacific to meet an emergency were still seen as more cost effective than deployments from Diego Garcia.[42]

However, the new Pentagon administration supported the Option B plan for an austere communications facility. It is said that the situation appeared fortuitous to the U.S. Navy in that particular period. Secretary Robert McNamara left and Clark Clifford became the new secretary of defense. However, the new defense secretary was too busy with Vietnam, and the deputy secretary of defense, Paul Nitze (1967-69), the ex-secretary of the navy (1963-67), took a favorable stand in regard to the naval plans for Diego Garcia. Dean Rusk, secretary of state, favored the modest naval buildup for an entirely different reason—he thought that a U.S. entry into the waters could act as an inducement for Great Britain to continue its presence east of Suez. A subsequent attempt by the analysts to stop the inclusion of the $26 million additional request failed, and the Defense budgets started requesting funds for the facilities on Diego Garcia.

In the calendar year 1969 (for fiscal year 1970), the navy requested new obligational authority of $9.6 million for the first increment of the naval construction plan for a total cost of the stated $26 million. [43] Like any other construction proposal, the request carried a security classification. The navy justified its request for the 1970 appropriation on the grounds that "An austere logistic support activity has become necessary to insure Navy readiness in the South Atlantic, Indian and Western Pacific Oceans."[44]

The request was approved by the Armed Services Committee of the Congress and by the House Appropriations Committee, but the Senate Appropriations Committee refused to allot money for such a base. This latter committee opposed the idea of a naval base in the Indian Ocean, believing that a sustained Indian Ocean deployment, leading to an arms race with the Soviets, was not in the interests of the United States. [45] The Military Construction Subcommittee and the full Armed Services Committee of the Senate deleted the Diego Garcia project completely from the 1970 Military Construction Appropriations bill. The Senate opposition prevailed, and the plan for the Diego Garcia buildup was shelved. [46] An oral agreement was reached, however, asking the navy to come back for a new appropriation and for only a communications station in fiscal year 1971. [47]

The navy duly requested the communications station in 1970 for fiscal year 1971. The rationale for the communications station appeared to be different in that the navy now sought to justify the station on the grounds that the United States would "probably have to withdraw from the main continent of Africa the large communications facility that the United States maintained at Eritrea, Ethiopia (Kagnew Station)."[48] In fact, the future of Ethiopia as one nation was itself doubted by the U.S. strategic planners at the moment. [49] The possibility of losing the station made the necessity of Diego Garcia seem logical.

Congress approved the request for $5.4 million as the first increment for an austere communications facility at Diego Garcia. In November 1971, for fiscal year 1972, Congress approved a second increment of $8.95 million toward the completion of the communications facility. In October 1972, Congress finally approved the $6.1 million requested as the third increment for the communications facility. Thus, in three appropriations, Congress approved $20.45 million for the communications station in the middle of the Indian Ocean.

Although Congress trimmed the navy's request for the original $26 million communications proposal as an unnecessary attempt to escalate U.S. presence in a new region, talk of a greater U.S. involvement in the Indian Ocean waters was already in the air

by the end of 1971. Melvin Laird, secretary of defense, asserted
in August 1971 that the United States would maintain an air and naval
presence in the Indian Ocean. He even viewed a search for additional bases and allied facilities as a possibility in the purported
U.S. attempt to maintain a posture of realistic deterrence in the
area.[50] Secretary of State Henry Kissinger sought to use gunboat
diplomacy during the India-Pakistan War in December 1971.
Although the attempt to influence events in the subcontinent did not
exactly lead to success, a formidable naval presence in the waters
came to be viewed as a visible backing for Kissinger's crisis diplomacy. A powerful naval deployment was seen as adding flexibility
to U.S. diplomacy while contributing to an increased sense of uncertainty on the part of the littoral countries about the possible course
of U.S. response toward developments. Two events in the area—the
alleged increase in the Soviet inroads into the subcontinent in the
aftermath of the India-Pakistan War and the possible opening of the
Suez Canal—were viewed in Washington as necessitating further U.S.
involvement in the waters.[51]

The Department of Defense started construction of the Diego
Garcia communications facility, after London's concurrence, in 1972.
Discussions with London on the matter led to the signing of an agree-
ment on October 24, 1972, which supplemented the agreement of
December 30, 1966.[52] The agreement, pursuant to paragraph 2(b)
of the initial agreement, dated December 30, 1966, approved in
principle the construction of a U.S. limited naval facility on Diego
Garcia.[53] Among other things, London approved that

> . . . the Government of the United States shall have the
> right to construct, maintain and operate a limited naval
> communications facility on Diego Garcia. The facility
> shall consist of transmitting and receiving services, an
> anchorage, airfield, associated logistic support and supply
> and personnel accommodation.[54]

As part of the increased U.S. involvement in the area, Washington sought to make MIDEASTFOR more impressive. The force
authorized five ships, but the United States had maintained only a
three-unit force. In the summer of 1972, the commandship La Salle
(14,000 ton Logistic Ship Deploy [LSD]) replaced the comparatively
much smaller Valcour (1,800 tons) as the flagship of MIDEASTFOR.
The newer ship was much better suited for representational purposes
and in all respects more prestigious. The destroyer escorts that
rotate as part of MIDEASTFOR were also made more visible with
newer ships.[55]

The United States signed an agreement in December 1971 with the sultan of Bahrain for a permanent naval station in the sultanate. The agreement was not publicly announced at the request of the Bahrain government.[56] The Bahrain government wanted the United States to take over part of the former British base as a way to ensure the territorial integrity of the sultanate against its stronger neighbors, Iran and Iraq, as well as to strengthen it against danger from internal revolutionaries. From Washington's point of view, the treaty only ensured the continuity of MIDEASTFOR, as a new treaty relationship with the independent government of Bahrain became necessary as soon as the British withdrew. An executive agreement signed by the United States and Bahrain, entitling deployment in Bahrain by the U.S. Middle East force, was effected by an exchange of notes and signatures at Manama on December 23, 1971.[57] MIDEASTFOR was henceforth updated, and personnel strength was increased from 200 to 260. The United States also leased the Juffir base, which was formerly used by British.

The Diego Garcia communications station became operational on March 23, 1973.[58] The Defense Department did not make any public announcement in order to allay the fears of the littoral states that this would begin big power rivalry. The communications post was billed as an essential development to "help control the future movement of American ships and planes through the area."[59] With the operation of the Diego Garcia station, the United States opened up a new chapter of its involvement in the Indian Ocean.[60] The communications installation at Diego Garcia became an important link in the Department of Defense's Worldwide Military Command and Control Systems.[61] The communications facility was designed to eliminate a long-felt gap in high frequency radio coverage in the area.[62] The Diego Garcia facility receives its information from the Defense Satellite Communications System to be relayed to the naval and air units in the region.[63]

The Middle East War of 1973 is portrayed by the Defense Department as a watershed in U.S. strategic thinking about the Indian Ocean. The war transformed the traditional view of the Indian Ocean, and it is now seen as having "the potential to influence major shifts in the global power balance over the next decade."[64] The oil embargo, which followed the Arab-Israeli War, and the economic impact of the embargo and the ensuing higher prices resulted in greater attention toward the Indian Ocean area. The interrelationships among the developments in those waters and the well-being of other nations in the world came to be perceived in clearer terms.[65] Admiral Zumwalt, during the course of testimony before the U.S. Senate Committee on Foreign Relations, admitted that the experience of the Mideast War of 1973 made it evident that "our interests in the

Indian Ocean are directly linked with our interests in Europe and Asia; and more broadly, with our fundamental interest in maintaining a stable worldwide balance of power."[66] In that context, the capability to deploy or provide an enhanced U.S. military power presence in the Indian Ocean became essential.[67]

Secretary of Defense James Schlesinger soon announced that the United States would establish a pattern of regular visits into the ocean, a presence that would be more regular and frequent than ever before.[68] The need for a demonstrable U.S. military presence also became the crux of the rationale for the proposed expansion of the Diego Garcia facility.[69] The few lessons of the Yom Kippur War taught the U.S. defense planners about the necessity for an expanded facility at Diego Garcia. The emergency dispatch of the carrier-based naval power during the height of the 1973 war failed to influence events in favor of the United States. The successful Soviet efforts at neutralization of the sudden U.S. naval augmentation, as evidenced in 1971 and 1973, suggested a regular U.S. presence in the vital waters. The refusal of the United States allies, except for Portugal, for U.S. overflights in the support of the Israeli war efforts intimated that the United States could not rely on friendly littoral countries for necessary support in the event of great necessity.

The logistics constraints in the efforts to support the American naval units in the Indian Ocean were felt to be formidable. The prospective opening of the Suez Canal as a result of the consequences of the Mideast War offered the possibility of greatly shortened lines of Soviet redeployment into the Indian Ocean, necessitating a U.S. response in regard to the expanded facility on the atoll. The possibility of MIDEASTFOR permanently leaving Bahrain also figured prominently in the calculations leading to the proposed expansion plans.[70] The sultan of Bahrain asked the United States to withdraw its MIDEASTFOR units as part of Arab opposition to the pro-Israel bias of Washington. (MIDEASTFOR is back, as the sultan rescinded his order sometime in 1974.)

Prompted by the Yom Kippur War experience, the U.S. defense planners put forward the plans for the Diego Garcia expansion on a priority basis and asked for the necessary authorizations under Military Procurement Supplemental for Fiscal Year 1974.[71] The Department of Defense asked for a $29 million authorization for the construction of the expanded facility. The justification was put as follows:

> Mission and Project: The Naval Communications Station
> provides Fleet broadcasts, tactical ship to shore and
> point to point communications, and is a critical link in
> the Defense Communication System. A new mission is

being assigned to this Station to support periodic presence
of an Indian Ocean Task Group. This project provides
facilities to improve Diego Garcia for logistically supporting the Task Group.

Requirement: Recent events in the Middle East, the en
energy crisis, and the potential for hostilities in an area
subject to chronic instability have necessitated a reevaluation of U.S. national interests in the Indian Ocean Area,
problems that may affect those interests, and the adequacy of the means now available for their protection.
These national interests which could require an occasional
increased Navy presence are: (1) free access to and transit in the Indian Ocean, (2) protection of U.S. nationals,
and (3) protection of sea lines of communication. These
events and interests are the basis of a requirement to
provide logistic support facilities to support a task force
operating in the Indian Ocean Area. Facilities to be provided are the minimum required to support surface and
air operations. . . .

Impact if not provided: If this project is not provided,
there will be no fixed site to support carrier task force
operations in the Indian Ocean Area. . . .[72]

The aim of the construction, the description and the scope of which
are listed as follows (see Table 5.2) was to transform Diego Garcia
into a modest support facility. During the course of his testimony
before the House Subcommittee on the Near East and South Asia of
the Committee on Foreign Affairs, James H. Noyes, deputy assistant secretary of defense for international security affairs (Near
Eastern, African, and South Asian affairs), described the proposed
expansion as a modest support facility for the effective operation of
U.S. naval forces in the Indian Ocean.[73] The navy's request for
the authorizations would have provided an expanded facility capable
of supporting a carrier task force. The House approved the supplemental request but the Senate rejected it.[74] The joint conferees
decided to defer the matter for a complete consideration of the
construction request under the 1975 Military Construction Bill,
without "prejudice to the merits of the project."[75]

The Fiscal Year 1975 Military Construction Authorization Bill
contained the $29 million request for the navy, which was refused
in the 1974 supplemental bill, along with the expected additional
$3.3 million for the air force to complete the first leg of the Diego
Garcia expansion into a logistics facility. The House Armed Services

TABLE 5.2

Diego Garcia Construction as per
Fiscal Year 1974 Supplemental Request

Description	Scope	Amount (thousands of dollars)
Fiscal year 1974 supplemental request		
Petroleum, oil, lubricant (POL) storage facilities	[Deleted]	6,834
Pier	750 feet of berthing	5,100
Parking apron	64,750 square yards	2,279
Runway extension	4,000 feet	2,264
Aircraft arresting gear		215
Hangar		440
Operations building addition	2,850 square feet	232
Overhaul paving train		250
Transit storage building	4,000 square feet	140
Subsistence building addition	3,517 square feet	393
Bachelor enlisted quarters	277 men	3,882
Bachelor officers quarters	32 men	1,360
Armed forces radio/TV station		96
Ready issue ammo magazine		220
Cold storage addition	4,190 square feet	466
General warehouse addition	26,385 square feet	1,251
Receiver building addition	1,250 square feet	131
Vehicle repair hardstand	1,110 square feet	40
Power plant expansion	2,400 kilowatts	2,265
Utilities		1,065
Navy Marines Construction Battalion(NMCB) camp		77
Total		29,000
Fiscal year 1975 request		
Parking apron	25,000 square yards	1,000
POL storage	[Deleted]	1,800
Ammunition storage	6,000 square yards	500
Total		3,300

Source: U.S., Congress, House, Subcommittee on the Near East and South Asia, Committee on Foreign Affairs, Proposed Expansion of U.S. Military Facilities in the Indian Ocean, 93d Cong., 2d sess., 1974, p. 25.

71

Committee approved the amount requested as usual, but the Senate
Armed Services Committee reduced the navy authorization to $14.8
million. The air force authorization was kept intact. The Senate
Armed Services Committee also inserted qualifying language in its
committee report:

> At the same time, the Committee included Section 612
> in the bill to preclude the obligation of any of these funds
> until the President of the United States has advised the
> Congress in writing that he has evaluated all military
> and foreign policy implications regarding the need for
> these facilities and has certified that this construction
> is essential to the national interest. Such certification
> must be submitted to the Congress and approved by both
> Houses of Congress. This will assure the opportunity for
> full debate on the expansion at Diego Garcia as a policy
> matter, in light of the most recent circumstances. [76]

The committee also believed that in light of the importance
and complexity of the issues raised by the proposed Diego Garcia
expansion, the administration should fully reevaluate the matter,
including an examination of the possibility of a mutual arms limitation agreement with the Soviet Union. [77] The matter went before
the joint conference and the conferees agreed to endorse the Senate
authorization of $14.8 million for the navy and the $3.3 million for
the air force with qualifying language, which, among other things
stated clearly:

> Sec. 613. (a) None of the funds authorized to be appro-
> priated by this Act with respect to any construction pro-
> ject at Diego Garcia may be obligated unless—
> (1) the President has (A) advised the Congress in
>   writing that all military and foreign policy im-
>   plications regarding the need for United States
>   facilities at Diego Garcia have been evaluated
>   by him, and (B) certified to the Congress in
>   writing that the construction of any such project
>   is essential to the national interest of the United
>   States;
> (2) 60 days of continuous session of the Congress
>   have expired following the date on which certifi-
>   cation with respect to such project is received
>   by the Congress, and
> (3) neither House of Congress has adopted, within
>   such 60-day period, a resolution disapproving
>   such project. [78]

The joint conference of the House and Senate Appropriations Committees agreed to delete the funds earmarked for the proposed expansion of the Diego Garcia facility with a caveat. If neither body adopts any resolution disapproving the proposed construction in accordance with the provisions of Section 613 of the Military Construction Authorization Act, 1975, then the navy and the air force would be able to utilize any construction funds that might be available to them under the appropriations act for the proposed expansion. [79] On May 12, 1975, President Gerald Ford sent the certification for the expansion proposal as required under Section 613 (a) (1) of the said act. The certification read:

> To the Congress of the United States:
> In accordance with section 613 (a)(1)(A) of the Military
> Construction Act, 1975 (Public Law 93-552), I have
> evaluated all the military and foreign policy implica-
> tions regarding the need for United States facilities
> at Diego Garcia. On the basis of this evaluation and
> in accordance with section 613 (a)(1)(B), I hereby
> certify that the construction of such facilities is
> essential to the national interest of the United States. [80]

On May 19, 1975, barely a week after the tart presidential certification, Mike Mansfield, Majority Leader of the Senate, as well as the chairman of the Senate Military Construction Subcommittee, introduced a resolution (Senate Resolution 160) disapproving the construction at Diego Garcia as per Section 613. The resolution read:

> S. Res. 160
> Resolved, That the Senate does not approve the pro-
> posed construction project on the island of Diego Gar-
> cia, the need for which was certified to by the Presi-
> dent and the certification with respect to which was
> received by the Senate on May 12, 1975. [81]

As the U.S. Senate was preparing to debate the Mansfield resolution (S. Res. 160), the Defense Department restructured its development plan for the Diego Garcia facility. With an estimated $37.8 million (an increase of $5.5 million from its original request under the 1974 supplemental and the 1975 budget as possible cost overrun), the Department of Defense listed the proposed construction for the expanded facility (see Table 5.3)

The Mansfield resolution was referred to the Senate Armed Services Committee, which was required to act on it by June 18,

TABLE 5.3

Restructured Diego Garcia Development Plan

Service/Project	Cost (thousands of dollars)
Fiscal Year 1975	
Navy	
POL storage (320,000 barrels)	5,492
Pier	4,000
Runway extension/parking apron	3,500
Power plant expansion	1,165
Substation	292
Subsistence building addition	393
Subtotal	14,802
Air Force	
Aircraft parking area (25,000 square yards)	1,000
POL storage, JP-4 (160,000 barrels)	1,800
Open ammunition protective storage	500
Subtotal	3,300
Total	18,102
Fiscal Year 1976	
Navy	
POL storage (160,000 barrels)	1,530
Power plant expansion	1,254
Aircraft parking apron/runway extension	1,173
Hangar	572
Operation building addition	265
Airfield transit storage	160
Bachelor enlisted quarters, 277 men	4,325
Bachelor officers quarters, 32 men	1,550
Ready issue ammunition magazine	251
Cold storage	531
General warehouse	713
Receiver building addition	149
Amphibious vehicle hardstand	46
Aircraft arresting gear	245
Utilities distribution system	927
Radio and TV station	109
Total	13,800
Fiscal Year 1977	
Navy: Various facilities (total, fiscal year 1977)*	5,900
Grand Total	37,802

*The precise facilities to be constructed have not been determined but, for the most part, they are troop-support facilities (such as chapel, club, recreational facilities, hobby shop, theater, library) that would be required to support the communications site even if there were no expansion.

Source: U.S., Congress, Senate, Committee on Armed Services, Selected Materials on Diego Garcia, 94th Cong., 1st sess., 1975, p. 6.

1975, under the Military Construction Act of Fiscal Year 1975. The Committee held its hearing on the matter on June 10, 1975. The chief defense witness, James Schlesinger, secretary of defense, testified on the urgency of the construction at Diego Garcia to make the station a much-needed support facility in the waters. Schlesinger also showed photographic proofs of a Soviet major base construction in Berbera, Somalia, which, on completion, would be able to act as a missile-handling and storage facility. The committee, in its subsequent hearing on June 17, 1975, voted against the Mansfield Resolution ten to six. The Senate took up the resolution on July 28, 1975, and after a five-hour debate, the resolution was defeated by a 53 to 43 vote, with 3 abstaining. [82]

While the amount authorized under the 1975 Military Construction Authorization Act was released with the defeat of the Mansfield resolution, the navy's request of $13.8 million for fiscal year 1976 for the Diego Garcia construction was held up during its final passage through the Senate. Senator John Culver of Iowa, who had opposed the base expansion from the beginning, successfully offered an amendment to the 1976 appropriations bill on November 6, 1975. [83] The amendment adopted by the Senate 51 to 44 sought to defer the spending of the additional amount allotted under fiscal year 1976 until July 1, 1976. [84] The intent of the amendment was to provide indications of the U.S. desire for restraint that "would be evident to nations of the region and which would improve the chances of a U.S. initiative toward negotiations." [85]

Since the House approved the amount under the 1976 fiscal request, the measure went to the Joint Conference Committee. Faced with the reluctance of the House conferees to prolong the Diego Garcia construction, the conference agreed to modify the Senate amendment "with the full expectation that the Administration will report" to the appropriate congressional committees "regarding negotiation initiatives before April 15, 1976." [86] The conferees' intent was specifically expressed: "to prohibit construction of projects on Diego Garcia using fiscal year 1976 funds before April 15, 1976 but not to delay planning of the procurement of long leadtime items." [87]

On February 25, 1976, the United States and the United Kingdom finally concluded an executive agreement that replaced the agreement constituted by the exchange of notes, October 25, 1972, concerning the limited naval communications facility on the Diego Garcia atoll. [88] The 1976 agreement permits the expansion of the existing communications facility into a logistics facility, the scope of which is stated to include an anchorage, airfield, support and supply elements and ancillary services, personnel accommodation, and transmitting and receiving services. [89]

The purpose of the facility is described as a means to provide an improved link in U.S. defense communications and to furnish support for "ships and aircraft owned or operated by or on behalf of either Government."[90] The specific areas allotted for the construction of the immovable structures, installations, and buildings for the facility are shown in Map 5.1. The additional construction plans of the U.S. government, subject to the availability of funds, are listed in Table 5.4.

The State Department transmitted the administration's report on the Indian Ocean arms limitation issue on April 15, 1976, as per the congressional amendment of December 1975, referred to above (Joint Conference report).[91] The administration clearly stated its view that such a U.S. initiative for an Indian Ocean arms limitation agreement would be inappropriate, particularly in the light of the Soviet involvement in Angola.[92] Such an initiative, the administration observed, "in a region immediately contiguous to the African continent might convey the mistaken impression to the Soviets and our friends and allies that we were willing to acquiesce in this type of Soviet behavior."[93]

The administration thus secured all the appropriations that it had asked for the expansion of the Diego Garcia facility. As Table 5.5 shows, the last installment for the completion of the Diego Garcia facility will be requested under the 1978 Military Construction Program. The final request by the U.S. Navy, as shown, will include a $5.9 million authorization to provide the final touch to the logistics facility at the strategically located atoll, which will be completed by 1980.

THE NEED FOR DIEGO GARCIA

The need for a logistics base facility in the Indian Ocean area has been felt by the Department of Defense for a considerable length of time, probably going back to late 1940s. The Long Range Objectives Group of the CNO detected "a vacuum of realistic planning to meet possible future national and navy needs in the Indian Ocean" even prior to 1960.[94] In fact, it was this early realization of the vacuum that led to the initiation of the political efforts that finally created BIOT and the subsequent base agreements that secured the Chagos Archipelago for U.K.-U.S. defense purposes for 50 years.[95]

The basic objective for Diego Garcia was to provide the United States with an inexpensive listening point and emergency support point covering a vast global area of great potential importance whose use would be free of encumbrances. The need for such an expanded facility has probably increased with the increase in the Soviet pres-

MAP 5.1

Diego Garcia Agreement 1976:   Construction Areas

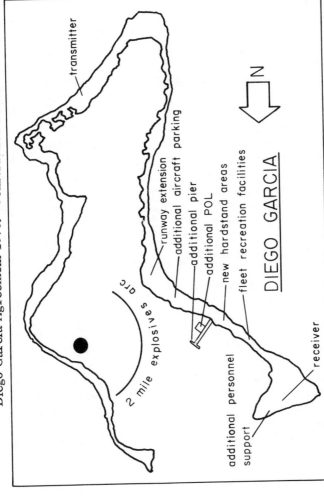

transmitter

2 mile explosives arc

runway extension
additional aircraft parking
additional pier
additional POL
new hardstand areas
fleet recreation facilities

additional personnel
support

receiver

N

DIEGO GARCIA

Source: U.S., Congress, Senate, Armed Services Committee, <u>Selected Materials on Diego Garcia</u>, 94th
Cong., 1st sess., 1975, p. 7.

TABLE 5.4

Additional Construction Under U.K.-U.S. Agreement

Item	Approximate Capacity or Size
Expanded dredging for fleet anchorage	4,000 acres
Fuel and general purpose pier	500 feet of berthing
Runway extension	4,000 linear feet
Aircraft parking apron	90,000 square yards
Hangar	18,000 suuare feet
Air operating building addition	2,900 square feet
Transit storage building	4,000 square feet
Aircraft arresting gear	—
Storage petroleum, oil, and lubricants	640,000 barrels
Power plant expansion	2,400 kilowatts
Vehicle repair hardstand	1,200 square yards
Subsistence building addition	3,600 square feet
Cold storage addition	4,200 square feet
Armed forces radio and TV station	1,200 square feet
General warehouse addition	13,000 square feet
Utilities	—
Ready issue ammunition magazine	2,000 square feet
Protective open storage area for munitions	6,000 square yards
Bachelor enlisted quarters	277 men
Bachelor officers quarters	32 men
Receiver building addition	1,300 square feet
Recreational facilities	(scope to be determined)
Shed storage	7,100 square feet
Flammable storage	2,700 square feet
Navy exchange warehouse	5,400 square feet
Crash fire station	7,300 square feet
Structural fire station	3,000 square feet
Aircraft washrack	(scope to be determined)
Aircraft ready issue refueler	(scope to be determined)
Public workshops	16,600 square feet

Source: U.S., Department of Defense, Office of the Assistant Secretary of Defense for International Security Affairs.

TABLE 5.5

Summary of Authorization and Appropriation Actions and Summary
of the Construction Program
(in thousands of dollars)

Diego Garcia Construction Program, Programming Summary

Fiscal Year	Description	Authorization	Appropriation
Navy			
1970	Naval facility (first increment)	9,556	
1971	Naval communications facility (first increment)		5,400
1972	Naval communications facility (second increment)	4,794	8,950
	Subtotal	14,350	14,350
1973	Dredging	6,100	6,100
1975	Expansion of facilities (first increment)	14,802	
1976	Expansion of facilities	13,800	13,800*
1978	Various facilities	5,900*	5,900
	Subtotal	54,952	40,150
Air force			
1975	Various facilities	3,300	†
	Total	58,352	40,150

Diego Garcia Construction Program—Construction Status
October 31, 1975

Fiscal Year	Project and Appropriation Amount
1971	Naval communications station (first increment), $5,400,000 Communications facilities—completed Personnel support facilities—underway, complete August 1976

	Fuel system—underway, complete December 1975
	Airfield—completed
	Waterfront facility—requirement canceled
	Utilities—underway, complete December 1976
1972	Naval communications station (second increment), $8,950,000
	Personnel support facilities—underway, complete July 1976
	Fuel system—underway, complete December 1975
	Airfield facilities—underway, complete December 1975
	Utilities, public works, maintenance facilities—underway, complete December 1976
1973	Dredging—underway, complete June 1976, $6,100,000
1974	None
1975	Expansion of facilities, $14,802,000
	POL facilities—February 1976 to April 1979
	Pier—June 1976 to February 1978
	Airfield pavement—November 1975 to April 1977
	Personnel support facilities—December 1975 to September 1976
	Power plant and utilities—June 1976 to March 1979
	Air force—parking apron, POL storage, ammunition storage—November 1975 to April 1979, $3,300,000
1976	Expansion of facilities, $13,800,000
	POL facilities—February 1976 to April 1979
	Airfield facilities—November 1975 to May 1978
	Personnel support facilities—March 1976 to November 1978
	Communication facilities—May 1977 to October 1978
	Supply facilities—October 1976 to February 1979
	Power plant and supporting utilities—June 1976 to March 1979
1977	None
1978	Expansion of facilities, $5,900,000
	Recreational facilities—July 1978 to March 1980
	Supply facilities—July 1978 to April 1980
	Land operational facilities—July 1978 to January 1980
	Airfield facilities—July 1978 to October 1979
	Maintenance facilities—July 1978 to December 1979

*Not yet approved.

†To be funded from available appropriations.

Source: U.S., Department of Defense, Office of the Assistant Secretary of Defense for International Security Affairs, Commander Gary G. Silk, Country Director for the Persian Gulf and Indian Ocean.

ence in the Indian Ocean waters. In addition to the increasing need of surveillance of the area, Diego Garcia also acquired extra importance when the sultan of Bahrain asked MIDEASTFOR to suspend its activities as part of the general Arab boycott against the United States that took place after the Mideast War of 1973.

The U.S. decision to increase its presence in the Indian Ocean in the aftermath of the 1973 Yom Kippur War also necessitated a secure place where fuel stocks would be available to U.S. naval units. Such an arrangement was also important because U.S. naval and air units could refuel in friendly countries of the area only with prior arrangement on a case-by-case basis.[96] The naval task force dispatched during the October War also faced substantial difficulties in catering to its logistics needs. With a logistics tail reaching as far back as Subic Bay in the Philippines, the task group found its flexibility impaired. It was also observed that had there been "another hot spot in the Pacific, we would have been in deep trouble."[97]

To reduce the logistics tail, and to reduce the cost from such overextended logistics support, the facility at Diego Garcia was seen by military planners as essential as well as cost effective.[98] The House of Representatives Armed Services Committee even found the facility necessary for the overall readiness of the United States.[99] Therefore, the expanded general-purpose facility at Diego Garcia was necessary for U.S. capability to respond to the requirements of foreign policy.[100]

The possibility of the closing of Subic Bay, or even the fact that Manila could control the use of the base facilities in the Philippines, also lent credence to the necessity of having Diego Garcia transformed into a logistics facility. The liberal terms under which the United States can use the base facility at the Diego Garcia make it profitable for the United States to build its own facility. The limitations placed on the use of the Utapo base and the final withdrawal of U.S. troops from Thailand also increase the importance of Diego Garcia for the surveillance of the Indian Ocean area.

Diego Garcia is planned only as needed help for units that would be present in the Indian Ocean at a given time. The expansion does not signify a U.S. decision for a permanently increased presence in the waters. The facility will provide the logistics support to the task forces that would be deployed into the waters at a lesser cost and greater efficiency.[101]

The necessity for stationing submarine tenders in the area calls for an expanded Diego Garcia facility. In spite of the nuclearization of the submarines, tenders are essential for restocking, rotating of crews, and even for repairs of submarines. Without Diego Garcia, the submarines are provided with these services only at Subic Bay or at Guam, a distance of 4,000 and 5,000 miles, respectively, thus losing deployment time.

The egresses and ingresses through the Malacca Straits have added to the problems of periodic submarine deployments in the Indian Ocean waters.* Routing of the submarines farther southward around Australia or Indonesia while on transit from Subic Bay or Guam adds thousands of miles in distance and makes any substantial presence in the Indian Ocean waters nearly impossible. The facility at Diego Garcia adds flexibility to U.S. strategic submarine deployments, and the tenders stationed off Diego Garcia will enable the United States to exploit fully the strategic advantage of submarine launced ballistic missile deployment in the Indian Ocean.

Along with strategy and tactics, logistics still plays an important role in ensuring such a presence. Dwight Eisenhower is quoted as making the broad statement that "You will not find it difficult to prove that battles, campaigns and even wars have been won or lost primarily because of the logistics."[102] Field Marshall Sir Archibald Percival Wavell also supported the importance of logistics. The availability of bases throughout the world also contributed positively in the Allied victory over the Nazis. World War II demonstrated the importance of bases in any scheme for security and balance of power.[103]

According to Admiral Zumwalt, the proposed expansion relates only to U.S. efforts to maintain a presence in the area for political and diplomatic reasons rather than contributing to a conventional war preparation against the Soviet Union.[104] Zumwalt also sees the U.S. presence as a stabilizing factor rather than as a bastion of U.S. interest.[105] However, the Diego Garcia facility will contribute to U.S. success in prevailing over any hostility in the area.[106]

The expansion of the communications station into a logistics facility is portrayed as a "prudent precautionary move" to enhance U.S. capability in an area that has increasingly become of great strategic significance.[107] The facility adds considerably to the U.S. Navy's reinforcement capability for contingency operations.[108] The expansion will "underline the U.S. interest in the peaceful development of the region."[109] At the same time, it is a signal of U.S. determination to ensure access to and transportation of the "crucial petroleum resources of the Middle East."[110] The added flexibility in logistics will contribute toward the U.S. attempt to fill the salient gap in the Indian Ocean naval deployment capability, which acquires greater importance in relation to the Soviet buildup, the

---

*With the adoption of the 12-mile territorial limit, some parts of the strait will become justifiably the territorial waters of Indonesia and Malaysia. Already, their claim for increased control over the strait has raised problems over Innocent Passage.

purported U.S. determination to use force to offset the crippling effect of a prolonged oil embargo in the future, [111] and the explosive situation in southern Africa.

THE ADVANTAGES OF DIEGO GARCIA

The Diego Garcia facility is an ideal way of meeting logistics support needs with a minimum of offsetting liabilities. [112] The 14-mile long and five-mile wide V-shaped atoll is centrally located, and its prominent location makes it the Malta of the Indian Ocean. Admiral Moorer noted also that the geopolitical prominence of the atoll attracted his attention as early as 1961. [113] The depopulated island provides "about as low a political profile" as could be attained. The strategic location, the liberal base rights guaranteed under the U.K.-U.S. agreement, and the unpopulated nature of the atoll make Diego Garcia the best possible choice for a U.S. logistics facility. Any alternative to Diego Garcia could have been much more costly in terms of political, diplomatic, and economic price.

Arrangements by the Pentagon for a land-based base and other such logistics facilities with some countries in the area could have meant much more than a mere economic price. The location of the facility (only 1,000 miles from any major littoral country) provides the United States with a place that enables it to utilize a "measured and discreet application of force," whenever needed. [114] Moreover, by looming large on the horizon, Diego Garcia presents a visible deterrent, yet its distance makes it relatively invulnerable to shore-based air forces of littoral countries. In case of refusal of over-flights by littoral countries, the United States hopes to use Diego Garcia to sustain its airborne help to its friends and allies in the region. The facility was used in the 1973 Mideast War for surveillance and P-3 reconnaissance flights to monitor the central Indian Ocean zone, including the Red Sea port of the Gulf of Aqaba, which was blockaded by the Arabs. [115]

In its role as a filling station, the atoll will not have stationing of U.S. naval units. [116] It will, however, help the U.S. naval units to stay longer in the Indian Ocean waters. The facility will not see any force-building exercise but will remain a service-oriented base for forces that pass through the area. [117]

The expanded Diego Garcia facility would facilitate an extended and semicontinuous American presence in the Indian Ocean. The 1,200-foot runway, the dredged harbor, and the lagoon will enable the United States to use the facility for strategic units. Although Pentagon officials disclaim any possibility of U.S. B-52s regularly using the atoll, the runway is adequate for periodic use. The

Pentagon maintains that because of its proximity to the equater, the runway will need an additional 50 feet in width, and an additional 10 inches in thickness for regular use by the B-52s.[118] However, according to expert opinions called upon by the United Nations, the runway can be used by almost any aircraft in the world, including the U.S. B-52 strategic bomber and the KC-135 refueling aircraft for B-52s, even if fully loaded.[119] The facility will also be able to accommodate a carrier task force.

These uses will enable the U.S. Navy to bring its power to bear in the region more quickly and effectively than could have been done during the past. The improvement of the facility on the atoll means "that a major American naval squadron will be able to operate more or less continuously in the Indian Ocean."[120] The P-3 Orion ASW aircrafts will be one of the primary users of the Diego Garcia facility.[121] The SR-71 reconnaissance aircrafts may also utilize the atoll.[122] The surveillance capability of the United States will enable the monitoring of the entire Indian Ocean area for both surface craft and submarines.[123] The atoll also provides the opportunity for servicing nuclear submarines. The base will be comparable in function to that at Subic Bay in the Philippines.[124]

Although the expanded facility is usually labeled as an austere logistics facility (a superfilling station for the fleet), the construction when completed would, in fact, turn the atoll into a decisive facility enabling the United States to "influence major shifts in the global power balance over the next decade."[125] The facility is viewed as offering increased options to U.S. deployment in the waters.[126]

The Diego Garcia facility, with its fuel reserves, can contribute substantially in the case of urgent redeployment of major naval forces between the Atlantic and the Pacific, especially in case of sabotage or other damage to the Panama Canal. (Carriers cannot transmit through the canal in any event.) Between the western Pacific and Europe, the Indian Ocean route is preferable to that around South America. If the United States provides a necessary refueling facility at the Ascension Island staging post, which the U.S. Navy had planned along with the Royal Air Force, the naval units refueled at the Diego Garcia facility can safely arrive at Spain without difficulty. The need for additional refueling on the route can also be taken care of if the United States decides to use South African facilities, a possibility long sought after by the U.S. Navy.[127] In the light of the evolving Panama Canal crisis, the Diego Garcia facility attains greater importance in the overall U.S. naval strategy.

NOTES

1. U.S., Congress, House, Subcommittee on the Near East and South Asia, Committee on Foreign Affairs, Proposed Expansion of U.S. Military Facilities in the Indian Ocean, 93d Cong., 2d sess., 1974, p. 174.

2. "Sino-Indian Conflict Draws Navy Eye," Christian Science Monitor, December 22, 1962, p. 5.

3. "A Dangerous Shield," New Times (Moscow) no. 6 (February 13, 1963): 22. In December 1963, the Seventh Fleet visited the Indian Ocean. For former Indian Prime Minister Jawaharlal Nehru's response, see Chapter 9.

4. Congressional Record, Senator Strom Thurmond, speech, 94th Cong., 1st sess., November 6, 1975, 121:S19462.

5. Washington Post, August 29, 1964, pp. 1, 6.

6. Washington Post, August 30, 1964, p. 8.

7. Christian Science Monitor, April 22, 1965, p. 11.

8. Ibid.

9. Phillip Darby, British Defence Policy East of Suez 1947-1968 (London: Oxford University Press, 1973), p. 265.

10. Washington Post, November 7, 1964, p. 9.

11. U.S. Department of State, "Availability of Certain Indian Ocean Islands for Defense Purposes," Treaties and Other International Acts, Series 6196, 1967.

12. Ibid., paragraph 4.

13. U.S., Government Accounting Office, Financial and Legal Aspects of the Agreement on the Availability of Certain Indian Ocean Islands for Defense Purposes, Report of the Comptroller General of the United States, B-184915, 1976, p. 1.

14. Ibid., pp. 1-2.

15. Ibid., p. 2.

16. Ibid.

17. Ibid., p. 3.

18. Ibid., p. 4. The House Appropriations Committee and the Senate Foreign Relations Committee were the only recipients of 1969 State Department intimation of the matter in 1969. However, by then $9 million in surcharges had already been waived. See U.S., Congress, House, Committee on International Relations, Diego Garcia, 1975: The Debate Over the Base and the Island's Former Inhabitants, 94th Cong., 1st sess., 1975, p. 45.

19. U.S., Government Accounting Office, op. cit., p. 4.

20. Devendra Kaushik, The Indian Ocean: Towards a Peace Zone (Delhi: Vikas Publications, 1972), p. 17. See also "Diego Garcia, The Islanders Britain Sold," Sunday Times (London), September 21, 1975, pp. 10-11.

21. U.S., Government Accounting Office, op. cit., p. 4.

22. Interview with Barber.

23. Approximately 45,000 barrels. Ibid.

24. For the nature of the opposition of the ecologists and the naturalists, see "Letter from London," NATO'S Fifteen Nations 13, no. 1 (February-March 1968): 17. See also United Nations, General Assembly (A/C. 159/1), annex V, 1974, p. 2.

25. Kaushik, op. cit., p. 18.

26. Interview with Barber, op. cit. Faced with the cost analysis (which the services regarded as a can of worms) brought to the Pentagon by Robert McNamara, the three services tried to provide a joint front, and thus the navy did not feel it wise to approach the secretary of defense for necessary appropriations for an Indian Ocean construction when the air force itself preferred to have no part in the navy stipulated plan. The detestation for McNamara's cost-effectiveness approach and the use of the International Business Machine computers in the Pentagon was such that the insiders of the services used to define IBM as truly meaning "I, Bob McNamara."

27. New York Times, November 11, 1965, p. 8.

28. Ibid.

29. Ibid.

30. Ibid.

31. U.S., Congress, House, Proposed Expansion of U.S. Military Facilities in the Indian Ocean, op. cit., p. 83.

32. Ibid.

33. Ibid., p. 82.

34. Interview with Barber.

35. Ibid.

36. Ibid.

37. U.S., Congress, House, Proposed Expansion of U.S. Military Facilities in the Indian Ocean, op. cit., p. 175.

38. Ibid.

39. Ibid., p. 83.

40. Ibid.

41. Ibid.

42. Ibid.

43. U.S., Congress, Senate, Committee on Appropriations, Second Supplemental Appropriations for FY 1974: Hearing on H.R. 14013, 93d Cong., 2d sess., 1974, p. 2114.

44. Ibid.

45. Ibid.

46. Ibid.

47. Ibid.

48. Ibid.

49. Interview with Michael H. Van Dusen, Washington, D.C., August, 1974.

50. Melvin Laird, interview, "Press Conference, U.S.A." Voice of America, Washington, D.C., August 11, 1971.

51. Hanson Baldwin, "The I.O. Contest. Part 2. Staking Their Claims," New York Times, March 21, 1972, p. 41.

52. U.S., Department of State, "Naval Communications Facility on Diego Garcia," Treaties and Other International Acts, Series 7481, (1972).

53. U.S., Department of State, Series 6196, op. cit. Paragraph (2)(b) of the December 30, 1966 agreement says that "Before either Government proceeds to construct or install any facility in the Territory, both Governments shall first approve in principle the requirement for that facility, and the appropriate administrative authorities of the two Governments shall reach mutually satisfactory arrangements concerning specific areas and technical requirements for respective defense purposes."

54. U.S., Department of State, Series 7481, op. cit., p. 2.

55. U.S., Congress, House, Subcommittee on the Near East and South Asia, Committee on Foreign Affairs, U.S. Interests and Policies Towards South Asia, 93d Cong., 1st sess., 1973, p. 105.

56. Lee Hamilton, "The Persian Gulf and the Indian Ocean," Congressional Record, 92d Cong., 2d sess., January 18, 1972, vol. 118: E36-37.

57. U.S., Department of State, "Deployment in Bahrain of the United States Middle East Force," Treaties and Other International Acts, Series 7263, 1972, p. 1.

58. New York Times, June 18, 1973, p. 3.

59. Ibid.

60. Ibid.

61. U.S., Congress, House, Committee on Armed Services, Full Committee Consideration of H.R. 12565, 93d Cong., 2d sess., March 18, 1974, p. 107.

62. Ibid.

63. Ibid.

64. U.S., Congress, Senate, Committee on Foreign Relations, Briefings on Diego Garcia and Patrol Frigate, 93d Cong., 2d sess., 1974, p. 2.

65. Ibid.

66. U.S., Congress, Senate, Briefings on Diego Garcia, op. cit., testimony of Admiral Elmo Zumwalt, p. 2.

67. Ibid., p. 3; U.S., Congress, House, Proposed Expansion of U.S. Military Facilities in the Indian Ocean, op. cit., p. 24.

68. U.S., Congress, House, Proposed Expansion of U.S. Military Facilities in the Indian Ocean, op. cit., p. 25.

69. U.S., Congress, Senate, Briefings on Diego Garcia, op. cit., p. 3.

70. Ibid., p. 23; U.S., Congress, House, Proposed Expansion of U.S. Military Facilities in the Indian Ocean, op. cit., p. 27.

71. See Military Procurement Supplemental FY 1974, on S.2999, 93d Cong., 2d sess., 1974, pp. 54-55. Some members of the Senate Armed Services Committee believed that the need for an expanded Diego Garcia facility was not so urgent as to be included in a supplemental.

72. U.S., Congress, Senate, Committee on Appropriations, Second Supplemental Appropriations for FY 1974, op. cit., p. 2115.

73. U.S., Congress, House, Proposed Expansion of U.S. Military Facilities in the Indian Ocean, op. cit., p. 54.

74. U.S., Congress, Senate, Committee on Armed Services, Selected Materials on Diego Garcia, 94th Cong., 1st sess., 1975, p. 3.

75. U.S., Congress, House, Committee of Conferences, Department of Defense Report No. 93-1064, 93d Cong., 2d sess., 1974, p. 9.

76. U.S., Congress, Senate, Committee on Armed Services, Military Construction Authorization, FY 1975, Senate Report 93-1136 accompanying H.R. 16136, 93d Cong., 2d sess., 1974, p. 7.

77. Ibid.

78. U.S., Statute, Military Construction Authorization Act, 1975 (Public Law 93-552), H.R. 16136, 93d Cong., 2d sess., December 27, 1974, pp. 22-23.

79. Ibid.

80. U.S., Congress, House, Committee on Armed Services, Message from the President of the United States, House Document No. 94-140, 94th Cong., 1st sess., May 12, 1975.

81. U.S., Congress, Senate, Senate Resolution 160, Congressional Record, 94th Cong., 1st sess., May 19, 1975, pp. S8651-652.

82. U.S., Congress, Senate, Committee on Armed Services, Disapproving Construction Projects on the Island of Diego Garcia, Report No. 94-00 to accompany S.R. 160, 94th Cong., 1st sess., 1975, p. 2.

83. Congressional Record, 94th Cong., 1st sess., November 6, 1975, vol. 121:S19465.

84. Ibid.

85. "Background to Indian Ocean Report," office of Senator John Culver release, April 21, 1976, release time 11 A.M. CST.

86. U.S., Congress, House, Committee of Conference, Military Construction Appropriations for FY 1976, Conference Report No. 94-655 to accompany H.R. 10029, 94th Cong., 1st sess., 1975, p. 7.

87. Ibid.

88. For the 1972 agreement, see U.S., Department of State, Series 7481, op. cit.

89. Note No. DPP 063/530/2, Foreign and Commonwealth Office, London, paragraph 1(a).

90. Ibid., paragraph 2.

91. U.S., Department of State, Report on Indian Ocean Arms Limitations, letter to Congress, office of Senator John Culver release, April 21, 1976, release time 11 A.M. CST.

92. Ibid.

93. Ibid.

94. U.S., Congress, House, Proposed Extension of U.S. Military Facilities in the Indian Ocean, op. cit., pp. 174-75.

95. Ibid.

96. U.S., Congress House, Full Committee Consideration of H.R. 12565, op. cit., testimony of Thomas H. Moorer, p. 10.

97. U.S., Congress, House, Military Authorizations, FY 1975, op. cit., testimony of Admiral C. D. Grojean, p. 563.

98. Ibid., p. 32.

99. U.S., Congress, House, Department of Defense Supplemental Authorization for Appropriations for FY 1974, Report No. 93-934, 93d Cong., 2d sess., 1974, p. 12.

100. Ibid., p. 15.

101. U.S., Congress, Senate, Disapprove Construction Projects on the Island of Diego Garcia, op. cit., p. 20.

102. Cited in Jonas L. Blank, "The Impact of Logistics Upon Strategy," Air University Review 24 (March-April, 1973): 10.

103. Fabian Publications, Fabian Colonial Bureau, Strategic Colonies and Their Future: The Problems of Hong Kong, Gibralter, Malta and Cyprus, Research Series no. 100 (London: Fabian, 1945), p. 4.

104. U.S., Congress, Senate, Briefings on Diego Garcia, op. cit., p. 25.

105. Ibid.

106. Ibid.

107. U.S., Congress, Senate, Selected Materials, op. cit., p. 40.

108. U.S., Congress, Senate, Briefings on Diego Garcia, op. cit., p. 7.

109. U.S., Congress, Senate, Selected Materials, op. cit., p. 41.

110. Ibid.

111. There has been a series of statements and articles discussed about the possible military action against a continued oil embargo against the Western industrial society. For statements by President Ford: exclusive interview, U.S. News and World Report, November 25, 1974, p. 24; exclusive interview, Time, January 20, 1975, p. 21; presidential news conference, January 21, 1975, cited in Department of State Bulletin, February 10, 1975, pp. 179-80; interview with NBC television and radio, January 23, 1975, cited in Department of State Bulletin, February 17, 1975, p. 220.

Secretary of State Kissinger's statements: exclusive interview with Newsweek, December 18, 1974, cited in Department of State Bulletin, January 20, 1975, pp. 61-62; exclusive interview with Business Week, December 23, 1974, cited in Department of State Bulletin, January 27, 1975, p. 101; press conference January 10, 1975, cited in State Department News Release, January 10, 1975, p. 6; interview for "Bill Moyer's Journal," January 15, 1975, cited in Department of State Bulletin, February 10, 1975, pp. 172-73; press conference, January 28, 1975, cited in State Department News Release, January 28, 1975, pp. 2-3.

Secretary of Defense Schlesinger's statements: television interview by Hugh Sidey, "Washington Straight Talk," January 7, 1974, cited in The Agency Library, USIA, August 1974, p. 35; news conference at the Pentagon, January 14, 1974, cited in Defense Department Press Release, January 14, 1974, pp. 2, 7-8, 9, 11; exclusive interview, U.S. News and World Report, May 26, 1975, pp. 38-39.

For articles in periodicals and so on: Robert W. Tucker, "Oil: The Issue of American Intervention," Commentary, January 1975, pp. 21-31; Ignotus Miles, "Seizing Arab Oil," Harpers, March 1975, pp. 45-62; Earl C. Ravenal, "The Oil-Grab Scenario," New Republic, January 18, 1975, pp. 14-16; I. F. Stone, "War for Oil?" New York Review, February 6, 1975, pp. 7-8, 10; William Fullbright, "1980 Middle East Scenario," Washington Star-News, July 13, 1975, pp. E-1, E-4.

For congressional interest: Oil Fields as Military Objectives. A Feasibility Study, CRS Study, for Special Subcommittee on Investigations, Committee on International Relations, House of Representatives. 94th Cong., 1st sess., 1975; Data and Analysis Concerning the Possibility of a U.S. Food Embargo as a Response to the Present Arab Oil Boycott, CRS Study, for the Committee on Foreign Affairs, House of Representatives, 93d Cong., 1st sess., 1973.

112. U.S., Congress, House, Military Construction Authorization, FY 1975, testimony of Grojean, op. cit., p. 561.

113. U.S., Congress, House, Full Committee Consideration of H.R. 12565, op. cit., testimony of Thomas H. Moorer, p. 34.

114. U.S., Congress, Senate, Disapprove Construction Projects on the Island of Diego Garcia, op. cit., p. 22.

115. U.S., Congress, Military Construction Authorization, FY 1975, testimony of Grojean, op. cit., p. 571.

116. Ibid., p. 567.

117. U.S., Congress, House, Full Committee Consideration of H.R. 12565, op. cit., p. 54.

118. Ibid., p. 32.

119. United Nations, General Assembly, Ad Hoc Committee on the Indian Ocean, Declaration of the Indian Ocean as a Zone of Peace, Report of the Secretary-General Pursuant to Paragraphs 6 and 7 of General Assembly Resolution 3080 (XXVIII) (A/AC. 159/1), p. 12.

120. Ibid.

121. U.S., Congress, House, Full Committee Consideration of H.R. 12565, op. cit., p. 104.

122. U.S., Congress, Senate, Military Procurement Supplemental, FY 1974, op. cit., p. 49.

123. United Nations, op. cit., p. 12.

124. Ibid.

125. U.S., Congress, Senate, Briefings, Zumwalt testimony, op. cit., p. 37.

126. U.S., Congress, House, Proposed Expansion of U.S. Military Facilities in the Indian Ocean, op. cit., p. 55.

127. President Ford clearly held out such possibility: If we could get Diego Garcia, which is in the middle of the Indian Ocean, . . . then we could take a look at these South African bases. . . . "Interview of the President, April 30, 1976, Dallas, Tex.

6

THE U.S. CONGRESS AND U.S. STRATEGY

American naval presence in the Indian Ocean is not, after all, to prepare for war. It is to emphasize our commitment to peaceful use of international waters by all nations.

> Senator Strom Thurmond speaking against Senate Resolution 160 disapproving Diego Garcia expansion, U.S., Congress, Senate, Congressional Record, 94th Cong., 1st sess., July 28, 1975, S13948.

The fact of the matter is, the U.S. Government is not interested in negotiations on the Indian Ocean. The fact of the matter is that the Pentagon, once again, is the driving force in American foreign policy in the post-Vietnam period.

> Senator John Culver, U.S., Congress, Senate, Congressional Record, 94th Cong., 1st sess., July 28, 1975, S13948.

The U.S. Congress sought to play an active role in the formulation of U.S. strategy in the Indian Ocean. There seemed to have been a general consensus in Congress that the area around the periphery was of modest strategic importance to the United States and that the general low level presence of the post-World War II years was sufficient.

When the navy asked for $26 million for an "austere naval base" under the classified proposal for a "Project Rest Stop" in the 1970 military construction requests, the Senate Appropriations Committee felt compelled to oppose any U.S. buildup and commitment to yet another ocean. The Military Construction Subcommittee and the full Military Appropriations Committee of the Senate deleted the request completely, although in the conference with the House, an oral agreement was reached to let the navy request a modified version for a communications station under the 1971 military authorization requests. [1]

The mood of Congress was evident from the fact that in spite of the attempts of the CNO, Admiral Thomas Moorer, to have the funds made available, the House-Senate Conference Committee refused to endorse any buildup effort in the ocean. Moorer, in his letter to John Stennis, chairman of the Senate Armed Services Committee, and in a memorandum to committee members, termed the deletion of the funds as leading to an "adverse strategic effect of major strategic importance," but the congressional leaders thought otherwise. [2] The navy bowed to the congressional advice and came back subsequently with the request for a limited communications proposal as a future replacement for the Asmara facility in Eritrea, Ethiopia.

The White House and the Department of State seemed to share the congressional belief that no naval expansion was necessary for the security interests of the United States in and around the ocean. [3] In a House hearing held during the middle of 1971 to discuss the political and strategic developments in the Indian Ocean area, there was general agreement that substantial augmentation of the U.S. naval presence in the waters was "premature and impractical." [4] The proposal for the communications station on the Diego Garcia atoll was supported as "an appropriate extension of the U.S. presence" in the area, but a greater emphasis was given to "diplomatic finesse rather than military power in dealing with the problems of the Indian Ocean area." [5] The administration itself constantly reassured Congress that there would be nothing more than a communications facility at the strategically located atoll of the Chagos Archipelago. As late as 1973, James Noyes of the Defense Department reiterated before Congress that "there were no plans to transform Diego Garcia into a base facility 'from which forces could be projected, or that would provide a location for basing of ships and aircraft.'"

In the light of these assurances, a subsequent administration request for an expanded facility at Diego Garcia took some members of Congress by surprise. Thus, when in early February 1974, Marshall Wright, the assistant secretary for congressional relations

(Department of State), wrote a few members of Congress about the administration's intention to expand the existing Diego Garcia communications station into a permanent base support facility, Congress felt impelled to hold extensive hearings to examine the efficacy of the request.[7] When the Defense Supplemental Bill of 1974 carried the request for the expansion authorization, Congress was anxious to know what new circumstances had emerged in the interim few months to warrant the request.[8]

As evident in Wright's letter, and from the various testimonies of administration witnesses, certain post-Yom Kippur War of 1973 developments were seen as factors necessitating an increased presence in the Indian Ocean.[9] The need to deter a Soviet buildup and possible threat to the vital oil and sea routes through a regular and augmented U.S. deployment was seen as requiring the logistics support that an expanded base at Diego Garcia could offer. The Department of Defense announced its desire to deploy a carrier task force into the ocean intermittently, and expansion was to provide support for a 30-day additional presence in the waters.

Although from the narrow perspective of logistics the expansion of the facility at Diego Garcia was seen as sensible for the regular deployment of the carrier task forces, Congress was not unanimous in agreeing about the need for the expansion.

The congressional reluctance to support the administration's request for the expansion was based on various reasons. Many members of Congress did not share the apocalyptic view about Soviet activities in the Indian Ocean. In its effort to justify the proposed expansion at Diego Garcia, the U.S. Navy apparently relied on the usual game called "the Russians are coming."[10] Admiral Zumwalt, for example, warned that the Soviet "tentacles are going out like an octopus into the Indian Ocean."[11] The Soviet moves in the Indian Ocean were portrayed as part of an overall Russian quest for increasing strategic mobility that could be used by Moscow to extend its political influence.[12]

The portrayal of the Soviet threat in the Indian Ocean was also seen as another indication of the U.S. Navy's belief that congressional appropriations for it would increase directly, if not geometrically, to the Soviet threat; thus, the more alarming the threat, the better the prospects for the navy.[13] The navy seemed to have accepted the official self-denigration process as an imperative for dealing with the congressional appropriations process.[14] As George Kennan, former U.S. ambassador to Moscow recently put it, a measure of exaggeration has become part of American reference to the greatly increased military strength, particularly naval and amphibious strength, of the Soviet Union.[15]

Senator Stennis found the trend of alarmist charges and speculation about the weaknesses of the U.S. Navy in comparison with the
Soviet counterpart as too disturbing, and branded the arguments as
false.[16] Refusing to believe in the myth of a "second-class U.S.
Navy," the chairman of the Senate Armed Services Committee
charged that "those who are overzealous or overconcerned or have
something to sell have oversold" the strength of the Soviets.[17] The
Soviet Union, in the face of its potential opponents, stands in a significantly disadvantageous position. In his annual report, Defense
Secretary James Schlesinger admitted that the naval forces of the
Soviet Union and its allies are not generally superior to those of the
United States and its allies, and that this should be perceived by
well-informed observers.[18]

The ascription of the "equipose" of the U.S. Navy with the
Soviet navy is already seen as affecting U.S. interests in terms of
third-party perception. In this context, the tendency for the concerned officials to characterize the Soviet presence in the Indian
Ocean as already far superior to that of the United States, and that
without the Diego Garcia base expansion the U.S. Navy would be
definitely in the weaker stance as compared to the Soviets, might
already have taken its toll in terms of perception of some of the
littoral countries of the region. The preoccupation with the Russian
buildup in the Indian Ocean, signified by the often-quoted "the Russians are coming," is already seen as paying dividends to the Soviets—if unbalancing an adversary is the goal of gunboat diplomacy.[19]

The extent of the Soviet naval buildup in the Indian Ocean, as
presented by the Defense Department officials, was questioned by
congressional members. The most commonly used indicator of the
respective presence in the waters is "ship-days," which is found
to be the lease accurate means of measurement of naval strength.
Ship-day totals are simply procured by multiplying the number of
ships in the waters by the number of days they spend in the area.
Thus, the ship-days will equate for its purpose an aircraft carrier
with a small destroyer by ignoring the actual nature of the ships,
their combat capabilities, and the level of sophistication available.[20]
As Soviet naval units are smaller, they generally provide for apparent increased weight in terms of ship-days as an indication of their
general capability in a given ocean.

The Soviet inability to establish a chain of shore-based logistics
and general-purpose support facilities also forces it to send large
numbers of support vessels to accompany its naval units. The result
has been the usual pattern of self-sufficient flotillas in forward
deployment, which, in terms of numbers and consequently in terms
of ship-days, automatically appears impressive. Thus, the number

of vessels and the duration of their stay in the Indian Ocean waters
show a tremendously impressive, albeit misleading, picture. As
Table 6.1 shows, in terms of ship-days, the United States stands
a distant second to the Soviets.

Witnesses for the navy significantly failed to provide any comparative data of Soviet and U.S. port calls to the Indian Ocean littoral
countries. In-port days, or the days and time spent by naval units
in any port of a littoral country, are often suggested as better indicators of naval power and influence in a given area.[21] Such in-port
days provide impressive visibility through direct contact with, and
presence in, the littoral ports, and the latter takes the former into
account in any foreign policy and strategic configuration.

Port calls consolidate ties between the littoral country and the
visiting power, and offer great opportunities to enhance the visiting
power's influence through the exploitation of politicomilitary and
sociopsychological events.

As Table 6.2 shows, the United States makes more port calls
and acquires greater visibility than its Soviet counterpart in spite of
the larger number of Soviet naval units in the area. The U.S. units,
although smaller in number, are, however, much more impressive.
No Soviet naval unit can provide a presence that could rival the U.S.
carrier task forces that have regularly visited the Indian Ocean in
the post-October (1973) Mideast War.[22]

U.S. access to littoral countries' ports and facilities is
accepted as greater than that of the USSR. In the light of the recent
changes in the Australian and New Zealand policies of allowing
nuclear-weapons-carrying naval units to make port calls, the U.S.
Navy gains further advantage.* Certain ports are not visited by the
United States of its own will, as it finds the entry rules and regula-
tions encumbrances. For example, the United States does not use
Indian ports because India requires all ships entering a port to
declare whether or not they have nuclear weapons on board.[23]

Deadweight tonnage is often used as an index for respective
sealift capabilities.[24] Although data on the tonnage of the respective navies in the Indian Ocean are not known precisely, it is believed
that the Soviets do not enjoy any advantage over the United States.[25]
Measurement of tonnage fails to reflect the combat and mission
capability of a navy, since smaller and lighter naval units with opti-

---

*The new Liberal-Country party government in Australia has
removed the restrictions that the outgoing Labour government had
placed on nuclear-weapons-carrying naval units' access to the
Australian ports. The Liberal government of New Zealand also
followed suit and removed similar restrictions that were placed by
the late Norman Kirk Labour government.

TABLE 6.1

U.S.-USSR Indian Ocean Ship-Days per Year,
1968-75

Year	USSR*	U.S.
1968	1,760	1,788
1969	4,066	1,315
1970	4,936	1,246
1971	4,023	1,337
1972	8,854	1,448
1973	8,895	2,154
1974	10,501	2,619
1975	7,171	1,921
1976	7,300	1,750

*The Soviet ship-days include special operations (such as the port-clearing operations in Bangladesh, which were in thousands).

Source: U.S., Department of Defense, Office of the Country Director for the Persian Gulf and Indian Ocean.

TABLE 6.2

Comparison of Port Calls to the Indian Ocean Littorals by
U.S. and USSR Navies, 1969-76

Year	U.S.	USSR
1969	152	11
1970	135	18
1971	177	18
1972	161	35
1973	154	100
1974	118	206
1975	108	113
1976	132	n.a.

Sources: 1969-73: Department of Defense, cited in U.S. Congress, House, Committee on Armed Services, Military Construction Authorization FY 1975, 93d Cong., 2d sess., 1974, p. 511. 1974 (USSR): Department of Defense, cited in U.S., Congress, House, Committee on International Relations, Diego Garcia, 1975: The Debate Over the Base and the Island's Former Inhabitants, 94 Cong., 1st sess., 1975, p. 24. 1975 (USSR): Department of Defense, Office of the Country Director for the Persian Gulf and Indian Ocean. 1974-76 (U.S.): Ibid.

mum flexibility can provide greater muscle to a navy than heavier
ships. Tonnage, by itself, also fails to measure the effectiveness
of the available units for different missions. [26] In the same light,
mere increase in terms of tonnage may not convey the enormous
versatility that augmentation with carrier task forces provides.

The force characteristics of U.S. and Soviet naval presence
in the Indian Ocean also signify the general inferiority of the Soviet
naval capability as compared to that of the United States. The Soviet
armadas are essentially less impressive and have less reach than
the U.S. carrier task forces, which have been regularly deployed in
the Indian Ocean waters since the Mideast War of 1973. [27]

The force characteristics—size, composition, and reach—are,
in fact, one of the most important indicators of naval strength, and
the United States maintains its superiority in overall naval might.

In terms of naval forces, the USSR does not have any advantage
over the United States. In the category of naval force, surface ships,
major combatants, auxiliaries, and the associated air supports, the
Soviet limitations in the ocean are apparent. [28] Particularly, the
lag in the capability for air support considerably handicaps the Russian navy in making any determined move in the region.

The Soviet staying power in the Indian Ocean is considerably
less than the overall U.S. staying power. The United States excels
in providing underway replenishment, while the Soviets are still on
the lookout for ways and means to achieve similar flexibility. The
Soviets, in the absence of units for underway replenishment, depend
on extensive moorings and buoys, which are generally placed in and
around waters off the Chagos Archipelago—Mauritius, Somalia, and
the Malagasy Republic. [29] However, Soviet efforts to acquire an
afloat-support capability have as yet to go a long way before Moscow
can relieve itself of the dependence on overseas facilities. [30] The
present disparity between the two navies' extended deployment (at
distant waters) capabilities is revealing, as indicated in Table 6.3.

The Soviet inability to provide underway replenishment leads
Moscow to rely more on base facilities in a given ocean. The Soviet
navy has diligently searched for secure access to the littoral coun-
tires' ports and facilities. The U.S. Defense Department provides
a picture of Soviet bases and facilities in the ocean that is generally
accepted as exaggerated. Retired Admiral Zumwalt, for example,
asserted that the Soviet infrastructure in the Indian Ocean is the
most impressive—"far, far superior to that of the United States."[31]
He even characterized the Soviet position as astride the "central
part of the West's energy jugular down to the Persian Gulf."[32]

In congressional hearings, witnesses from the Defense Department, especially from the Department of the Navy, have alleged to
a chain of Soviet bases in the Indian Ocean. Such allegations of

TABLE 6.3

Comparison of U.S. and USSR Extended Distant
Naval Deployment Capability

Units	U.S.	USSR
Aircraft carriers	13 (2n[a])	1/2 Building[b]
	2 Building (n)	2 Helicopter
	6 Reserve	carriers
	1 Training	
Underway replenishment ships	49	26
	2 Building	
	14 Reserve	
Fleet support ships	78	5
	8 Building	
	19 Reserve	
Sealift ships	28	64
	13 Reserve	

[a]n = nuclear.

[b]40,000-ton displacement.

Source: Jane's Fighting Ships, 1976-1977 (New York: Franklin Watts, 1976), pp. 522-24, 684-85.

Soviet bases in various countries in the region persisted, although it was admitted that "the Russian do not have bases per se."[33] The Soviet Navy was said to have three well-developed bases at Umm Qasr (Iraq), Aden (South Yemen), and Berbera (Somalia). Some witnesses, in fact, had suggested the existence of Soviet special rights and facilities in various other countries—India, Sri Lanka, Mauritius, and Bangladesh—which made the Soviet navy predominant in the Indian Ocean.[34]

During the course of a press conference (August 28, 1974), President Ford said, "The Soviet Union already has three major naval operating bases in the Indian Ocean." The Defense Department identified the three bases as Berbera, Umm Qasr, and Aden.[35] The three countries, however, strongly denied the accusation that they had any Soviet bases. The Soviet Union itself called the Ford allegation a regrettable error.[36]

Congressional skepticism of the Department of Defense's projection of Soviet capability in the Indian Ocean was reinforced by the testimony of the head of the Central Intelligence Agency, William

Colby. Testifying before the Subcommittee on Military Construction
of the Senate Armed Services Committee, Colby denied that the
Soviet Union had any major operating base in the ocean. He characterized the Soviet buildup in the ocean as limited, and branded the
allegation of Soviet major operating facilities in these littorals as
inaccurate. [37]

Recent Soviet activities in Berbera, Somalia, attracted wide
attention, and Congress was persuaded to agree with the Department
of Defense's contention that Berbera had become an important Soviet
facility in the Indian Ocean. The Department of Defense apprised
Congress of the developments in Berbera, and Defense Secretary
James Schlesinger even called the Berbera expansion a process of
"establishing a significant new facility capable of supporting Soviet
naval and air activities in the northwest Indian Ocean."[38] The
defense secretary identified the types of construction at Berbera as
port facility, housing facilities, communications facility, POL storage expansion, new airfield construction, and construction on the missile storage and handling capability that is just about operational. [39]
Schlesinger also produced photographs taken earlier (latter part of
April 1975) by reconnaissance planes and termed the facility as "far
larger than the facility intended at Diego Garcia" in terms of manpower and in "terms of certain types of facilities."[40]

The Somalian government vigorously denied the allegation and,
through its ambassador in Washington, Abdullahi A. Addou,
invited members from the Armed Services Committee of both houses
of Congress to visit Somalia and see for themselves the inaccuracy
of the charge. [41] The invitation was accepted and a Senate and House
delegation visited Somalia during the first week of July 1975. [42]
Senator Dewey F. Bartlett, the only senator to have visited Berbera,
publicly confirmed the Schlesinger allegation of a "significant" new
Soviet air-cum-naval facility in Somalia. [43] Bartlett's congressional
counterparts agreed with the senator that the Berbera construction
represented "a very significant enhancement of Soviet capabilities
to operate in the Indian Ocean."[44] The professional members accompanying Bartlett also stated that the facility at Berbera would be a
strategic plus factor to the Soviet navy in the Indian Ocean. [45] In the
light of these "confirmed" developments, the need for an expanded
U.S. facility at Diego Garcia acquired new urgency.

With the reopening of the Suez Canal, it was thought that the
Soviet navy would quickly enhance its capability for rapid Indian
Ocean deployment. [46] This, in turn, would add urgency to U.S.
expansion of its Indian Ocean facilities. As Map 6.1 shows, the
reopening of the Suez Canal has substantially affected the fleet
mobility augmentation distances, particularly of the Soviet Baltic
Sea and Black Sea fleets. All naval units of the Soviet navy can

MAP 6.1

Comparison of U.S. and USSR Fleet Mobility Augmentation Distances with and without the Suez Canal

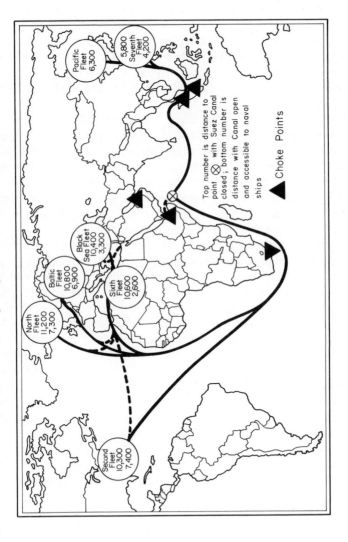

*Note: Top number is distance to point "X" with Suez Canal closed; bottom number is distance with Canal open and accessible to naval ships.

Source: U.S., Congress, House, Subcommittee on the Near East and South Asia, Committee on Foreign Affairs, Proposed Expansion of U.S. Military Facilities in the Indian Ocean, 93d Cong., 2d sess., 1974, p. 42.

traverse the canal, while U.S. aircraft carriers, one of the major
factors of U.S. naval prowess, cannot use the canal because of their
length and topside overhangs.

However, the advantages of the Soviet navy are more than met
by the advantages that the U.S. Navy enjoys from the reopened canal.
Although the Soviet home fleets are closer to the Indian Ocean with
a working canal, the fact is that the canal, if used, could shorten
the augmentation distances for both navies[47] (see Table 6.4). The
U.S. carriers cannot traverse the canal, but the U.S. helicopter
carriers can use the canal easily, and the navy has seven such
carriers as compared to two in the Soviet navy.* Moreover,
transiting the canal during a crisis is risky since the canal can be
closed easily. In the event of such a closure, the Soviet naval units
can be trapped in the canal.

Lack of flexibility in the European theater also stands in the
way of maximum Soviet utilization of the reopened canal for Indian
Ocean augmentation. Because of the higher priority that the Soviet
navy ascribes to the Mediterranean and its need to maintain a strategic reserve in the Black Sea, the Soviet navy will continue to rely on
its Pacific Fleet for Indian Ocean deployments.[48] A reordering of
Soviet priorities to make the reopened canal more valuable in the
context of its Indian Ocean presence seems remote.[49]

The Soviet presence in the Indian Ocean is not overwhelming.
The combined Western presence in the ocean far surpasses that of
the USSR.[50] The Western access to the littoral ports and facilities,
as has been indicated earlier, clearly disproves the alarming notion
of a Soviet headway in the Indian Ocean infrastructure. As the list
of the major facilities of the two superpowers and those of the United
Kingdom, France, and China indicates, the Soviet navy still remains
a distant second in the necessary wherewithal for any upsetting of
the "military equilibrium," as U.S. naval officials often hyperbolize.
Port visits by U.S. civilians and combatants during the last three
years, as Tables 6.5 and 6.6 indicate, dispel any notion that the
Russians have acquired considerable headway in the region at the
expense of the United States. A substantial increase in the Soviet
naval presence in the Indian Ocean could probably be expected only
if the United States builds up its Indian Ocean strength substantially.[51]
In this context, the expanded Diego Garcia facility might defeat its
purpose.

---

*The two Moskva-class Soviet helicopter carriers have a dis-
placement capability of 15,000 tons each. The U.S. helicopter
carriers (LPH Iwo Jima class), on the other hand, displace 17,500
tons each. While the USSR tonnage equals 30,000, the U.S. combined
tonnage is 122,500.

TABLE 6.4

Comparative Steaming Times
for USSR and U.S. Fleets
(in days)

To the Persian Gulf[a]	
USSR	
From the Mediterranean anchorages	9
From Sevastapool	11
From Vladivostok	17
U.S. (approximately)	
From the Sixth Fleet (Mediterranean)	
(through the Suez with no carriers)	7.5
From the Seventh Fleet[b]	6
To the Red Sea	
USSR	
From Sevastapool	8
From Vladivostok	17
U.S. (approximately)	
From the Sixth Fleet	6.5
From the Seventh Fleet	7.5
To Diego Garcia	
USSR	
From Sevastapool	13
From Vladivostok	14
U.S. (approximately)	
From the Sixth Fleet	11
From the Seventh Fleet	6

[a]The high overall average speed is taken as 16 knots, and one steaming day is taken as lost while transiting the Suez Canal. The U.S. carriers are too big to pass through the canal.

[b]The carrier task force at full speed can cover 600 nautical miles a day.

Sources: For USSR: U.S., Congress, Senate, Committee on Armed Services, Military Construction Authorization, FY 1975, 93d Cong., 2d sess., 1974, p. 167. For U.S.: U.S., Congress, House, Subcommittee on the Near East and South Asia, Committee on Foreign Affairs, Proposed Expansion of U.S. Military Facilities in the Indian Ocean, 93d Cong., 2d sess., 1974, p. 42.

TABLE 6.5

Port Visits by U.S. Civilian Flag Vessels
in the Indian Ocean,
1973 to June 15, 1975

Country	Port
Bahrain	Sitra Island, Minasulman
Bangladesh	Chalna, Chittagong
Diego Garcia	Diego Garcia
United Arab Republic	Port Suez
Afars and Issas	Dijibouti
Ethiopia	Assab, Massawa
India	Bombay, Calcutta, Cochin, Kandla, Madras, Mangalore, Quilon, Visakhaptham
Iran	Bandar Abbas, Bandar Mahshar Banda Shapurr, Kharg Island
Jordan	Aqaba
Kuwait	Nina Al Ahmadi, Kuwait, Menasaud, Shuaiba
Kenya	Mombasa
Mozambique	Lorenço Marques, Mozambique Port, Nacala, Beira
Pakistan	Karachi
Malagasy Republic	Tamatave
Qatar	Ummsaid, Halul Island
Reunion Island	Reunion
Sri Lanka	Colombo, Tricomalee
Saudi Arabia	Dammam, Jiddah, Ras Tanura
South Africa	Durban, East London, Port Elizabeth
Sudan	Port Sudan
Tanzania	Dar es Salaam, Tanga
United Arab Emirates	Abu Dhabi, Dubai, Das Island, Jebel Dhanna
Yemen	Modeidah, Makha
South Yemen	Aden
Oman	Muscat, Quoin Island

Source: U.S., Congress, Senate, Committee on Armed Services, Disapprove Construction Projects on the Island of Diego Garcia, on S.R. 160, 94th Cong., 1st sess., 1975, p. 65.

TABLE 6.6

Port Calls by U.S. Combatants
in the Indian Ocean,
1973-75

Country	Port	1973	1974	1975
Afars and Issas	Dijibouti	X	X	X
Bahrain	Damman	X	X	X
	Bahrain	X	X	X
Diego Garcia	Diego Garcia	X	X	X
Ethiopia	Assab	X	X	X
	Massawa	X	X	X
Indonesia	Surabaya	X	X	—
Iran	Bandar Abbes	X	X	X
	Bandar Shapur	X	X	X
	Kharg Island	X	X	X
Kenya	Monbasa	X	X	X
Kuwait	Kuwait	X	X	—
Malagasy Republic	Diego Suarez	X	X	—
Maldives	Male	—	X	—
Mauritius	Port Louis	X	X	X
Mozambique	Lourenco Marques	X	X	—
Muscat/Oman	Khor Kuwai	X	X	X
Pakistan	Karachi	X	X	X
Reunion	Reunion	—	X	—
Saudi Arabia	Jidda	—	X	X
Seychelles	Victoria	X	X	X
Sri Lanka	Colombo	X	X	X
United Arab Emirates	Abu Dhabi	X	X	—
	Dubai	X	X	—
Egypt	Port of Suez	—	—	X
Yemen	Hodeida	—	—	X

Source: U.S., Congress, Senate, Committee on Armed Services, Disapprove Construction Projects on the Island of Diego Garcia, on S.R. 160, 94th Cong., 1st sess., 1975, p. 66.

POLITICAL AND DIPLOMATIC COSTS

One reason Congress objected to the expansion of the Diego Garcia facility was that such an expansion would be costly in political and diplomatic terms. Karl von Clausewitz observed long ago that military policy must at all times be completely subservient to political interests. The apprehension is that the United States has allowed military policy to acquire a life of its own, "without attempting to tie it very closely to political and economic interests."[52] The late senator Richard Russell spoke of the possible consequences of congressional laxity with the military: "If we make it easy for the military to go places and do things, we will always find them going places and doing things."[53]

Congressional reluctance was also influenced by the realization of the problems that an overseas base entails. Full-time occupation of an overseas base generally proves to be provocative, and the United States already had many bases overseas.[54] Diego Garcia was seen as another small seed that, in time, would become too big, causing complications and troubles to the United States.

The Executive branch agreed with Congress that the nature of the challenges in the Indian Ocean required a political rather than a military response. A political and diplomatic initiative was thus favored in the region. One of the administration's witnesses pointed out that while "military instruments can contribute to political solutions; they cannot serve as solutions in any of themselves."[55] Although it was admitted that a military presence can support effective diplomacy without its ever having to be used, an overtly militaristic approach toward the Indian Ocean region was seen as unnecessary and costly. The area's sensitivity to external military presence was seen as dangerous to long-term U.S. interests and influence in the region. Indeed, the repercussions of the external powers' thrust for solutions of Asian problems often generate only more dissension and trouble.[56]

Thus, in the initial stages, many Americans, while welcoming a communications station at Diego Garcia, thought it inappropriate and inopportune to construct a major base facility there. They regarded an Indian Ocean fleet or substantial augmentation of naval forces in the waters as premature and impractical. Emphasis was placed on the need for Washington to rely more on diplomacy than on military visibility in its dealings with the prospective problems in the area. Viewing strategy in its broader connotation as something much more than the science of military command, Congress emphasized the need for politicodiplomatic means to secure and enhance U.S. influence in the Indian Ocean region.

The administration, however, advocated an expansion of the communications facility into a logistics base and secured belated congressional approval for the same. The United States thus became the first country to start strategic base building in the Indian Ocean. The administration's refusal to adhere to the wishes and the desires of the Indian Ocean littoral countries for keeping the ocean as a "zone of peace," as expressed in repeatedly endorsed UN resolutions to that effect, was seen by some congressional leaders as detrimental to long-term U.S. interests by contributing to the intensification of the big-power arms rivalry that the littoral countries hoped to avoid. The U.S. action was seen as disturbing the peace and the possibility for a rivalry-free Indian Ocean order. The American insistence on matching the so-called asymmetrical Soviet position in the waters by building strategic bases was seen as a flat rejection of the wishes and aspirations of the littoral countries to keep the ocean free of the vagaries of external power politics.

Chester Bowles, former United States ambassador to India, states that much of the trouble for the United States in Asia is the result of American inability and unwillingness to adjust its views to the changing Afro-Asian scene.[57] In his view, Diego Garcia symbolizes a new example of unprovoked U.S. interference in Asia, for Diego Garcia is not a minor upgrading of a remote military base for passive purposes, but "a new incursion by America into waters it does not need and cannot protect."[58] The implied intention of the base as a deterrent to the Soviets was also seen as foolhardy and a laughable gesture.[59] Bowles, with his experience in Asia, could forewarn that past experience should dissuade the United States from demonstrating its continued "interest in Asia by setting up shop on Asian turf."

The administration's request for funds for the permanent support facility at the strategically located atoll effectively changed the earlier low profile of the United States in the ocean. Some of the members of Congress thought that the change was unnecessary, and one representative even remarked that, in the light of Vietnam, only those who liked Vietnam would love Diego Garcia.[60] U.S. insistence on using the concepts of vacuum and balance of power, which the littoral countries rejected as no longer applicable to the area, was also seen as part of the continued U.S. display of the great powers' sense of omnipotence and grandiosity. In fact, the emphasis on the effective naval presence even at high political and diplomatic costs is interpreted by some as not beneficial to the long-term interests of the United States.[61] Rather, political and diplomatic initiatives would have helped to enhance and preserve U.S. interests and influence in the ocean.

The administration viewed the littoral opposition to U.S. plans for the expansion of the Diego Garcia facility into a logistics base as pro forma. [62] The political and diplomatic cost of ignoring the overwhelming littoral objection itself was portrayed as minimal. It was pointed out that only one factor, U.S. national interests, ought to determine the course of U.S. action. The littoral concerns and wishes had nothing to contribute to the trend of U.S. thinking. Admiral Grojean observed: "If the United States finds it essential to move into the Indian Ocean out of its national interest then it will."[63]

The administration also believed that the real views of the greater number of the littoral countries were in reality at variance with their stated views against the proposed expansion. The public views of support of the UN-sponsored and -supported resolution for the Indian Ocean to be a zone of peace were portrayed as more for public consumption, while the private support for the U.S. proposals for expansion of its Indian Ocean presence was advanced as the real point of view. The apparent discrepancy between the stated public and private views of the littoral countries that belonged to the nonaligned bloc was characterized as the most prominent. [64]

In his testimony to the Senate Armed Services Committee, Schlesinger characterized the littoral opposition to the U.S. buildup in the waters by saying "talk is cheap."[65] He stated that many of the littoral countries hoped that the United States would not take their views seriously and would move into the ocean in great force, as such a U.S. presence would be helpful to their own stake in the area. Schlesinger branded the zone-of-peace resolution as nothing more than a showpiece for domestic and international political considerations. [66] The Department of State, in fact, expressed surprise at the mildness of the protests from the littoral countries against the proposed expansion of the Diego Garcia facility. [67]

In spite of the public opposition from all the littoral countries (see Table 6.7), the administration maintained that, in fact, in private many a country encouraged the United States to move into the ocean. [68] Indeed, in Executive sessions, administration officials observed that the only opposition to the "Diego Garcia buildup was coming from some 'nuts' in India and some ultra-leftists in America who were trying to 'gut' American national defense."[69]

The administration justified the expanded base facility for foreign policy and diplomatic reasons. When confronted by Senator John Culver about the immense political and diplomatic costs of the expansion in the face of the opposition of the littoral countries, George Vest, director of the Bureau of Politico-Military Affairs, Department of State, said that specific policy reasons of the freedom of the seas and the need to maintain the balance of power justified U.S. State Department's support to the Defense Department's plans

TABLE 6.7

Responses of 31 Littoral Countries to the Proposed
Expansion of the U.S. Facility in Diego Garcia
(percent of total number of countries)

	Official			Press/Public		
	1973	1974	1975	1973	1974	1975
Favorable	23	10	—	10	—	—
Unfavorable	23	29	35	29	39	42
Balanced	13	3	13	26	16	10
No reaction	38	52	10	32	42	6
None known	3	6	42	3	3	42

Source: Department of Defense and Department of State survey, cited in U.S., Congress, House, Subcommittee on the Near East and South Asia, Committee on Foreign Affairs, Proposed Expansion of U.S. Military Facilities in the Indian Ocean, 93d Cong., 2d sess., 1974, p. 45; U.S. Congress, Senate, Armed Services Committee, Military Procurement Supplemental, FY 1974, 94th Cong., 1st sess., 1975, pp. 50-51; U.S., Congress, Senate, Committee on Armed Services, Selected Materials on Diego Garcia, 94th Cong., 1st sess., 1975, p. 11.

for expansion.[70] Vest also refuted the charge that State Department support was another case of U.S. militarized foreign policy—the tail wagging the dog.[71] Schlesinger also observed that specific foreign policy issues strongly argued in favor of the Diego Garcia expansion.[72]

U.S. justification of the base expansion, even in the face of the strong opposition from all the littoral countries, may prove to be shortsighted. Because of a narrow view of security that does not take into account the aspirations of the littoral states, this view is seen as ultimately running the risk of defeating the aims pursued by the traditional strategists of the great powers.[73] The Department of Defense seems to identify with an earlier observation that the smaller countries may complain publicly about gunboat diplomacy, but privately there is a good deal of satisfaction that more than one country's gunboats are around.[74]

CONGRESSIONAL APPREHENSION OF AN ARMS RACE

The opposition in Congress to the Diego Garcia expansion proposal was the result of the apprehension that an arms race would

ensue in yet another ocean. The Indian Ocean had remained among
the very few areas without a big-power arms rivalry. Concern
among the opponents of the Diego Garcia expansion centered around
the fear that a U.S.-led arms buildup would automatically result in
a Soviet response, thus causing a costly arms rivalry in the area.
The concerned members of the Senate tried to halt the expansion of
the Diego Garcia facility through the Mansfield Amendment (Senate
Resolution 160). The resolution represented a widely held feeling
against a step that was seen as a sure contributor toward the unwanted
arms rivalry.

Senate Majority Leader Mike Mansfield was visibly emotional
in warning against the unnecessary escalation in yet another area of
the world. The senior senator from Montana branded the joint
navy and air force request for the $17.1 million (navy, $14 million
and Air Force, $3.1 million) as only a down payment for a much
bigger Indian Ocean base in the future. The senator felt compelled
to warn against the dangers of another Vietnam in the making. He
likened the initial authorization for the Diego Garcia expansion to
another Gulf of Tonkin resolution. [75] He asked Congress to be cir-
cumspect in allowing an enlargement of the existing facility at the
Diego Garcia atoll. He wondered about the wisdom of allowing a
naval buildup in another volatile area of Asia when even the wounds
of Vietnam were still raw. [76]

Originally, congressional leaders supported the communications station on Diego Garcia as an alternative to the station in Eritrea,
Ethiopia. The communications station at Asmara, Eritrea, Ethiopia,
was viewed as dangerous in the light of the developments in the area;
and many a senator, in fact, applauded the navy's move to shift the
facility into the British-owned atoll in the ocean. [77] The Kagnew
station was seen as costly as well as dangerous. U.S. support to
the 40,000-man Ethiopian army as a price for the Kagnew facility
had cost Washington over $160 million over the past decade. [78]
The Senate found the proposal for the communications station at
Diego Garcia both timely and cost effective, as it would permit the
withdrawal of U.S. personnel from a potentially dangerous area
(Ethiopia) and would also save certain costs. [79]

Senator Claiborne Pell warned Congress not to provide the
Soviet military with a reason for escalation and expansion in the
Indian Ocean. U.S. plans for the Diego Garcia expansion were seen
as exactly such a dangerous reason for a prospective Soviet expansion. [80] Senator Pell observed further that the lessons from the Cold
War ought to have made it clear than an arms race was an exercise
in futility. The expansion of the Diego Garcia atoll was also seen as
totally in opposition to the Nixon doctrine; in fact, with its emphasis
on confrontation before negotiation, the expansion proposal was seen
as turning the Nixon doctrine 180 degrees. [81]

Congressional concern that the proposed Diego Garcia expansion would cause an action-reaction cycle was also shared by William Colby. Colby observed that whenever the United States increased its naval strength in the ocean, the Soviet Union followed suit. He also believed that the pace of the Soviet buildup in the Indian Ocean would squarely depend on U.S. moves: if the United States pressed forward with an expansion of its presence in the waters, then the Soviets would be compelled to respond accordingly. [82]

Some administration officials and a considerable segment of Congress, however, refused to believe the argument that the expansion would lead to a Soviet response and finally an arms race in the ocean. An Arms Control and Disarmament Agency's witness before a House hearing on the issue thus disassociated the $30 million Diego Garcia expansion from any repercussions leading to an arms race. He asserted that the Diego Garcia expansion would not have any "significant impact for or against arms control" because the question of arms control between the United States and the Soviet Union "depends on a great many other factors—the size of the forces, the threat which might be thought to pose to each other, and also our global relationships with them."[83]

President Ford observed that the expansion would in no way effect an arms race in the Indian Ocean. In his letter to Congress, in pursuance of his certification of the Diego Garcia expansion, the president observed that the growth of the Soviet naval presence in the Indian Ocean "can most convincingly be ascribed to the pursuit of their own national interests—including the continuing expansion of the Soviet Navy in a global 'blue water' role—rather than to U.S. force presence as such."[84]

The majority of the members of the Senate Armed Services Committee also believed that the expansion of Diego Garcia would not in any way lead to an arms race in the area. They observed that the proposed expansion would only enhance U.S. capability for deployment of naval units. [85] Drawing on past experiences, the members observed that Soviet expansion in the ocean would proceed regardless of U.S. restraint. [86]

The basic premise of some of the administration's officials, as well as that of some members of Congress, was that with a long association in the ocean the United States could not be accused of leading an arms race in the area. With an association with the ocean as a visible entity for over 25 years, the United States refused to be branded as any "Johnny-come-lately" and be ascribed the responsibility of leading an arms race in the area. [87]

An expanded Diego Garcia facility was, in fact, portrayed as a possible "trump card" in any future arms limitation talks with the Soviets. [88] According to Owen Zurhellen, the expanded facility would positively contribute toward the preservation of the East-West balance of power and would, in turn, contribute toward the arms control efforts.[89] Senator Bartlett represented the views of many of his colleagues when he said that with the expanded Diego Garcia facility a balance would be attained with the Soviets in the Indian Ocean area and such a situation alone could provide the essential atmosphere for arms talks.[90] The Diego Garcia base was seen as an essential factor in providing the atmosphere of equilibrium necessary for such arms talks.

The reluctance of the United States to enter into arms limitation talks with the Soviet Union until the base was fully expanded was based on the apprehension that, without a base facility in the ocean, the United States would stop the buildup with the Soviets occupying a better position. Admiral Grojean observed that the Soviets would be predominant in the Indian Ocean in the event of a U.S. decision to forego the base expansion.[91] In the absence of the expanded facility, the limitations on the U.S. efforts to project its political, economic, and military presence would be telling and would prove to be costly for Washington.[92] A naval presence in peacetime is essential to protect and support U.S. national interests in the region. The Russian offer for arms limitation talks on the Indian Ocean issue was itself suspected as being motivated by a Soviet desire for an interim peace. That desire was seen as one of expediency in the light of the remark by Lenin favoring the signing of the Brest-Litovsk Treaty, where he observed that "history has taught us that peace is an interval of war, and war is the means to achieve a better peace."[93]

Part of the Western reaction to possible Soviet intentions in the Indian Ocean presence was influenced also by the changes in the Soviet strategic concepts and policies. The Brezhnev-Kosygin rejection of the Khruschev revision of the accepted Russian strategic thinking about war has greatly affected the West's perception of Moscow's strategic priorities. The original strategic precept of Moscow was that of von Clausewitz, as endorsed by Lenin, which said that war was a continuation of politics (policy) by other (violent) means.

Soviet theory had adhered to the principle until the realization of the dangers of the nuclear war forced Khrushchev to modify it.[94] Beset by the problem of acknowledging the dangers in admitting or pursuing a strategic nuclear policy for political gain and influence, Khrushchev came to admit the "general and mutually distructive nature" of nuclear war.[95] However, in the post-Khrushchev era, the emphasis was seen as based on the assumption that the Soviets would not only be able to survive a nuclear war but would also win such a war. In that context, the Soviet desire to exploit nuclear parity for political advantage even at high risks is often accepted as a plausible phenomenon.

Thus, a Soviet buildup in the Indian Ocean was seen as part of the present Soviet effort to deploy military power for political gain. Such efforts for enhanced influence and leverage in the area were viewed as costly to Western societies. A corresponding U.S. buildup became a must for the preservation of Western interests.

The doubts about the sincerity of Soviet desires in regard to the Indian Ocean arms talks was heightened by the purported lukewarm response to Washington queries in the aftermath of the Brezhnev announcement expressing the necessity of such a reduction. [96] The Department of State therefore told Congress that the possibility of arms talks to cover the Indian Ocean would take place only when the Soviet Union showed an equal interest. [97]

Some congressional leaders, however, saw a deliberate attempt on the part of the administration not to pursue any fruitful talks for an Indian Ocean arms reduction. Even by its own account, the administration admitted that it had not initiated any discourse with the Soviets for that purpose. [98] The only attempt on record was the casual perusal of the matter in the aftermath of the Brezhnev speech indicating the Soviet desire for such naval arms reduction talks. The administration's attempt to stonewall all pleas from Congress for such arms reduction talks led many to believe that the United States would never sit down with the Soviets to pursue the possibility.

The U.S. Navy's opposition to any meaningful naval arms talks with the Soviets is often ascribed as the reason for the administration's lukewarmness. [99] The navy has always desired to be dominant in each ocean for the creation of a Mare Americanum per Mundum. [100] The navy's shifting rationales for an expanded Indian Ocean presence betray the true motives that have guided its outlook toward the Indian Ocean. At first, when the Soviets were not a naval power with any "blue water" capability, a base at Diego Garcia was wanted as a means "to fill the vacuum created by the waning British presence."[101] Admiral John S. McCain talked of four-ocean navies and openly advocated an Indian Ocean fleet with full-fledged bases in the ocean. He believed that the Indian Ocean would be the future testing ground of the U.S. resolve to keep secure its access to the scarce raw materials and sea-lanes of the region. [102] The location of Diego Garcia, a "pinprick in the middle—in the precise middle of the Indian Ocean," suited the U.S. Navy best for controlling all access points to the ocean from both the Pacific and the Atlantic as well as from the Mediterranean through the Suez. [103] He believed that, based on the strategically located atoll, the U.S. Navy would be able to project its panoply throughout the entire area. [104] Admiral Arleigh Burke, who was instrumental in providing the idea of the British Indian Ocean Territory to British authorities, also believed that an Indian Ocean presence with all its armor would be essential for the United States. [105]

When the Suez Canal was closed during the 1967 Arab-Israeli War, the advocates for a U.S. naval presence in the Indian Ocean used the closure for their case. They advocated that an American presence in the Indian Ocean became essential because the ocean was less accessible to U.S. forces.[106] In the light of the decade-old navy desire to be in the Indian Ocean, the often-used rationales—the Soviet buildup, the threat to oil and the sea-lanes, the opening of the Suez Canal offering additional advantages to the Soviet navy, the necessity of a staging post to enable overflight to a beleagured Israel—appear (to the opponents of the Diego Garcia plans) as nothing more than parts of the shifting rationales that the navy has used to secure its goal.

In the process of persuading Congress for the necessary author- izations for the Diego Garcia expansion, the navy built up frightening scenarios. Admiral Elmo Zumwalt, for example, in line with the domino theory of the Vietnam context, warned Congress that in the absence of a viable U. S. naval presence, the Soviets would be able to "Finlandize" the greater part of the Afro-Asian littoral nations.[107] In projecting such a picture, the admiral conveniently forgot that the United States made more port calls than the Soviets or that the number of U.S. combatant units was higher than that of the Soviets.[108] If one takes into account the French and the British, the combined Western presence and position in the Indian Ocean easily over- shadows that of the Soviets. The Diego Garcia expansion is not related to any tactical requirement, since the United States enjoys tactical superiority in the ocean even without such a base.[109]

The removal of the indigenous population from Diego Garcia is also cited as an indication of the long-term plans for the base by the U.S. Navy. Depopulation was undertaken to make the atoll ideal for a strategic base warranting maximum security.

Congressional concern about the base expansion proposal was deeply associated with the apprehension that the navy would use the expansion as the first installment of an eventual Indian Ocean fleet. The navy's desire for an independent Indian Ocean fleet and for a carrier force of 15 ships is long standing. The concept of the Indian Ocean fleet was openly sounded after the Sino-Indian War of 1962.[110] The first visit of a U.S. carrier into the waters took place in December 1963.[111]

Government officials, particularly those from the Department of the Navy, ensured Congress that there would be no request for a carrier force to cover the additional responsibility of an Indian Ocean presence. It was said that the Indian Ocean deployment would be taken from the Pacific and that the existing 12-carrier force would remain adequate.[112] However, any possibility of diverting a sizable portion of the Pacific-based Seventh Fleet for the Indian

Ocean duty seems remote, because such a diversion would affect
the navy's main mission in the Pacific. [113] The desire to provide a
carrier presence in the Indian Ocean without serious dislocations
in other deployments could be ensured only with additional units.
To maintain a continuous Indian Ocean deployment, the navy would
have to add three more carriers to its fleets, for three carriers
are needed in the inventory to maintain one on such distant waters.[114]

Such an addition would also require adjustments in the accompanying escort vessels, support ships, and air supports, which
would involve substantial additional costs. By a conservative estimate,
the full cost of the additional naval units would be between $5 and $8
billion. [115] The addition of these units to the navy would raise the
overall operating cost by about $800 million. [116]

The possibility of an Indian Ocean Fleet with independent carriers for continuous deployment in these waters was even acknowledged by Admiral Zumwalt. The admiral openly admitted that since
the Pacific Fleet would not be able to cover exigencies in the Indian
Ocean without causing "a dangerous vacuum in U.S. presence throughout the Western Pacific region" in the event of an extended crisis
in the Indian Ocean, the United States would have little option but to
spend considerable sums in providing a matching presence. [117]

The logic of an expanded Indian Ocean presence in the form of
an Indian Ocean fleet or a continued presence of carriers would
essentially lead to further expansion of the Diego Garcia facility.
Diego Garcia, by the navy's account, remains an "austere logistics
facility."[118] To transform it into a strategic base, the navy would
require $10.1 million to upgrade the airstrip to accommodate per-
manent deployment of B-52s. [119] In the existing locale, there would
be no permanent air presence on the facility. The air force authorization is expected to be spent only for contingency-related requirements: tankers supplying in-flight refueling; staging point for supply
missions to Israel, Iran, and so on; and tactical deployments, such
as fighters and reconnaissance. [120] However, in the event of an
exigency requiring added U.S. augmentation, the forewarning that the
United States might become a hostage of Diego Garcia, "a cause for
greater expenditures, and the enlargement of a commitment in another part of the world going in direct violation of the excellent Nixon
Doctrine" may come true. [121] Admiral Zumwalt might have reflected
the truer pattern of things to come when he asserted that "a permanent presence is mandatory" in the Indian Ocean. [122]

The congressional concern about an arms race in the Indian
Ocean led to various attempts to impress upon the administration
the need for approaching Moscow for mutual restraints. It was
believed that an approach to Moscow, which has occasionally expressed
support for an arms limitation in the Indian Ocean, could lead

to the prevention of costly, and dangerous, developments in the area. The need for such an approach also would express U.S. responsiveness at least to one aspect of the littoral wishes and desires that the ocean be spared the pitfalls of a big-power rivalry.

As early as March 19, 1974, Senator Edward Kennedy introduced Senate Concurrent Resolution 76, expressing the desire of Congress that the administration seek negotiations with the Soviet Union to avoid a competitive naval arms race in the Indian Ocean. The repeated refusal of the administration to proceed toward the stated congressional desire for the arms reductions led Kennedy to introduce Senate Resolution 117 to persuade the Executive branch to start talks on a bilateral or a multilateral level. [123] Kennedy referred to the Military Construction Appropriation Act of 1974 that embodied the provision that the president evaluate all the military and foreign policy implications of the proposed expansion of the Diego Garcia facility (Section 613, Public Law 93-352) and observed that the time was ripe for an attempt at an arms reduction in the Indian Ocean. [124]

The Kennedy-Pell-Javits resolution became an amendment to the Economic Foreign Assistance Bill for fiscal 1976. However, the House did not carry a similar amendment. When the bill arrived before the House and the Senate Conference Committee, the amendment was dropped inasmuch as a presidential certification under Section 613, Public Law 93-352, had already been made. [125]

After their trip to Moscow for the U.S.-USSR Parliamentary Conference, Senators John Culver, Gary Hart, and Patrick Leahy wrote to Secretary of State Henry Kissinger asking that the State Department pursue the possibility of an Indian Ocean naval arms talk with Moscow more vigorously. [126] The senators expressed their belief that Moscow would respond favorably to such an attempt for an Indian Ocean naval arms limitation agreement. Robert McCloskey, the assistant secretary of state for congressional relations, replying on Kissinger's behalf, maintained that after the Soviet lukewarmness to an earlier U.S. query on the same subject, the department had been persuaded not to pursue naval arms limitation talks (NALT) until sometime in the future. [127] McCloskey, however, maintained that after the construction of the Diego Garcia logistics facility, the possibility of negotiations for such an arms limitation in the ocean would increase. [128]

Opponents of the U.S. buildup in the Indian Ocean tried to underscore the importance that they attached to the arms control talks through an amendment to the 1976 Appropriations Bill that carried the second installment of the Diego Garcia expansion authorization. Senator Culver, the crusading spirit behind the pro-NALT congressional group, proposed the amendment to give the Executive branch another opportunity to negotiate the arms restraint that Congress hoped for.[129] The amendment read: "Sec. 112. None of the funds appropriated in this Act may be used prior to July 1, 1976, for the purpose of carrying out any military construction project on the island of Diego Garcia."

The administration reported that the State Department was ready to talk to the Soviets about the mutual limitation of the super-power presence in the Indian Ocean after the Senate voted to fund the Diego Garcia expansion.[130] It was, in fact, reported that "consultations on how best to approach the Russians are now going on in the department and National Security Council in the belief that the subject is bound to be raised repeatedly in the next six months in Congress and by U.S. allies."[131] It was, however, revealed that the Soviets had shown coolness to the prospect of the arms reduction talks, as they were on the verge of enlarging their own presence in the ocean. The Soviet momentum for the Indian Ocean buildup, it was said, was deliberately kept slow with a view toward letting the U.S. Senate defeat the Diego Garcia expansion request, and that, with the failure of the Senate to do so, the Soviets saw no reason to slow the pace.[132]

However, the letter of Senators Culver, Hart, and Leahy to the Department of State (Kissinger) maintained that their inquiries in Moscow made them think that the Russians would be positive toward an arms talk plan.[133] The Department of State, in its reply to the senators' letter, stated clearly that the administration had not pursued the possibility for such talks at all.[134] In spite of the public feeling that such an attempt was being sought after, as newspaper articles lead one to think, in reality, the administration had not pursued the matter since 1971.[135] Congress required that the administration furnish a report of its attempts on that score before the deadline of April 15, 1976 (under Amendment No. 9, House Report No. 94-655).

A Soviet presence in the Indian Ocean area is essentially defense oriented. Moscow wants to ward off the advantages that the United States might gain from a Polaris-Poseidon deployment in the Indian Ocean. In that context, some authorities believe that "the initiative in renouncing a strategic role in the Indian Ocean should belong to the U.S.A."[136] The possibility for naval arms limitation talks in the Indian Ocean exists because, with the new generation of submarine launched ballistic missiles with incredible range, "a nuclear disengagement in the Indian Ocean would hardly be a great sacrifice" for either the United States or the USSR.[137]

A U.S. decision to ignore the possibility of such arms reduction talks would naturally lend strength to the Soviet military. Although a Soviet naval surge in the Indian Ocean may not be auto-

matic, as the Soviet navy has to convince a host of other services
before a favorable naval decision is taken, a Soviet response of
some kind can be safely expected. The congressional leaders, advocating arms reduction talks, had hoped to counteract the pressure
on the civilian leaders in the Kremlin by the Soviet military for an
arms buildup. As Senator Pell narrated the story, the Soviet leaders
were also concerned by the possible pressures for bigger defense
outlays and buildups that the military demanded in its desire to
match the U.S. military almost everywhere. [138]

The congressional expectation that the administration would
at least make an honest attempt to reduce the dangers of an unnecessary naval arms race through a mutual agreement with Moscow did
not materialize. The State Department, in its reaction to the congressional amendment, simply stated that

> although we might want to give further consideration to
> some arms limitation initiative at a later date and per-
> haps take up the matter with the Soviet government then,
> any such initiative would be inappropriate now. [139]

The possibility of any initiation of such naval arms limitation
talks looks dim for the present, since the administration openly
states that unless the Soviets cease their "unrestrained" behavior
in the African continent, there could be no such negotiations. [140]

The Indian Ocean has come to be closely associated with the
past and future events on the African mainland, and, with the developments in the region, there seems to be no reason for hope in the
immediate future. While the Soviets have reiterated their desire
for such talks on the basis of equal bargain, the United States has
made it clear that any naval arms limitation talks "might convey
the mistaken impression to the Soviets" as well as to "our friends
and allies" that the United States has acquiesced to the Soviet activities in Africa. [141] Since the Soviets insist on the rightness of their
actions in Angola and in the other parts of southern Africa, there
seems to be no viable hope that the superpowers will find a common
basis for such talks.

NOTES

1. U.S., Congress, Senate, Committee on Appropriations,
Second Supplemental Appropriations for FY 1974; Hearing on H.R.
14013, 93d Cong., 2d sess., 1974, pp. 2114-115.
    2. Ibid.

3. For testimonies, see U.S., Congress, House, Subcommittee on National Security Policy and Scientific Developments, Committee.on Foreign Affairs, The Indian Ocean: Political and Strategic Future, 92d Cong., 1st sess., 1971; see also U.S., Congress, House, Subcommittee on the Near East and South Asia, Committee on Foreign Affairs, Proposed Expansion of U.S. Military Facilities in the Indian Ocean, 93d Cong., 2d sess., 1974, testimony of Admiral Gene LaRocque, p. 7.

4. U.S., Congress, House, The Indian Ocean, op. cit., p. v.

5. Ibid.

6. Cited in Senator Claiborne Pell testimony, U.S., Congress Senate, Committee on Appropriations, Military Construction Appropriations FY 1975, 93d Cong., 2d sess., 1974, p. 415.

7. For text of the Wright letter, see U.S., Congress, House, Proposed Expansion of U.S. Military Facilities in the Indian Ocean, op. cit., pp. 167-68.

8. Ibid., p. v.

9. Ibid., pp. 167-68.

10. "The Indian Ocean: A New Naval Arms Race?" Defense Monitor 3, no. 4 (April 1974): 4.

11. Cited in Senator Claiborne Pell testimony, U.S. Congress, Senate, Committee on Armed Services, Military Procurement Supplemental FY 1974, 93d Cong., 2d sess., March 1974, p. 154.

12. U.S., Congress, House, Proposed Expansion of U.S. Military Facilities in the Indian Ocean, op. cit., testimony of James H. Noyes, p. 53.

13. David Holloway, "The Post-Vietnam Navy," Proceedings, p. 58.

14. Edward Luttwak, American Naval Power in the Mediterranean, Part I: The Political Application of Naval Force (Newport, R.I.: Naval War College, 1973), p. 47.

15. "Detente and Military Power," Defense Monitor 3, no. 10 (December 1974): 7.

16. Ibid.

17. Ibid. For a comparison of U.S. and USSR naval shipbuilding as indicative of the respective standings of the navies, see Jane's Fighting Ships, 1976-1977 (New York: Franklin Watts, 1976). See also U.S., Congress, Congressional Research Services, Comparison of U.S. and U.S.S.R. Naval Shipbuilding, March 5, 1976, by Alva M. Bowen.

18. U.S., Department of Defense, Annual Defense Department Report, FY 1976 and 1977, 1976, p. 1-21.

19. C. L. Sulzberger, "The Russians Are Coming," New York Times, May 5, 1971, p. 47.

20. U.S., Congress, House, Proposed Expansion of U.S. Military Facilities in the Indian Ocean, LaRocque testimony, op. cit., p. 105.

21. U.S., Congress, House, Subcommittee on the Near East and South Asia, Committee on Foreign Affairs, Means of Measuring Naval Power with Special Reference to U.S. and Soviet Activities in the Indian Ocean, CRS, 93d Cong., 2d sess., May 12, 1974, p. 4.

22. The deployments have been primarily from the Seventh Fleet units. For a sample of the task group composition, duration, and port calls, see U.S., Cong., House, Diego Garcia: The Debate Over the Base and the Island's Former Inhabitants, 94th Cong., 1st sess., 1975, p. 33.

23. U.S., Congress, House, Committee on Armed Services, Military Construction Authorization, FY 1975, 93d Cong., 2d sess., 1974, testimony of Rear Admiral C. D. Grojean, p. 566; see also U.S. Congress, Senate, Military Construction Appropriations, FY 1975, Pell testimony, op. cit., pp. 495-46.

24. U.S., Congress, House, Means of Measuring, op. cit., p. 3.

25. Ibid.

26. Ibid., pp. 3-4.

27. On December 1, 1973, Schlesinger announced that the United States would reestablish the pattern of regular visits disrupted by the Vietnam War, and he said that "we expect that our presence there will be more frequent and more regular than in the past." Cited in U.S., Congress, House, testimony of Seymour Weiss, Proposed Expansion of U.S. Military Facilities in the Indian Ocean, op. cit., p. 25.

28. See Jane's Fighting Ships, op. cit.

29. For the locations of U.S. and USSR major facilities in the Indian Ocean, see United Nations, General Assembly (A/C.159/1), Annex 1, 1974.

30. Michael MccGwire, "Current Soviet Warship Construction and Naval Weapons Development," in Soviet Naval Policy: Objectives and Constraints, ed. Michael MccGwire, Ken Booth, and John McDonnell (New York: Praeger, 1975), p. 444.

31. U.S., Congress, Senate, Military Construction Appropriations FY 1975, op. cit., p. 399.

32. U.S., Congress, Senate, Military Construction Authorization FY 1975, Pell testimony, op. cit., p. 416.

33. U.S., Congress, House, Proposed Expansion of U.S. Facilities in the Indian Ocean, LaRocque testimony, op. cit., p. 510.

34. U.S., Congress, Senate, Second Supplemental Appropriations for FY 1974, op. cit., testimony of Elmo Zumwalt, pp. 2118-

120. However, the list of the Soviet support facilities that the U.S. Navy submitted to the Subcommittee on Military Construction of the Senate Armed Services Committee provides a different picture. See U.S., Congress, Senate, Military Construction Authorization FY 1975, op. cit., p. 15.

35. U.S., Congress, House, Diego Garcia: The Debate, op. cit., p. 9.

36. Washington Star-News, September 1, 1974, p. B-1.

37. U.S., Congress, Senate, Military Construction Authorization, FY 1975, op. cit., testimony of William Colby, pp. 163-65.

38. U.S., Congress, Senate, Committee on Armed Services, Disapprove Construction Projects on the Island of Diego Garcia, S.R. 160, 94th Cong., 1st sess., 1975, p. 11.

39. Ibid., p. 13.

40. Ibid., p. 21. On May 4, 1976, former ambassador to Saudi Arabia, James E. Akins, testifying before the Senate Subcommittee on Multinationals, told the senators that during the same period, Saudi Arabia offered to pay for the necessary amount of aid for a Washington effort to reduce Soviet influence in Somalia. Akins told the Senate subcommittee that Saudi Arabia was prepared to offer the amount of economic aid that the Soviets were offering to Somalia, and also offered to pay for arms sales by Washington to Somalia in an effort to reduce Somali dependence on the Soviets. However, on the face of the Department of Defense's opposition, which was relying heavily on the alleged Soviet buildup in Berbera for the congressional passage of its Diego Garcia expansion plan, the Department of State did not respond to the Saudi offer. The administration's refusal to accept the Saudi offer was seen by many as indicating that it (the administration) was not serious in reducing Soviet inroads in the area, since such an attempt might make an expanded Diego Garcia facility look not absolutely essential. See Robert M. Smith, "Ex Envoy Charges U.S. Ignored an Offer on Soviet Somalia Role" and "Kissinger's View on Somalia Asked," New York Times, May 5, 1976, p. 3; May 6, 1976, p. 8.

41. See U.S., Congress, House, Armed Services Committee, House Report of the Special Subcommittee to Inspect Facilities at Berbera, Somalia, 94th Cong., 1st sess., 1975, p. 2; also Senate, Visit to the Democratic Republic of Somalia, July 14, 1975, Report by the Members of the Fact-Finding Team (Expert Report), 94th Cong., 1st sess., 1975, p. 4.

42. For respective viewpoints, see U.S., Congress, Senate, Armed Services Committee, Soviet Military Capability in Berbera, Somalia, report of Senator Dewey F. Bartlett, 94th Cong., 1st sess., July 1975, p. 2; U.S., Congress, Senate, Visit to Somalia, op. cit. Only Bartlett visited the alleged missile-handling and storage facility. However, his summation was based on the assumptions of the "expert"

supplied by the Department of Defense. Other reports accept the senator's summation as valid and accurate. See Congressional Record, July 28, 1975, Robert L. Legget speech, pp. H7654-655.

43. U.S., Congress, Senate, Soviet Military Capability, op. cit., p. 29.

44. U.S., Congress, House, House Report, op. cit., p. 9.

45. U.S., Congress, Senate, Visit to Somalia, op. cit.

46. See Marshall Wright's letter, U.S., Congress, House, Proposed Expansion of U.S. Facilities in the Indian Ocean, op. cit., p. 167. References to the reopened Suez Canal are numerous in Defense Department testimonies; see, U.S., Congress, House Proposed Expansion of U.S. Facilities in the Indian Ocean, op. cit.; U.S., Congress, Senate, Military Construction Authorization FY 1975, op. cit.; U.S., Congress, Senate, Military Construction Appropriations, FY 1975, op. cit. For a general discussion, see Arnold Hottinger, "The Reopening of the Suez Canal: The Race for Power in the Indian Ocean," The Round Table, no. 256, October 1974, pp. 393-402; and Shlomo Lonim, "Suez and the Soviets," U.S. Naval Institute Proceedings 101 (April 1975): 37-41.

47. U.S., Congress, House, Committee on Foreign Affairs, The United States Role in Opening the Suez Canal, 93d Cong., 2d sess., 1974.

48. U.S., Congress, Senate, Military Construction Authorization FY 1975, Colby testimony, op. cit., p. 165.

49. Ibid.

50. Congressional Record, speech by John Culver, 94th Cong., 1st sess., July 28, 1975, 121: S13936.

51. U.S., Congress, Senate, Military Construction Authorization FY 1975, Colby testimony, op. cit., p. 165.

52. U.S., Congress, House, Committee on Foreign Affairs, New Perspectives on the Persian Gulf, 93d Cong., 1st sess., 1973, p. 71.

53. Cited by Mike Mansfield, U.S., Congress, Senate, Military Construction Appropriations FY 1975, op. cit., pp. 360-61. Originally expressed by Russell in opposing the first deployment logistics. Lord Salisbury warned against the tendency of the military to expand military requirements: "if they were allowed full scope they would insist on the importance of the moon to protect us from Mars." Cited in Ken Booth, The Military Instrument in Soviet Foreign Policy 1917-1972 (London: Royal United Services Institute for Defence Studies, 1973), p. 62. President Dwight Eisenhower, in his farewell address on January 17, 1961, also warned the American people against the dangers of the military-industrial complex.

54. According to Pell, there were 1,800 U.S. bases overseas; 300 of them stationed more than 500 personnel (U.S., Congress,

Senate, Military Construction Appropriations FY 1975, Pell testimony, op. cit., p. 421). In the post-Vietnam years, the number has gone down, but, by Mansfield's account, some "25 percent of all U.S. military forces are still stationed on foreign soil." As he laments, "Not since the time of the Roman Empire have so many ventured so far from [home] in peacetime" (Congressional Record, July 28, 1975, op. cit., p. S13930).

55. U.S., Congress, House, New Perspectives on the Persian Gulf, op. cit., Noyes testimony, p. 38.

56. Norman Kirk, prime minister of New Zealand, "System for 'Security' or for Aggression and Expansion?" Peking Review, no. 52, December 28, 1973, p. 7.

57. U.S., Congress, House, The Indian Ocean, op. cit., testimony of Chester Bowles, p. 53.

58. New York Times, May 13, 1974, p. 31.

59. Bernard Weinraub, "The Value of Diego Garcia," New York Times, January 2, 1974, p. 5.

60. Congressional Record, July 28, 1975, Leggett speech, op. cit., p. H7656.

61. U.S., Congress, House, The Indian Ocean, op. cit., p. 10.

62. Warren Unna, "Kissinger Down South," New Republic, March 9, 1974.

63. U.S., Congress, House, Military Construction Authorization, FY 1975, Grojean testimony, op. cit., p. 565.

64. Ibid., p. 563.

65. U.S., Congress, Senate, Committee on Armed Services, Disapprove Construction Projects on the Island of Diego Garcia, on S.R. 160, testimony of James Schlesinger, 94th Cong., 1st sess., 1975, p. 53.

66. Ibid.

67. Interview with George Churchill, director, Office of International Security Operations, Department of State, March, 1976.

68. U.S., Congress, Senate, Disapprove Construction, Schlesinger testimony, op. cit., p. 53.

69. U.S., Congress, House, Committee on Armed Services, Full Committee Consideration of H.R. 12565, statement of Otis Pike, 93d Cong., 2d sess., March 18, 1974, p. 267.

70. U.S., Congress, Senate, Disapprove Construction, op. cit., p. 45.

71. Ibid. Senator Culver sarcastically observed, "We should give that Secretary of Defense Schlesinger double pay because he is doing two men's jobs. He is Secretary of Defense and of State." Congressional Record, July 28, 1975, op. cit., p. S13936.

72. U.S., Congress, Senate, Disapprove Construction, op. cit., p. 53.

73. Dieter Braun, "The Indian Ocean in Afro-Asian Perspective," The World Today 28 (June 1972): 249.

74. U.S. News and World Report, January 24, 1972, p. 34.

75. Congressional Record, May 19, 1975, pp. S8651-654. During the Senate debate on the Mansfield resolution to disapprove the construction of the Diego Garcia facility, the supporters of the resolution referred to the Gulf of Tonkin resolution repeatedly. They saw a parallel with the Tonkin resolution and warned their colleagues about the possible Vietnam-type consequences out of the Diego Garcia authorization. See Congressional Record, July 28, 1975, op. cit., pp. S13926-72.

76. U.S., Congress, Senate, Committee on Appropriations, Department of Defense Appropriations, FY 1972, Part 3, Navy, 92d Cong., 1st sess., pp. 28-32.

77. Ibid.

78. Ibid., p. 28.

79. U.S., Congress, Senate, Armed Services Committee, Military Construction Appropriations, H.R. 11418, 92d Cong., 1st sess., p. 225.

80. U.S., Congress, Senate, Military Construction Appropriations, FY 1975, op. cit., p. 414.

81. Ibid.

82. U.S., Congress, Senate, Military Construction Authorization, FY 1975, Colby testimony, op. cit., p. 165. Senator Stennis, chairman of the Senate Armed Services Committee, voiced similar concern: "If we are going to have a big buildup over there that would call for another fleet, a great augmentation, at least, of what we have, why couldn't that area by the subject of negotiations or agreements of some kind. I am sure that if we go to building, the Soviets are going to go to building" (ibid., p. 506). For similar opposition, see Barry M. Blechman, senior defense analyst, the Brookings Institution, "Establishing a Base on Diego Garcia," Washington Post, July 20, 1975, p. C-6.

83. U.S., Congress, House, Proposed Expansion of U.S. Military Facilities in the Indian Ocean, op. cit., testimony of J. Owen Zurhellen, Jr., p. 13.

84. "Justification for the Presidential Determination on the Construction of Limited Support Facilities on Diego Garcia," cited in U.S., Congress, Senate, Committee on Armed Services, Disapprove Construction Projects on the Island of Diego Garcia, 94th Cong., 1st sess., 1975, p. 8.

85. Ibid., p. 14.

86. Ibid.

87. U.S., Congress, House, Proposed Expansion of U.S. Military Facilities in the Indian Ocean, op. cit., pp. 11, 22.

88. Robert Manning, "Diego Garcia: The Pentagon's Trump Card," Far Eastern Economic Review, no. 7, 1975, pp. 27-29.

89. U.S., Congress, House, Proposed Expansion of U.S. Military Facilities in the Indian Ocean, op. cit., p. 18.

90. Congressional Record, 94th Cong., 1st sess., November 6, 1975, 121: S19457.

91. U.S., Congress, Senate, Military Construction Authorization, 1975, op. cit., p. 158.

92. Ibid.

93. Cited in David Holloway, "Strategic Concepts and Soviet Policy," Survival, November 1971, pp. 364-69.

94. Ibid.

95. Ibid.

96. Brezhnev's speech to his constituents in June 1971: "We have never regarded and do not regard as being ideal a state of affairs in which the navies of the great powers cruise for long periods miles and miles away from their shores. Indeed, we are prepared to tackle this problem but to tackle it on an equal basis," cited in G. Svyatov and A. Kokoshin, "Naval Power in the U.S. Strategic Plans," International Affairs (Moscow), no. 4, April 1973, p. 62.

97. U.S., Congress, Senate, Committee on Foreign Relations, U.S. Commitment to SEATO, 93d Cong., 2d sess., 1974, p. 8.

98. U.S., Congress, Senate, Disapprove Construction, op. cit., p. 39.

99. U.S., Congress, House, Proposed Expansion of U.S. Military Facilities in the Indian Ocean, op. cit., p. 180, Senator Culver agrees—see Congressional Record, July 28, 1975, op. cit., p. S13936.

100. U.S., Congress, Senate, Second Supplemental Appropriations FY 1974, op. cit., p. 2164.

101. Ibid., Pell testimony, p. 2163. Also interviews with Barber, McCain, Admiral Burke.

102. Interview with McCain.

103. Ibid.

104. Ibid.

105. Interview with Burke.

106. U.S., Congress, Senate, Second Supplemental Appropriations, FY 1974, Pell testimony, op. cit., p. 2163.

107. According to Zumwalt, the Soviets, with a series of exercises (military) both within their borders and with the fleet off Scandinavia, are trying "to provide a combination of power and at the same time policy inducements to move Finland from the status she has today to that of Latvia and to move, over time, Sweden into the status of Finland, and to move, over time, Norway into the status of a

Sweden" (U.S., Congress, Senate, Military Construction Appropriations, FY 1975, op. cit., p. 402). George Kennan, however, considers the Finlandization idea to be absurdly overdrawn and unsuitable. See George F. Kennan, "Europe's Problems, Europe's Choices," Foreign Policy, no. 14, Spring 1974, pp. 3-16.

108. U.S., Congress, Senate, Military Construction Appropriations, FY 1975, Pell testimony, op. cit., p. 417.

109. U.S., Congress, House, Committee on International Relations, Diego Garcia, 1975: The Debate Over the Base and the Island's Former Inhabitants, Culver testimony, 94th Cong., 1st sess., 1975, p. 39.

110. Christian Science Monitor, December 22, 1962, p. 5.

111. India (Republic), Parliament, Lok Sabha Debates, vol. 24, 1963.

112. U.S., Congress, Senate, Military Construction Appropriations, FY 1975, op. cit., p. 409.

113. Holloway, op. cit., p. 59.

114. Barry M. Blechman, The Control of Naval Armaments: Prospects and Possibilities (Washington, D.C.: Brookings Institution, 1975), p. 71.

115. Ibid. According to Rear Admiral (Ret.) LaRocque of the Center for Defense Information, Washington, D.C., the cost of keeping one carrier in the Indian Ocean would be $9 to $10 billion, since one new carrier with associated ships and aircraft costs about $3 billion in the current estimate. See his testimony, U.S., Congress, Senate, Military Construction Authorization, FY 1975, op. cit., p. 507.

116. The Control of Naval Armaments, op. cit., p. 71. The amount is based on the possible addition of three carriers, ten escorts, two support ships, and two air wings of eighty aircraft each to the fleet.

117. U.S., Congress, Senate, Military Construction Appropriations, FY 1975, op. cit., pp. 397-98.

118. U.S., Congress, Senate, Military Construction Authorization, FY 1975, op. cit., p. 154.

119. Ibid.

120. Ibid.

121. U.S., Congress, Senate, Second Supplemental, FY 1974, Pell testimony, op. cit., p. 2164.

122. U.S., Congress, House, Proposed Expansion of U.S. Military Facilities in the Indian Ocean, op. cit., p. 93.

123. Congressional Record, 94th Cong., 1st sess., March 22, 1975, 121:S4916-922.

124. Ibid., p. S4916.

125. U.S., Congress, House, Foreign Relations Authorization Act, FY 1976, Conference Report No. 94-660, to accompany S. 1517, 94th Cong., 1st sess., 1975, p. 32.

126. Congressional Record, 94th Cong., 1st sess., July 17, 1975, 121:S12855-56.

127. Ibid.

128. Ibid.

129. Congressional Record, 94th Cong., 1st sess., November 6, 1975, 121:S19451.

130. "U.S. Ponders Indian Ocean Superpower Limit," Christian Science Monitor, July 31, 1975, p. 15.

131. Ibid.

132. Ibid.

133. Congressional Record, July 17, 1975, op. cit.

134. Ibid.   Also interview with Churchill.

135. Ibid.

136. "World Armaments and Disarmament," SIPRI Handbook 1973, p. 395.

137. Ibid.

138. U.S., Congress, Senate, Military Construction Appropriations, FY 1975, op. cit., p. 414. Pell observed that Kosygin himself opened a discussion with him (Pell) and Senator Frank Church in Moscow with the remark: "What can I do to control my own military people in Moscow so they don't want to respond to yours?"

139. "Report on Indian Ocean Arms Limitation, April 15, 1976," Congressional Record, 94th Cong., 2d sess., May 6, 1976, 122:S6626.

140. Ibid.

141. Ibid.

CHAPTER

7

THE SOVIET RESPONSE

We have never thought and do not think now that it is an ideal situation when the navies of great powers are sailing for a long time at the other end of the world (Indian Ocean), away from their native coasts. We are ready to solve this problem but to <u>make an equal bargain</u>. [Emphasis added]

> Leonid Brezhnev, Election Eve Speech, June 11, 1971. Cited in Dusk Doder, "Brezhnev Asks Talk on Navies: Indian Ocean, Mediterranean Limits Urged," <u>Washington Post</u>, June 12, 1971, pp. 1, 14.

The Russian response toward U.S. strategy in the Indian Ocean is the result of various interests and factors—historic, economic, and strategic—that have influenced Soviet policies toward the same waters.

The historic desire for an outlet to the all-weather, warm-water ports of the Indian Ocean is characterized as one of the primary determinants of the Soviet outlook toward the ocean. The present interest in the Indian Ocean is partly "an extension of the old Czarist thrust for an outlet to the south, dating from the time of Peter the Great."[1] The czarist desire for an outlet to the warm waters of the Indian Ocean has evidently, though not surprisingly, survived the Bolshevik Revolution. Thus, in 1940, the Soviet desire for the warm waters to the south prominently featured in the Russo-German talks. Article 4 of the Secret Protocol of the talks clearly said that

"The Soviet Union declares that its territorial aspirations center south of the national territory of the Soviet Union in the direction of the Indian Ocean."[2] The pattern of recent Soviet activities in the Indian Ocean reflects the stated interests of the draft protocol.[3]

The Indian Ocean has come to figure prominently in Soviet economic calculations. The Soviet presence in the Indian Ocean is indicative of Russia's growing economic ties with the region. The commercial and trade relations with the Indian Ocean countries necessitate a show of Soviet presence in the waters, and, as Tables 7.1 and 7.2 show, Soviet aid to and trade with the area countries are increasing substantially. The Indian Ocean sea-lanes, that is, a secure and steady access to them, have become an important part of the Soviet Union's Indian Ocean configurations.

The Soviet merchant marine, one of the largest in the world, operates regularly in the Indian Ocean.[4] The Soviet emphasis on a global merchant marine commensurate with its size and position as a superpower is also motivated by economic factors. The availability of its own transport to carry on the increasing trade with the Indian Ocean area countries not only saves foreign exchange but also helps the Soviet Union in bargaining terms of sales and purchases from other maritime powers.[5] As the Soviet trade expanded in volume and in geographic extent, the Soviet merchant marine increased commensurately.

The Indian Ocean has also attained importance as the all-weather route for the Soviets between their eastern and western provinces.[6] With the intensification of Sino-Soviet rivalry, the necessity for a secure all-weather, ice-free, east-west route has become paramount. The Trans-Siberian Railroad is already overburdened, and Indian Ocean sea-lanes now provide the best alternative in connecting the Black Sea with Vladivostok. The sea route has been extensively used for shipment of "bulk goods and essentials."[7] As Siberia develops and traffic between the eastern and the western parts of the Soviet Union increases, the ice-free Indian Ocean route will attain even greater importance.

The extent of Soviet dependence on these sea-lanes is evident from the fact that hundreds of ships use these lanes every month carrying cargo, oil, and other essentials from one Soviet port to another.[8] In fact, it is being said that the southern sea-lanes have become Soviet lifelines, almost as vital as they are for Japan.[9] Izvestia also asserted that the Indian Ocean is the "natural way over which our ships can travel the year round between our western and eastern ports."[10]

The Indian Ocean, rich in food potential, particularly fish, attracts wide attention from the Russians. Moscow already catches a substantial amount of its fish from the ocean. The significance of

TABLE 7.1

Soviet Union Exports to and Imports from
Selected Indian Ocean Countries, 1972-73
(in millions of dollars)

Country	1972 Exports	1972 Imports	1973 Exports	1973 Imports
Afghanistan	46.1	37.3	45.5	46.4
Bangladesh	10.6	9.4	58.7	13.2
Burma	4.7	3.3	2.6	0.7
Egypt	322.0	299.6	374.2	356.3
Ethiopia	1.9	2.5	2.2	3.0
India	167.6	185.6	300.8	494.1
Indonesia	3.2	8.2	3.6	5.7
Iran	115.6	162.1	185.4	185.9
Iraq	109.0	74.5	191.0	257.3
Kenya	0.8	0.8	0.3	—
Kuwait	17.5	—	10.7	—
Malagasy Republic	—	1.4	—	0.4
Malaysia	1.2	70.7	1.2	130.5
Mauritius	NR	NR	NR	NR
Mozambique	NR	NR	NR	NR
Nepal	0.7	0.7	0.9	0.4
Pakistan	21.2	22.6	17.0	32.1
Saudi Arabia	5.4	—	3.9	—
Singapore	5.3	5.6	8.6	4.3
Somalia	14.2	3.5	15.5	1.5
South Yemen	7.9	Negligible	15.5	0.1
Sudan	20.7	1.3	3.4	—
Tanzania	0.7	1.0	0.8	3.4
Thailand	3.4	3.9	2.8	3.2

NR = not recorded.

Source: U.S., Department of State, Bureau of Intelligence
and Research, Communist States and Developing Countries: Aid
and Trade in 1974, Report no. 298, January 27, 1976, pp. 35, 87.

TABLE 7.2

Soviet Union Credit and Grants (Economic) and Military
Aid to Selected Indian Ocean Countries
(in millions of dollars)

Country	Economic (1954–74)	Military (1955–74)
Afghanistan	826	490
Bangladesh	241	35
Burma	16	n.a.
Egypt	n.a.	3,450
Ethiopia	103	n.a.
India	1,943	1,400
Indonesia	114	1,095
Iran	750	850
Iraq	549	1,600
Kenya	48	n.a.
Kuwait	n.a.	n.a.
Malagasy Republic	n.a.	n.a.
Malaysia	n.a.	n.a.
Mauritius	n.a.	n.a.
Mozambique	n.a.	n.a.
Nepal	20	n.a.
Pakistan	652	60
Saudi Arabia	n.a.	n.a.
Singapore	n.a.	n.a.
Somalia	90	115
South Yemen	15	80
Yemen (Sana)	98	80
Sudan	64	65
Tanzania	20	5
Thailand	n.a.	n.a.

Note: Only about 5 percent of total economic aid represents
grants. Data as available until the end of September 1975.

Source: U.S., Department of State, Bureau of Intelligence and
Research, Communist States and Developing Countries: Aid and Trade
in 1974, Report no. 298, January 27, 1976, pp. 21-23, 28-30.

this source of food can be gauged by the fact that 70 percent of Soviet protein requirement comes from fish. The Soviet fishing fleet, one of the most modern in the world, uses the ports and facilities of various Indian Ocean littoral countries with which Moscow has entered into fishing agreements. [11] Strategic considerations occupy a pivotal position in the Soviet response toward the U.S. Indian Ocean presence and policies.

The Indian Ocean has come to acquire greater strategic importance for the Soviets today. With the increasing use of missiles and nuclear warheads, the ocean (the strategically located and third largest body of water) has come to be viewed as a "vast launching pad for missile-firing submarines."[12] The submarine, a major technological creation and a major facet of modern sea power, has indeed made every ocean a deployment area and the waters have simply become a "continuum of threat." The third largest ocean forms the soft underbelly of the Soviets, and thus naturally figures centrally in its superpower strategic configurations.

Since the early 1960s, the Soviet Union has been attempting to respond to the U.S. submarine-based strategic offensive. By the late 1960s, the Soviets officially recognized the potency of the seaborne threat. The Soviet Defense Ministry publication History of Naval Art stated that, in line with the U.S. and NATO policies of according greater prominence to seaborne strategic forces, the Soviet navy would also opt for increased forward deployments. [13]

The Russians are aware of the fact that sea-based strategy offers the United States better advantages, as Moscow still lags behind in the race. The Indian Ocean, particularly the waters around the Persian Gulf, the Arabian Sea, and the Bay of Bengal, are soft spots so far as Soviet security is concerned. Although the Soviets initiated antisubmarine warfare, the American lead in underwater strategy kept Moscow off balance. With its major concentration on the military uses of the sea, the United States is well ahead of the Soviet Union in sea-based defense studies. The United States, for example, had "floating underwater nuclear bases" as early as the mid-1960s. [14] Russian concern about the U.S. strategic seaward headway was apparent from a Morskoi Sbornik warning that the "struggle with the main forces of the enemy fleet" has acquired an "immeasurably greater significance" with the U.S. move to make the world oceans into a "vast arena containing the launch points for highly mobile, secretive vehicles carrying strategic missiles."[15]

Introduction of the Polaris A-3 (successfully tested in October 1963) and later the Poseidon, with a range of 2,500 nautical miles, made the northern Indian Ocean, particularly the Arabian Sea, an extremely favorable area for such missiles. The vulnerability of Soviet cities considerably increased from such an Indian Ocean deployment. As Tables 7.3 and 7.4 show, the distances of six selected Soviet cities from hypothetical launch points make the Indian Ocean, particularly the northwest region of the Arabian Sea, as ideal as the Mediterranean for such deployment purposes. Polaris A-3 missiles can cover a target at a hypothetical distance of 1,000 miles inland, with a sea room of over 8,242,500 square miles.[16] Tridents I and II offer the United States far more flexibility, and consequently Soviet vulnerability increases in great proportion.

TABLE 7.3

Range of U.S. Strategic SLBMs
(in nautical miles with kilometer equivalence)

Name	Launch Platform (Tubes/Launchers)	Range, Nautical Miles (Km)	Year of Initial Deployment	Character
Polaris A-2	"Lafayette" (16) submarines	1,500 (2,775)	1962	Thermonuclear; being replaced by Poseidon
Polaris A-3	"Ethan Allen," "George Washington" submarines (16)	2,500 (4,652)	1964	Thermonuclear; MRV warhead
Poseidon C-3	"Lafayette" submarines (16)	approx. 2,500 (4,625)	1971	Thermonuclear; MIRV warhead
Trident (I) C-4	"Ohio" submarines (24)	approx. 4,000 (7,400)	1978 (expected)	Thermonuclear; MIRV and MARV warhead
Trident (II) D-5	Trident submarines (24)	approx. 6,000 (11,100)	1982 (expected)	Proposed

Source: Jane's Fighting Ships, 1976-77 (New York: Franklin Watts, 1976) pp. 522-38.

TABLE 7.4

Distances to Six Selected Soviet Cities from
Hypothetical Launching Points
(great circle distances)
(in nautical miles)

City	Mediterranean[a]	Atlantic[b]	Indian[c]
Kiev	890	1,780	1,960
Moscow	1,240	1,990	2,100
Odessa	660	1,820	1,830
Sverdlovsk	1,750	2,215	1,840
Tashkent	1,820	3,400	1,050
Volgograd	1,000	2,310	1,940

[a]Launch point at 35 °N, 30° E.

[b]Launch point at 45 °N, 15° W.

[c]Launch point at 25° N, 60° E

Sources: For missile deployment and ranges: U.S., Department
of Defense; for distances: The Great Circle Globe, U.S., Library of
Congress, Map Division, Alexandria, Va.

As the tables show, the new missiles, before the end of a decade,
could hit anything within a 6,000-miles radius. The plans to pin
Moscow through such deployments in the Indian Ocean were apparent
from various developments. A communications chain around the Indian
Ocean area was the visible indication of the American decision to deploy
such strategic submarines in the waters. The United States can also
steal the initiative from the Soviet Union by deploying the sea-based anti-
ballistic missile intercept system in the Indian Ocean to knock out Russian oncoming missiles as soon as they take off from the central Russian silos.

As early as 1963, U.S. intentions were made clear from the way
North West Cape, Australia, was chosen over the Marian Islands for
a very low frequency communications station. This communications
station is one of the most important links in the U.S. global defense
network. According to official brochures, the base, while serving
several purposes, will primarily work to maintain reliable communications with submarines of the U.S. fleet serving in "this area of

the world" (that is, the Indian and western Pacific Oceans) and, in particular, will "provide communication for the U.S. Navy's most powerful deterrent force—the nuclear powered ballistic missile submarine."[17]

The Soviets charged that the era of superpower confrontation in the ocean was introduced by the United States in building this station.[18] The New Times (Moscow) warned that the powerful transmitters installed at North West Cape "would enable U.S. submarines to dart to and fro in the Indian and Pacific Oceans to train their lethal Polaris missiles on diverse targets."[19] The addition of Kagnew Base in Asmara, Ethiopia, was taken as a definite indication of U.S. plans to deploy strategic submarines in the northern Indian Ocean area around the Persian Gulf, the Red Sea, and the Arabian Sea.[20]

The United States is said to have deployed Polaris A-3 submarines in the Indian Ocean in 1964. Although no official declaration of such deployment was ever made, it is currently accepted by U.S. officials without any denials. A House Committee on Armed Services report included a map of the world that showed that a part of the Indian Ocean was used by U.S. submarine launched ballistic missiles.[21] By the latter part of the 1960s, the main naval activity of the United States in the waters consisted of the movements of parts of the Polaris-Poseidon force in the Arabian Sea and the Bay of Bengal, controlled by the communications station at North West Cape, together with stations at Asmara, Ethiopia, and Peshawar, Pakistan.[22] Another observer also wrote that the United States directed its anti-Russian Indian Ocean nuclear submarine fleet from Exmouth, North West Cape.[23]

In fact, even if the United States has not deployed any strategic submarines in the northern Indian Ocean area, the nondeployment cannot be used as a relevant argument against Soviet concerns. The fact is that the northern part of the Indian Ocean is one of the best areas for U.S. strategic submarines. Moscow will naturally be concerned about any U.S. move in the waters and would accordingly respond to its capacity. The Soviet presence in the waters itself is seen as one of such responses to the Polaris presence in the area. The U.S. strategic deployments thus forced the Soviets to provide a presence in the waters as part of a way to deter an American attack from the Indian Ocean. A Soviet presence in the waters is seen only as defensive, as Moscow does not possess the capability to deploy strategic submarines carrying missiles that could reach any target in the United States.[24]

The Soviet fear of its vulnerability of such Indian-Ocean-based missile-carrying submarines is genuine. The Soviets believe that the U.S. strategy for the area proceeds "not from present day realities but from a strategy devised during the Cold-War years which aimed to guarantee for the United States a dominant position in the Indian Ocean."[25] The Soviet planners are not flattered even if the strategic submarines are not permanently deployed at present. They are certain that in due course the Indian Ocean will be used for that purpose. As they see it, one of the Indian Ocean's attractions for the United States is the absence of the Soviet navy, and this is the only factor in the situation that is in their (Soviet) power to remedy.[26] Soviet deployment in the Indian Ocean thus appeared essential if not for any other offensive capability but to remove the temptation for an all-out U.S. deployment in those waters.[27]

The threat of the 1960s increased in the 1970s as the United States started deploying Poseidons, and the specter of Indian-Ocean-based Tridents still hangs over the Soviet Union.[28] The Soviet leaders suspect that the United States and NATO have been increasingly looking also toward the ocean in their attempts for strategic superiority. The possibility of a three-ocean-based missile system enabling the United States to launch a second strike in the event of war between the countries was, of course, perceived as a danger. Accusing the United States of militarizing the Indian Ocean, a Soviet analyst thus observed:

> The Indian Ocean is assigned a prominent place in the
> global strategic plans of the United States and Britain
> which want to turn this ocean, too, into a giant
> launching site for American strategic missiles, place
> the area fully under control, and ensure all conditions
> for pursuing a "policy of strength." . . .[29]

The utilization of the Indian Ocean by the U.S. sea-based strategic-missile-carrying submarines has indeed strengthened the American nuclear advantage considerably.[30] The Soviet quest of strategic parity necessitated a counterresponse to the United States-initiated Indian Ocean threat.

The Russian concern about danger from the Indian Ocean has brought about a concerted effort for a Soviet presence in the area. With its oceanographic activities, politicodiplomatic overtures, and naval buildup, the Soviet Union has sought to lay the groundwork for a well-orchestrated and formidable counterpresence of its own.

The Soviet shift to a posture of forward deployment is said to be defense-oriented.[31] It is the response to the threat of a sea-based strategic offensive from the West that the Soviets feared even in the early 1950s. On Navy Day in 1952, Pravda, for example, warned the nation of Russian vulnerability from its sea borders "extending over 40,000 kilometers."[32] George Kennan also wrote about the Soviet sensitivity about this weakness. He observed that the Russians have shown almost a pathological degree of sensitivity about maritime frontiers, "which they are unable to protect by the usual device of a belt of puppet states."[33]

The Russian realization of the sea as the weak link in its defense also has historic basis. The Russian defeats in the Crimea (1854-56) and in the Russo-Japanese War (1904-05) came from amphibious attacks.[34] Thus, the Russian sensitivity to its strategic soft underbelly, the Indian Ocean, can be easily understood. This danger becomes increasingly greater to Moscow as the United States increases its buildup in the ocean.

The present expansion of the Diego Garcia facilities is seen in Moscow as a confirmation of Soviet apprehensions that the atoll would be a home port for strategic-missile-carrying submarines.[35] The recent decision of the United States to build an Omega radar station in Australia is also seen as part of the myriad developments aimed at making the Indian Ocean waters a vital part of U.S. strategic deployment. Moscow knows that the present communications facility at Diego Garcia, along with the facility on the island of Reunion, can already act as guidance stations for nuclear-missile-carrying submarines as well as aircraft.[36]

Moscow opposed the initial entry of U.S. carriers in 1961. The U.S. decision to fill the gap that existed between its Atlantic and Pacific fleets, and the entry of the first U.S. carrier task force into the Indian Ocean, ostensibly for familiarization, led to vehement opposition from Moscow. While the U.S. naval presence was welcomed as a potential reassurance against China's possible blackmail of its southern neighbors, Moscow bemoaned the possibility of Washington extracting valuable bases and additional rights from the important littoral countries like India, as the price for the proposed nuclear umbrella.[37] Active U.K.-U.S. support of India was seen as a prelude to India's granting bases and facilities to the U.S. Navy. In fact, there were accounts of New Delhi's agreement to grant base rights to the U.S. Navy on the islands of Andaman and Nicobar.[38]

Some of the Soviet defense analysts even went further and talked of a chain of U.K.-U.S. bases in the Indian Ocean.[39] Soviet leaders feared that such facilities would enable the U.S. Navy to base tenders for permanent deployment of its submarines. Without such bases for tenders, the logistics and technical constraints limit the deployment period of the U.S. strategic submarines in the Indian Ocean. With such facilities, the submarines can be permanently based instead of making intermittent visits or patrols.

Moscow attempted to persuade the littoral countries to refuse any privileges to the West. The Soviet leaders increasingly identified with the solidarity of the Afro-Asian Indian Ocean littoral countries and tried to encourage the concept of a nuclear-free zone for the ocean. Encouraged by the general opposition of the littoral countries toward external power bases, the Soviets themselves offered to respect the littorals' desire to lessen tensions by keeping the ocean free from a volatile arms race.

In 1964, Moscow even submitted a memorandum to the United Nations entitled "On Steps to Further East International Tension and to Limit the Arms Race."[40] Under Section 3 of the state memorandum, the Soviet Union proposed that the military bases on foreign soil be liquidated. In it, Moscow also condemned the U.K.-U.S. attempts "to establish new military bases in the Indian Ocean despite the clearly expressed will of the peoples of the region."

In a joint Sri Lanka (Ceylon)-Soviet communique of the same year, the Soviet leaders reemphasized their belief that the exclusion of big-power rivalry from the Indian Ocean was to be desired to the utmost. Moscow considered that the implementation of the rivalry-free Indian Ocean idea was closely "connected with the indispenable dismantling of foreign military bases in that region," and stated that the Soviet Union had no intention "of obstructing in any way peaceful and mutually beneficial international cooperation in the area of the Indian Ocean."[41]

The Soviet leaders also tried to counter U.S. headway in the Indian Ocean by launching an offensive to acquire politicodiplomatic influence among the littoral countries.[42] The Soviet politicodiplomatic offensive in the Indian Ocean area is essentially a post-Stalinist phenomenon. During the Stalinist period, the ideological purity and the monolithism of communism did not give way to realpolitik.

In the early years of the Cold War, with a bipolar world, the Indian Ocean littoral countries were seen as part of the imperialist bloc and thus pariahs to the Communists. Africa was still a colony of the Western nations. The few Asian nations that became independent of their West European, primarily English, overlordship appeared as mere appendages of the "metropolies." In spite of their anti-imperialist credentials, most of the national leaders remained suspect in the Communist capitals; Stalin even called some of them "lackeys of imperialists." Soviet political indifference was matched by strategic indifference toward the region. Only to Iran, a country with both coastlines on the Indian Ocean and a common border with the Soviet Union, did Russia show any interest.[43] However, Stalin's attempt to create a puppet regime in part of Iran (Azerbaijan) failed in the face of Western opposition.

The post-Stalin era saw considerable change in the Soviet attitude toward the countries that have come to be called the third world. Premier Khrushchev's de-Stalinization at home was accompanied by a new Soviet flexibility in external relationships. It is difficult to say what single factor could have contributed to the

change in the Soviet attitude toward Afro-Asia. External developments as well as internal revisions of the Marxist-Leninist philosophy heralded a new Soviet attitude toward foreign policy, in general,
and state-to-state relationships, in particular; also, the intensifying
Cold War and attempts to contain Russia with a ring of bases and
allies forced the Russian leaders to make countermoves.

Although the Warsaw Pact attempted to respond to the threat
from NATO, the Soviets had to look for additional avenues to respond
to SEATO and CENTO. The Soviet political and diplomatic defense
against the Western effort at encirclement led to the recognition
of the importance of the Indian Ocean littorals in the political and
diplomatic arena where the East-West struggle itself was moving.

The first official Soviet visit to any of the Afro-Asian Indian
Ocean littorals took place in 1955. That year, Khrushchev, accompanied by Nikolai Bulganin, made a prolonged visit to India, Burma,
and Afghanistan. It opened up a diplomatic policy of aid and assistance to the important littoral countries. This policy of aid to, for
example, Nasser of Egypt, Nehru of India, and Sukarno of Indonesia,
not only opened up some of the key capitals of the Indian Ocean
region but also enhanced the importance and standing of the non-
alignment policy that consistently championed for an Indian Ocean
area free from external powers.

Support and the encouragement to the non-aligned nations
against their aligned neighbors were motivated by the Soviet desire
to lessen Western influence in the area. And in that the Soviets
succeeded considerably. At least in according the policy of non-
alignment a valuable recognition, the Soviet leaders came to acquire
diplomatic standing among some of the important leaders of the
Indian Ocean region. The fact that John Foster Dulles, U.S. secretary of state, did not regard non-alignment as even an honest foreign
policy in the struggle against communism provided added weight to
the Soviet acceptance of it as a viable and peace-oriented policy.

Although all Afro-Asian littoral countries acquired an importance in Soviet diplomacy, it was South Asia that was continuously
given the greatest attention, particularly to India, the most populous
and powerful of the littoral countries. While the Soviet goal was to
expand its influence over the entire area, India acquired the central
position in that drive. Moscow realized the potential role of India
in matters affecting Asia and gave due attention to its India policy. [44]

Moscow's perception of the importance of South Asia, especially India, also increased as the Sino-Soviet Cold War intensified.
The initial Soviet efforts to gain a political and diplomatic leverage
at the cost of the West transformed into an intensified struggle with
a trilateral configuration. Today, Moscow's desire to acquire influence is directed as much against the People's Republic of China as it

is against the United States. In the triangular configuration—United States, USSR, and China—Moscow sees Soviet gains as essentially losses to Peking and Washington.

Since the day the Spirit of '76 landed in Peking, Moscow has come to see a Washington-Peking unholy alliance against it. Thus, India, the centrally located and politically one of the most important countries of the Indian Ocean region, came to acquire added importance in Soviet efforts to counter the joint Peking-Washington axis. In India, Moscow saw at least a "partial balance to the political influence and potential military weight of China."[45]

Soviet diplomatic successes in other parts of the Indian Ocean region have also been considerable. In southern and eastern Africa, the Russians have actively sought and gained influence. The unequivocal Soviet identification with the struggle for majority rule in South Africa and Rhodesia has brought Moscow nearer to the important African leaders. Moreover, while the United States continued to provide tacit support to the Portuguese rule in Mozambique and Angola, the Soviet Union had always supported the national liberation struggle against the Portuguese. Moscow regards such liberation struggles as a fundamental right of subjugated peoples and as one always to be supported by the USSR. Khrushchev, for example, while denouncing world wars for the terrible costs to human lives and incalculable miseries, asserted that "Communists fully support national wars of liberation as just wars and march in the front rank with people waging liberation struggle."[46] The Soviets have close relationships with Somalia where the Russians are reported to have built a major base for Indian Ocean operations. Moscow also has close relations with the "progressive" elements of the area, such as Iraq, South Yemen, and Mozambique.

Russian efforts to increase their political influence in the region are, however, affected by the extension of the Sino-Soviet rivalry. In the aftermath of Angola, confronted by the perceived Soviet successes at the cost of Peking as well as Washington, both Peking and Washington have shown signs of yet closer efforts to checkmate any Soviet advance in the strategic southern Africa.

Also, Moscow's identification with the radical elements have cost considerably in terms of diplomatic gains in and around the Persian Gulf region. In this area, which is considered one of the most strategic spots of the future, Moscow is shunned by the majority of kingdoms. The Soviet Union has normalized relations with Iran, and Soviet-Irani trade and relationships have grown favorably in the recent years. However, the shah does not hide his opposition to communism, and the threat from the north is often played upon as a reason for the frenetic Iranian military buildup. The Azerbaijan incident (1946) always acts as a reminder of Soviet intentions toward Iran.

Additionally, the Soviet Union is still a pariah among the oil-rich conservative sultanates, and Moscow still lacks diplomatic relationships with Saudi Arabia, the United Arab Emirates, Bahrain, and the lesser sultanates of Oman and Qatar. These sultanates are strongly entrenched in the Western camp, and their newly-found oil wealth has given them power as well as influence—which they are using in many instances to combat the influence of Moscow among fellow Arab countries.

The United States, in fact, has sought to build up the two primary kingdoms of the region, Saudi Arabia and Iran, to preserve and further American interests. In terms of checkmating the Soviet advances in the vital Persian Gulf region, the American efforts have paid off considerably. The recent Soviet losses in Egypt could be an indication, since the Egyptian turnabout with Moscow is also greatly influenced by Anwar el-Sadat's desire to secure monetary aid from Saudi Arabia and the other sheikhdoms. [47]

While the pragmatic and businesslike diplomatic pursuit has earned for Moscow much in terms of Afro-Asian friendship, the economic constraints considerably limit the scope of the Russian offensive. Moreover, the Indian Ocean littoral countries provide a checkered field for a uniform regional policy. To the chagrin of Moscow, the closer Sino-American relationships and the identity of their interests in reducing Soviet inroads have come to restrict Moscow's flexibility considerably. In South Asia itself, the Soviets have not been successful in bringing about closer relationships among the nations, particularly between New Delhi and Islamabad, which Moscow makes great effort to do. An improvement of the relationship between India and Pakistan would lessen Peking's influence on Pakistan and open an opportunity for the Soviet Union. However, the Chinese attempts to keep Pakistan away from good relations with India and Moscow's Asian Collective Security concept bespeak of the limited Soviet success in the region. [48]

The Soviet diplomatic offensive had only limited effect also in keeping the United States from having a base in the Indian Ocean and was probably aimed toward political and propaganda ends. The Soviet Union, it should be noted, has not supported the littoral countries' proposal for a zone of peace. * The entire effort seemed to have been guided by the motive to bring home the fact that the United States unilaterally extended its naval presence into an ocean that was free from the vagaries of external power rivalry. The

---

*Moscow opposes the concept of the zone of peace as enunciated in the United Nations General Assembly resolutions as in contravention of the traditional international legal right of the freedom of the seas.

Soviet motive also must have been to make way for a Soviet presence
in the waters as a response (albeit unwilling) to U.S. penetration of
the vital Indian Ocean. Such a motive seems clear from the fact
that the Soviets, after pursuing a political and diplomatic route for a
decade, entered the Indian Ocean on its own at a time when the existing
external power, Great Britain, was announcing its decision to withdraw
from east of Suez.

THE SOVIET ENTRY INTO THE INDIAN OCEAN

In March, 1968, two months after the British announcement of
its withdrawal, the Soviet Union entered the Indian Ocean in strength.
With four warships detached from the Vladivostok-based Pacific Fleet,
the Soviets started its first flag-showing trip around the region. The
flotilla consisted of a Sverdlov class cruiser, a Kashin class destroyer,
and a Kruppy class guided-missile destroyer—an impressive formation
for flag-showing purposes. [49] The ships, during the course of the four-
month visit, called on ports in the subcontinent, the Persian Gulf, and
in East Africa.

The Soviet entry into the ocean on the very wake of the British
decision to withdraw from the area is seen as part of a calculated
Soviet move to fill the vacuum created by the British withdrawal. It
has even been alleged that the Soviets waited for the British announcement of the withdrawal before making their own naval deployments into
the ocean, as Moscow did not want to provide an excuse for Great
Britain to stay. It is conceivable that an early Soviet deployment into
the Indian Ocean would have strengthened the position of those Labour
and Conservative leaders in London who wanted to prolong the British
presence east of Suez. [50]

However, the timing of the Soviet entry appears more as a
coincidence, since the first Soviet naval combat units appeared in the
waters in 1967. In that year the combat units escorted the Soviet
vessels sent to the northwest Indian Ocean for the recovery of space
capsules. [51] The British presence itself was too modest to deter the
Soviets from entering into the ocean. The speed and the extent of the
Soviet entry do, however, indicate prior planning and preparation. [52]
And the time was opportune, with the British engaged in the withdrawal
and the United States too busy fighting in Vietnam. The groundwork
for the "goodwill visits" to some of the littoral countries was being
prepared with years of political, diplomatic, and military relationships in terms of aid and assistance. [53]

Since their flag-showing entry in 1968, the Soviet naval units
have been regularly deployed in the waters. While the first visit was
relatively short (March 22 to July 15, 1968), the second visit was

almost twice as long (November 4, 1968 to April 29, 1969). The
second deployment started with the Kynda, Kotlin (with surface-to-
air missile launchers), and the submarine tender Ugra, with a supply
ship and tankers. They were later joined by Krupnyj accompanying
two northern fleet F-class submarines along with tankers and lifting
ships from the Baltic en route to join the Pacific Fleet.[54] Two more
deployments took place in the latter part of the year. Subsequent
deployments were regular and prolonged. In terms of ship-days, the
Soviet presence seems to have progressed somewhat geometrically.

PATTERN OF SOVIET NAVAL DEPLOYMENTS

The Soviet naval presence in the Indian Ocean has come a long
way since the first entry of the squadron of three warships in March
1968. Today, Soviet deployments in these waters are characterized
as steady-state deployments. At the beginning, normal Soviet presence was an average of four to six surface warships. They were
accompanied by two or three submarines. Since 1970, however, a
typical pattern of deployments is either one or two destroyers (possibly with surface-to-air missiles), two fleet minesweepers, two
oilers, two to four supply ships, and two hydrographic (or oceanographic) ships or one cruiser (Sverdlov, Kresta, or Kynda class), one
or two destroyers, two oilers, two to four supply ships, and two
hydrographic (or oceanographic) ships.[55]
Soviet deployment takes place in a six-month rotational cycle.
This results in an increase in Soviet naval units for the time span
when the new units enter the ocean and the old units prepare to leave.
Normal deployments during the winter period (November to April)
are usually higher, with the inclusion of a cruiser, than that of the
other deployment period. In midyear, Soviet deployment is lower,
and no missile-equipped ship is deployed during this period.[56] The
pattern, however, changes when there is tension in the area, and
the Soviets may send additional naval units to counter an increase in
the Western presence. Thus, in both 1971 and 1973, when the United
States augmented its naval forces to influence the developments
relating to the Indo-Pakistani War and the Mideast War, respectively,
the Soviets followed suit.
When the U.S. Task Force 74, headed by the nuclear-powered
Enterprise, was ordered into the Bay of Bengal, the Soviets had
only four warships in the Indian Ocean. None of the units was equipped with surface-to-surface missiles. The largest of the Soviet naval
units was an old destroyer. However, the Soviets promptly augmented
their naval strength by sending 16 additional warships. Thus, during
January 1972, as long as the U.S. task force stayed in the Indian

Ocean, the Soviet naval strength consisted of twenty combat units. Thirteen of these twenty were surface units and seven others were submarines. The Soviet additional force left the ocean as soon as the Enterprise and the task force left.

During the 1973 Mideast crisis, the Soviets again augmented their presence from the usual of less than six (including two hydrographic research ships) to a total of fourteen (ten were surface warships and four were submarines). The additional reinforcements consisted of one cruiser with surface-to-surface and surface-to-air missiles, one destroyer with similar missiles, two destroyers, three submarines (one of which was nuclear), two supply ships, and one oiler. [57]

Soviet naval units generally concentrate in and around Aden and Somalia. The Soviet concentration in the northwest part of the ocean leads to various interpretations. It is said that they fear the strategic threat from this part of the Arabian Sea the most. During the period 1968-71 alone, of a total 162 ship visits, 96 were to ports in the Horn of Africa, the Red Sea, and the nearby area. Of the same visits, 57 took place to the Indian subcontinent and the Persian Gulf. [58] Recent Soviet visits are also concentrating in the same area. The Somali port of Berbera has become a point of special Soviet attention. The Soviet objectives are seen as centering around two possibilities: the Soviet desire to familiarize itself with the Arabian Sea area against the "postulated future Polaris/Poseidon deployment" and/or the Soviet desire to maintain a visible presence in an area near the Mideast. [59]

It is also said that the area around Socotra offers the best possible site for the Soviets to shadow the U.S. ballistic-missile-carrying submarines deployed in the Arabian Sea. [60] Soviet deployment of naval units with cruise missiles as a deterrent against U.S. strategic-missile-carrying submarines essentially centers around the Arabian Sea. These cruise missiles need constant checkout and adjustment. The Soviet desire to have a base in Somalia or in Socotra may reflect its need to have a facility in the area to provide the extra care that cruise missiles warrant.

The pattern of the Soviet naval deployment in the Indian Ocean reflects the Soviet decision to have a low profile in the area. The early Soviet deployment consisted of modest naval units, although few of them were highly visible. The fact of its presence was felt, although the nature of the deployments did not generate any sense of awe or displeasure on the part of the littoral countries. [61] The deployments with the large and unusually visible Sverdlov cruiser did, however, catch Western attention. On the whole, the Soviets were successful in attaining a visibility without inviting littoral ire and a forceful U.S. response. Moscow did not want to provide any excuse for a U.S. escalation in the area. The Soviet deployments were

essentially defense oriented, to provide a counterpresence to the U. S.
Indian-Ocean-based strategic forces. A larger deployment would have
led to the possibility of a frenetic U. S. naval buildup in the area, and
thus would have been self-defeating.

The trend of the Soviet deployments shows that much of the
Soviet naval stay is on the high seas. The Soviet navy has built up a
chain of conventional facilities around the Indian Ocean waters. It has
often relied on its own fleet anchorages and buoys, which are mainly
concentrated in the northwest. The largest number of the buoys,
clearly marked in both Russian and in English as "the property of the
USSR," and the anchorages are seen within the Durban-Madagascar-
Seychelles triangle. [62] Allegations of Soviet bases and allied facilities
in various littoral countries have been essentially denied by the countries concerned, as well as by Moscow itself. Thus, Iran, Yemen,
and Somalia have denied that Umm Qasr, Aden, and Berbera are Soviet
naval bases. [63] Other countries, such as India, Sri Lanka, Pakistan,
Mauritius, and Bangladesh, have also been named as having provided
the Soviet navy with base facilities. However, all these countries
have refuted the allegations. The ports and facilities of these countries
are available to both the United States and the Soviet Union. [64]

The pattern and the type of naval units in Soviet naval deployments may reflect the nature of the constraints under which the
Soviet navy finds itself in regard to forward deployments. The Soviet
navy, which started its first forward deployment in 1964 in the
Mediterranean, is still not in a position to sustain a presence in
distant waters. The logistics constraints are formidable. The naval
units take an unusual beating in the course of such deployments. As
a Soviet rear admiral admits, the navy is inadequately prepared for
forward projections. [65] The ships that were part of the initial deployment in the Indian Ocean also face similar problems of inadequate
deployable and logistics capability, which will continue for a few years
at the least.

In the existing situation, the Soviet leaders will augment their
naval presence in the Indian Ocean only when such bolstered presence
becomes essential. Such instances will arise as and when Moscow
sees its interests affected by Western, particularly U. S., attempts
at power diplomacy, similar to the attempts made during the 1971
Indo-Pakistani crisis and the Mideast War of 1973. Any Indian Ocean
augmentation causes undue constraints in the Soviet deployments elsewhere, especially in the Pacific Fleet, which had been sending its units
to the Indian Ocean. The opening of the Suez Canal may facilitate
Soviet augmentation of the Indian Ocean presence from the Mediterranean or the Baltic Sea, but the resultant constraints will be felt
nonetheless. Devoid of capability and in the absence of shore-based

facilities to service its modern naval units, the Soviet presence in the
Indian Ocean will remain modest, but visible.

THE IMPLICATIONS OF THE SOVIET ENTRY

The Soviet entry into the Indian Ocean introduced a new external
power into the waters. Geographically, the Soviet Union partially
belongs to Asia, but in the Indian Ocean context it is an outside power.
The Soviet entry into the Indian Ocean provides an alternate force to
the traditional external powers—Great Britain, France, and the United
States—adding a new visibility to the littoral countries' vision of external power presence. In an area infested with constant strife and crisis,
the impact of external powers can be multifaceted, and opportunities
for considerable enhancement of Moscow's influence exist.

The potency of the Soviet presence as a possible counteracting
force to Western efforts of a power play has already been manifested.
Thus, in both the Indo-Pakistani War of 1971 and the Mideast War of
1973, U.S. attempts to influence events through manifest naval buildups
proved unproductive. In both cases, the Soviet Union was capable of
augmenting its naval presence and providing a potent counterpresence
that effectively neutralized U.S. efforts at gunboat diplomacy. The
Soviet naval presence has also enabled Moscow to influence events
positively, to show support to friends, and to bolster friendly regimes.
The Soviet naval presence in Somalia in April 1970, for example,
bolstered the friendly military regime of President Siyad Barre against
an announced "imperialist backed plot." [66] During the Iraqi-Kuwaiti
border dispute in March 1973, the Soviet navy made visits to Iraq,
possibly to show support as well as to insulate Iraq from outside interference. [67]

In spite of its increasing visibility, the Soviet entry into the
Indian Ocean reflects the overall Soviet naval strategy, which,
according to Robert Herrick, is deterrent and defensive[68] and at most
a political move on the part of Moscow. The security-oriented strategic posture is counter to any notion of planned Soviet expansion. [69]
The Soviet leaders fear U.S. strategic deployment in the Indian Ocean.
Moscow already sees great danger in the continued U.S. forward
deployment in the Mediterranean and Europe, on the one hand, and the
Pacific, on the other. Faced with a stronger Western naval presence,
the Soviet navy will have to think very carefully before it transforms
its normal presence to something beyond a peacetime political gesture.
Because, in any event of combat, the fate of its naval units "would be
similar to that of the German cruisers back in 1914." [70]

The successful naval deployments in the Indian Ocean indicate
that the Soviet navy, visible on the high seas only for a decade, has

acquired "blue water" capability. A worldwide projection becomes a natural concomitant of the navy, second only to that of the United States. Soviet leaders have long aspired for a global navy as a part of big-power status. As far back as July 28, 1945, Stalin said that "the Soviet people wish to see their fleet grow still stronger and more powerful."[71] Although Stalinist Russia emphasized the over-all importance of the army and the Soviet Union remained a continental power, the foundation for naval development was, however, laid by Stalin himself. It was Khrushchev, however, who is credited with transforming Russia into a formidable naval power.[72]

Khrushchev provided the leadership for a Russian naval buildup, the pace and extent of which surprised the world. In the course of his leadership, Khrushchev transformed the Soviet Union from a mere continental power into a global one. Outgrowing its continental shell, the Soviet Union started asserting its influence and interests universally.

The Soviet navy today is much more than an appendage of the ground forces. It is a force of its own. As Sergey Gorshkov, the Soviet navy chief, boasted, the Soviet navy, with its "blue water" capability, can take upon itself the task of protecting the far-flung Soviet national interests. A sense of pride is evident in Gorshkov's observation that

> Soviet navymen . . . do not want to be satisfied with their Motherland occupying the position of a second rate sea power. They are well aware of the impor-tance of sea power for strengthening the international prestige of our country, to its military power, to the defenses of the immense maritime boundaries, and to the protection of the state interests of the Soviet Union on the sea and oceans, hence are constantly seeking ways in which to strengthen its military might.[73]

On April 16, 1970, the Soviet army journal Red Star also commented proudly that "the age-old dreams of the Russians have become reality. . . . The pennants of the Soviets' ships now flutter in the most remote corners of the seas and oceans."[74]

The OKEAN exercise of the same month (April 1970), an exer-cise called the "first for anyone in the history of naval art," lent credence to the Soviet claim of "blue water" capability. Soviet Defense Minister Andrey Grechko himself observed that OKEAN demonstrated the Soviet naval preparedness "to repel any aggression against our country from the sea and inflict decisive blows on the enemy."[75]

With its global status, the Soviet navy has come to acquire greater prominence within the Russian military hierarchy. In a way, it has outgrown its originally assigned coastal duties. [76] Among the new missions of the Soviet navy are the battles that the navy will fight to destroy the naval forces of the enemy at the sea and their bases. [77] The elevation of Admiral Sergey Gorshkov to the CPSU Central Committee and to the post of the deputy minister of defense signifies the increasing importance given to the navy. Admiral Gorshkov continues to emphasize the increasing role of the navies in general in present-day strategic parlance. He exhorts the Soviet leaders for an increased emphasis on the global posture of the navy on four counts:

> One, military power determines the outcome of inter-
> national inter-actions; Two, lack of naval power has in
> the past allowed Russia's enemies to dictate the out-
> come of events in areas of primary concern to her;
> Three, navies have an increased importance in war;
> and Four, in peacetime navies are the most effective
> means of projecting military and other forms of state
> power and influence beyond a country's borders. [78]

Soviet military leaders envied the admirable "flexibility and tremendous power" that Washington displayed in influencing events throughout the world. The capability of the flexible overseas deployment of Washington's naval prowess is indeed enviable. The Soviet navy has at last secured a share of the same capability. Admiral Gorshkov proudly said that today the flag of the Soviet navy proudly flies over the oceans of the world, and that "sooner or later the United States will have to understand that it no longer has mastery of the seas." [79] Russian leaders have clearly assigned to their global navy the role of a restraining counterpresence in times of need. Admiral Gorshkov quoted Denis Healey, former British minister of war, as admitting that "as a result of the presence of the Soviet naval forces, the countries of the West will not easily decide to intervene as they did at the time of the Lebanese Crisis in 1958." [80]

The Soviet navy is accepted as capable of preventing "American sea power from getting at its shore objectives." [81] During the Indo-Pakistani crisis of 1971, for example, the U.S. dispatch of the Enterprise-headed Task Force 74 was successfully challenged by the Soviets with additional naval augmentation. In fact, a relevant CIA report is quoted as showing that the Soviet ambassador to India, Nikolai M. Pegov, promised (December 13, 1971) that the Soviets would not allow the U.S. Seventh Fleet to intervene in the subcontinent. [82]

The Russian response to the policies of the United States in the Indian Ocean will probably continue to show this trend: the Soviet buildup in the ocean will move at a moderate pace, reflecting the over-all constraints faced by the Soviet navy; however, if confronted with any augmentation of American naval forces in those waters, the Soviets will augment their strength commensurately. The pattern of Soviet response toward past instances of U.S. augmentation reflects a Soviet penchant for parity in the Indian Ocean. Their apparently positive response to proposals for an Indian Ocean arms limitation agreement will continue, not out of any inherent Soviet desire for peace but for the benefits that such an agreement would bestow. In addition to legitimatizing Soviet naval parity, such an agreement would also have the advantage, from the Soviet perspective, of limiting the flexibility of U.S. strategy in the area.

NOTES

1. A. J. Cottrell and R. M. Burrell, "The Soviet Navy and the Indian Ocean," Strategic Review, Fall 1974, p. 24. However, for a contrary view refuting the so-called Soviet historic interest in the Indian Ocean, see Patrick Rollins, "Russian Fictitious Naval Tradition," U.S. Naval Institute Proceedings, January 1973, pp. 66-71; and Martin Edmonds and John Skitt, "Current Soviet Maritime Strategy, and NATO," International Affairs (London), January 1968, pp. 27-32.

2. R. J. Sontag and J. S. Beddie, eds. Nazi-Soviet Relations 1939-1941. The Documents from the Archives of German Foreign Office (Washington, D.C.: Department of State, 1948), p. 257.

3. For a detailed analysis, see T. B. Millar, "The Indian and Pacific Oceans," Adelphi Papers, no. 57 (London: International Institute for Strategic Studies [IISS], 1969).

4. For a discussion of the Soviet merchant marine, see David Fairhall, "Soviet Merchant Marine," Brassey's Annual, 1973, pp. 131-46; Philip Hanson, "The Soviet Merchant Marine," Survival, May 1970, pp. 165-73; Anthony C. Sutton, "The Soviet Merchant Marine," U.S. Naval Institute Proceedings, January 1970, pp. 34-43; and David Fairhall, Russia Looks to the Sea: A Study of the Expansion of Soviet Maritime Power (London: Deutsch, 1971). See also B. Oddvar, The Soviet Union in International Shipping (Bergen, Norway: Institute for Shipping Research, 1970).

5. Hanson, op. cit., p. 170.

6. Admiral James Holloway, CNO, USN, also agreed that "the Indian Ocean is an all-weather transit route for the Soviet Navy between European and Asiatic Fleets." See U.S., Congress, Senate, Armed

Services Committee, <u>Selected Materials on Diego Garcia,</u> 94th Cong.,
lst sess., 1975, p. 16.

7. U.S., Congress, House, Committee on Foreign Affairs, <u>The
Indian Ocean: Political and Strategic Future,</u> testimony of Howard
Wriggins, 92d Cong., lst sess., 1971, p. 210. George Vest, director
of the State Department's Bureau of Politico-Military Affairs, also
stated that the Indian Ocean is "the natural trade route" for the Soviets,
"being largely landlocked, this (the Indian Ocean) is their natural
transit point." In testimony, House Committee on International
Relations, hearings before the Special Subcommittee on Investigations,
June 5, 1975, typed transcript, p. 3.

8. William P. Bundy, testimony, ibid., p. 3.

9. Ibid., p. 4.

10. Cited in Christopher S. Wren, "Soviet Affirms Right to
Send Ships to Indian Ocean," New York <u>Times,</u> May 9, 1974, p. 3.

11. The Soviet Union has fishing agreements with India, Indonesia, Egypt, Mauritius, Kuwait, Somalia, Sri Lanka, Pakistan,
South Yemen, Tanzania, and Sudan. For an informative discussion
on Soviet deep-sea fishing, see Norman Polmar, <u>Soviet Naval Power</u>
(New York: National Strategy Information Center, 1972), pp. 59-62.

12. Hanson W. Baldwin, "The I.O. Context. Part 1. The
Soviet Union's Increasing Interest," New York <u>Times,</u> March 20, 1972,
p. 37.

13. Cited in Shinsaku Hogen, "The Present State of the Indian
Ocean," in <u>The Indian Ocean: Its Political, Economic, and Military
Importance,</u> ed. Alvin Cottrell and R. M. Burrell (New York: Praeger,
1972), p. 385. The publication observed: "In view of the way the
navies of the United States and NATO are being utilized in the military field, it is becoming increasingly evident that the main role they
are to be given in a future war tends to be the one as means of deliv-
ering strategic strikes. . . . The fact that one third of the overall
nuclear missile striking power of the United States is being concentrated in nuclear submarines and aircraft carrier forces, with the
prospect that this level will be increased to one half by 1970, signifies that above mentioned tendency is there to stay. . . . The primary
mission of the Soviet Navy with its flotillas equipped with nuclear
missiles, if required, are capable of destroying important land
targets anywhere in the enemy territory."

14. For reports of extensive research in advancing undersea
warfare systems, see Keith Critchlow, <u>Into the Hidden Environment,
Oceans: Lifestream of Our Planet</u> (London: Phillip & Sons, 1972),
pp. 116-18.

15. "Morskoi prazdnik Sovetskogo naroda" (Naval Holiday of the
Soviet People), <u>Morskoi Sbornik,</u> July 1966, p. 5.

16. J. O. Naugle, "The Allied Command Atlantic Submarine Challenge," NATO's Fifteen Nations 17, no. 1 (February-March 1972): 66-67.

17. Welcome Aboard the U.S. Naval Communications Station Harold E. Holt, a booklet for personnel newly assigned to North West Cape, preface, pp. 10-11, cited in Desmond Ball, "U.S. Bases in Australia: The Strategic Implications," Current Affairs Bulletin (Sydney) 51 (March 1975): 6. The recent addition of an Omega station at North West Cape allows submarines with missiles not only to locate their stations at sea but also to perform the valuable task of in-flight course correction for missiles. Interview with Rear Admiral Gene La Rocque, USN (Ret.), director, Center for Defense Information, Washington, D.C.

18. Maj. Gen. D. K. Palit, Indian army (Ret.), "An Alibi in the Indian Ocean," Overseas Hindusthan Times, May 2, 1974, p. 7.

19. "A Relevant Question, International Notes," New Times (Moscow), no. 20 (May 22, 1963): 23.

20. Y. Shvedkov, "Bases in Pentagon's Strategy," International Affairs (Moscow), May 1964, pp. 56-61.

21. U.S., Congress, House, Committee on Armed Services, Military Posture and H.R. 11500, Part 4 of 5 parts, 94th Cong., 2d sess., 1976, p. 61. The U.S. Navy League magazine Sea Power also acknowledged in early 1974 that the communications station at North West Cape sends "classified messages to Polaris/Poseidons" while the units are deployed in the Indian Ocean (February 1974, p. 5).

22. Hedley Bull, "Security in the Indian Ocean," Modern World, Annual Review of International Relations 7 (1969): 61.

23. Paul Webster, "What's Russia's Aim In Indian Ocean?" Toronto Globe & Mail, January 5, 1972, p. 11.

24. United Nations, General Assembly (A/C. 159/1), 1974, p. 7.

25. A. D. Portnyagin, "Criticism of Pentagon's Plans in Indian Ocean," USA: Economic, Politics, Ideology (Moscow) February 10, 1975, pp. 74-75.

26. G. Jukes, "The Soviet Union and the Indian Ocean," Survival, November 1971, p. 372.

27. Ibid.

28. The maximum range that the Trident provides will allow the submarines a sea room "10 to 20 times the total ocean area available to today's SSBNs while maintaining the most vital targets within range." Such enormous sea room allows the Trident the flexibility of selecting its own deployable area "of prevailing seasonal storms, high biological noise or other phenomena to counter attempts of ASW sensors to detect Trident." U.S., Congress, House,

Committee on Armed Services, Military Posture and H.R. 11500, 94th Cong., 2d sess., 1976, p. 61.

29. Yuri Tomilin, "U.S., Britain Intend to Militarize Indian Ocean," Tass International Service, August 10, 1971, monitored in FBIS, III, August 11, 1971, p. B1.

30. Hanson Baldwin, Strategy for Tomorrow, op. cit., p. 223.

31. See Robert Waring Herrick, Soviet Naval Strategy: Fifty Years of Theory and Practice (Annapolis, Md.: U.S. Naval Institute, 1968).

32. Cited in Anthony Sokol, "Naval Strategy Today," Brassey's Annual, 1958, p. 38.

33. Ibid., p. 40.

34. Ibid.

35. Aleksey Leontyev, commentary, "Imperialism Stands Accused," Moscow in English to South Asia, September 25, 1974, monitored in FBIS, SOV, 74, 188, September 26, 1974, pp. A6-A8.

36. L. Chirkov, "Shadows Over the Ocean," Sovetskaya Rossiya (Moscow), March 3, 1975, p. 75. Cited in FBIS, SOV, III, March 10, 1975, p. 3L.

37. See "A Dangerous Shield," New Times (Moscow), no. 6, February 13, 1963, pp. 22-23.

38. Y. Konovalov, "The Tenacles of Bases Strategy," International Affairs (Moscow), July 1963, pp. 52-57.

39. Andaman and Nicobar islands, the Seychelles, the Maldives, and Mauritius were listed as possible locations. See I. Andronov, "Wanted: A Desert Island," New Times (Moscow), September 16, 1974, p. 11; see also "More Bases," international notes, New Times (Moscow), May 29, 1963, p. 25.

40. See Pravda, December 8, 1964, pp. 1, 4.

41. "Commentary," Times of India, October 12, 1964, p. 6.

42. Hanson Baldwin, however, sees in this Soviet offensive a "grand design" to dominate the entire area. Baldwin, Strategy for Tomorrow, op. cit., Ch. 8.

43. Geoffrey Jukes, "Soviet Policy in the Indian Ocean," in Soviet Naval Policy: Objectives and Constraints, ed. Michael MccGwire, et al. (New York: Praeger, 1975), p. 309.

44. See Geoffrey Jukes, The Soviet Union in Asia (Berkeley: University of California Press, 1973). Also see Chester Bowles, "America and Russia in India," Foreign Affairs, April 1971, pp. 636-51. The importance of South Asia was recognized even by Lenin when he said, "In the last analysis the future will be determined by the cold fact that Russia, China and India represent a crushing majority of the people of the world. The shortest route to Paris runs through Calcutta and Peking." (Cited in U.S., Congress, House, The Indian Ocean, op. cit., testimony of Chester Bowles, p. 53).

For an informative discussion of the Russo-Indian relations of these years, see Arthur Benjamin Stein, India and the Soviet Union: The Nehru Era (Chicago: University of Chicago Press, 1969).

45. Bowles, op. cit., pp. 637-38; see also J. A. Naik, Soviet Policy Towards India from Stalin to Brezhnev (Delhi: Vikes Publications, 1970).

46. Cited in David R. Cox, "Sea Power and Soviet Foreign Policy," U.S. Naval Institute Proceedings, June 1969, p. 34; see also Jan A. de Plessis, "The Soviet Union's Foreign Policy Towards Africa: 1956-1973," Bulletin of the Africa Institute 7 (1974): 105-11, 115.

47. See Oles M. Smolansky, "Soviet Policy in the Persian Gulf," in Soviet Naval Policy, op. cit., pp. 278-86.

48. For a discussion of the Brezhnev concept of Asian Collective Security, see V. Kudryavtsev, "Problems of Collective Security in Asia," commentary in International Affairs (Moscow), December 1973, pp. 94-98.

49. For a discussion of the nature and capability of particular units of the Soviet navy, see Jane's Fighting Ships, 1976-1977 (New York: Franklin Watts, 1976).

50. Jukes, "Soviet Policy in the Indian Ocean," op. cit.

51. United Nations, op. cit., p. 8.

52. Cottrell and Burrell, "The Soviet Navy and the Indian Ocean," op. cit., pp. 24-25.

53. Jukes, "Soviet Policy in the Indian Ocean," op. cit.

54. Ibid.

55. United Nations, op. cit., pp. 8-9.

56. Ibid.

57. Ibid., p. 9.

58. For details of the Soviet naval visits to the Indian Ocean area, see Michael MccGwire, "Foreign-Port Visits by Soviet Naval Units," in Soviet Naval Policy, op. cit., pp. 387-418.

59. Jukes, ibid., p. 315.

60. Ravi Kaul, Indian Navy (Ret.), "The Indo-Pakistan War and the Changing Balance of Power in the Indian Ocean," U.S. Naval Institute Proceedings, May 1973, p. 180.

61. Geoffrey Jukes, "The Indian Ocean in Soviet Naval Policy," Adelphi Paper no. 87, May 1972, pp. 11-12.

62. United Nations, op. cit., p. 14.

63. Ibid., revision 1, pp. 7-8.

64. Ibid., p. 14.

65. V. S. Sysoyev, "Approach to Ethiopia," Morskoi Sbornik, July 1966, pp. 18-22.

66. James M. McConnel, "The Soviet Navy in the Indian Ocean," in Soviet Naval Developments: Context and Capability, ed. Michael

MccGwire, (Halifax, Canada: University of Dalhousie, 1973), pp. 355-56.

    67. Anne M. Kelly, "The Soviet Naval Presence During the Iraqi-Kuwait Border Dispute," in Soviet Naval Policy, op. cit., pp. 287-306.

    68. Herrick, op. cit.

    69. Andrew Wilson, Observer (London), September 12, 1971, p. 29.

    70. Jurg Meister, "Spotlight on the Indian Ocean," Swiss Review of World Affairs 24, no. 12 (March 1975): 19.

    71. Cited by Polmar, op. cit., p. 30.

    72. According to Admiral Gorshkov, the decision to create a modern navy, capable of dealing with the "latest innovations in the enemy camp . . . in any part of the globe" was taken in the mid-1950s. Pravda, July 26, 1964, cited in Smolansky, op. cit., p. 369. However, Premier Khrushchev was cautious in giving in to navy demands for more defense outlays. For an account of Khrushchev's views toward the navy, see Strobe Talbott, ed., Khrushchev Remembers, vol. 2 (Boston: Little, Brown, 1974).

    73. Cited in Polmar, op. cit., p. 43.

    74. Cited in Major E. Vanveen, "Soviet Naval Infantry—A Coming Weapon?" NATO's Fifteen Nations, February-March 1973, p. 85.

    75. N. I. Shabilkev, M. B. Novikov, and I. M. Panov, eds., "Introduction," Okean, Maneuvers of the U. S. S. R. Navy Conducted in April-May 1970, translated by Joint Publication Research Service, U. S. Department of Commerce, no. 52844, April 19, 1971, p. 6.

    76. For an analysis of the changed role of the Soviet navy in Russian strategy, see V. D. Sokolovsky, Military Strategy (New York: Praeger, 1963); see also Herrick, op. cit.

    77. Herrick, op. cit., p. 233.

    78. Cited in Michael MccGwire, "The Evolution of Soviet Navy Policy: 1960-1974," in Soviet Naval Policy, op. cit., p. 537. Although the global reach of the Soviet navy has brought about greater importance and appreciation, it still ranks low among the services. While the U. S. Navy, in pursuance of the Nixon doctrine, has come to acquire a primary role in U. S. global strategy, the Soviet navy, in spite of Admiral Gorshkov's efforts, has remained at the lowest rank in order of the services. The ground forces no longer occupy the top position, but the navy still retains its position on the lowest rung of the ladder. As it stands today, the respective order of the services is the strategic rocket forces, the ground forces, the air-defense forces, the air forces, and then the navy. For Admiral Gorshkov's argument for assigning the Soviet navy an active and coequal role in the Soviet strategic parlance, see his 11 installments

on "Navies in War and Peace," originally published in Morskoi Sbornik (Moscow), February 1972-February 1973. Translations of all the installments appeared in the U.S. Naval Institute Proceedings January through November 1974.

79. Cited in Anthony Harrigan, "Pentagon's Civilian Planners Think 'Little' When It Comes to U.S. Fleet," Sea Power 11 (August 1968): 19-20.

80. Pravda, July 30, 1972, monitored in FBIS, III SOV, August 1, 1972, p. M-7.

81. George P. Steele, USN (Ret.), "A Fleet to Match Our Real Needs," Washington Post, May 16, 1976, pp. C-1, C-5.

82. Frank Starr, "U.S. Vessels End Indian Ocean Duty," Chicago Tribune, January 11, 1972, quotes Jack Anderson of Anderson Papers fame, p. A16. See also New York Times, January 11, 1972, p. 1.

8

RESPONSES FROM
THE LESSER POWERS

CHINA

Of the lesser superpowers—China, Japan, and Western Europe—China could be expected to oppose a U.S. naval buildup in the Indian Ocean. While Japan and Western Europe view the Indian Ocean in terms of economic opportunities, China views it from ideological, strategic, and political perspectives. The Chinese response to U.S. naval expansion in the Indian Ocean reflects the essential change in Chinese strategic thinking over the last few years. The perception of the Soviet Union as a threat has come to be the single main factor in Chinese strategic thought since the latter part of the 1960s.[1] Chinese foreign policy, based on three anti's—anti-imperialism, antihegemonism, and antiequilibrium—has come to be more anti-Soviet than anything else. The immediate value to an opening with Washington was perceived by Peking as an added restraint on Moscow.[2]

Peking's response to the U.S. Indian Ocean policy is founded on the belief that the Soviet Union is trying to establish hegemony in the strategic Indian Ocean area. The Peking Review noted that "following the old imperialist 'gun-boat policy,' Soviet revisionist social-imperialism is sending its fleet to the Mediterranean, the Indian Ocean, the Pacific and the Atlantic in a bid for world hegemony."[3] Peking accused Moscow of trying to fill the vacuum in the Indian Ocean that was created by the British withdrawal.[4] China sees Russian attempts to obtain a dominant position in the Indian Ocean as part of the overall Soviet strategy "to encircle China from the sea."[5] Although Peking characterizes the Soviet attempts at encirclement as an attempt to "push a stone mortar uphill,"[6] it sees the U.S. presence as opportune and acknowledges the effectiveness of the United States as a deterrent to Soviet plans for expansion. Since the day the Cold War between Moscow and Peking erupted in hot skirmishes on the borders around the Amur River, Peking has accepted the belief that any Soviet gain means a loss to China.

The Peking-Washington thaw has now reached such proportions that there have been deliberations regarding a probable Chinese-American collaboration to contain the Soviet Union. [7] Both capitals find it desirable to contain Soviet gain in the Afro-Asian region. Following the oft-proclaimed doctrine that "your enemy's enemy is your potential friend," Peking has encouraged Washington to act as a counterforce to the Soviets in the ocean. The Chinese belief in the advantage of an alignment with the United States is so strong that Peking of late has become the most virulent critic of the purported American low profile in Asia. Peking's concern is based on the belief that such a shrinking of U.S. involvement would encourage the Soviets to expand their hold in the area. The Chinese leaders seem to be more worried than some American leaders about a soft attitude toward Moscow, and have expressed their dissatisfaction at the naivete and amateurism that, in their opinion, characterize American dealings with Moscow.* Peking's concern has reached such proportions that China has become a leading advocate of a continued American presence in Asia. [8]

However, this does not reflect the entire Chinese response to Indian Ocean developments. Peking's long-term desire is to see the Indian Ocean empty of the other big powers, thus allowing for expansion of Chinese influence. China is the only permanent member of the U.N. Security Council to support the U.N. Declaration on the Indian Ocean as a zone of peace. Peking is also represented in the ad-hoc committee that was appointed to work out the details of the zone-of-peace concept.

The long-range Chinese desire to see the Indian Ocean as an area free from both superpowers is evident from the purported Chou En-Lai remark that China would always work for the liberation of the Indian subcontinent and the Indian Ocean from the two superpowers. [9] In the immediate context, however, Peking sees the need to counterbalance the increasing Soviet presence in the ocean as of paramount importance. The Chinese leaders realize that only the United States can offer such a counterbalance.

----

*An increased antagonism between the superpowers is viewed by Peking as favorable to its interests. In the light of the Chinese proverb "sit on the mountain and watch the tigers fight," aggravation of U.S.-Soviet rivalry may be a conscious policy option of the present Chinese leaders.

The superpower attempts at maritime hegemony are consistently viewed by Peking as being detrimental to its long-term interests.[10] During the U.N. General Assembly debate on the 1972 draft resolution of the peace-zone proposal, Peking's representative observed "that the intensified pursuance of gunboat policy by the two super powers under the signboard of the so-called 'freedom of the sea' is the principal root cause of the threat to the peace and security of the Indian Ocean."[11] China also believes that, for the ocean to be a zone of peace, all modes of external power presence should be removed from the region.[12]

China's desire to play an important role in the Indian Ocean stems from both its historic association and its view of the waters as an area of vital national interest. China's long-term interests in the Indian Ocean are both economic and psychological. China wishes to be visible enough in the strategic waters to help in projecting its power and influence to areas that are not contiguous geographically and not susceptible to border intrusions. In areas like the Persian Gulf, East Africa, and the Indian Ocean islands of South and Southwest Asia, China can project itself securely only through a sustained and strong naval presence.

The People's Republic of China has actively pursued a political and diplomatic program that reflects its dual purpose. On the one hand, the program is aimed at countering the perceived Soviet design against Peking; on the other, Peking views its politicodiplomatic moves as a means to gain increased influence among the littoral countries.

Chinese efforts to develop a sphere of influence have been visible throughout the entire Indian Ocean region, most prominently in East Africa. The initial Chinese losses after the Chou En-lai remark in Somalia that "Africa is ripe for revolutions" have been successfully repaired.[13] Today, China ranks as the dominant external source of aid and assistance for many of the East African littoral countries.[14] The TanZam Railway, often described as the Aswan Dam of Africa, built with a Chinese interest-free loan of over $400 million, stands as the prime example of Chinese visibility in the area.[15] Chinese support to Frelimo's successful struggle against Portuguese colonial rule has earned the goodwill of the Mozambique leaders. Chinese influence in Tanzania is often described as immense; in fact, China has built a naval base facility in the port of Dar es Salaam.[16] The Tanzanian navy is being built by China, and the naval facilities of Tanzania are expected to be used by Peking for its intercontinental ballistic missiles tests in the near future.*

---

*Since the ICBM cannot be tested within the confines of China, the speculation continues that the 6,000-nautical-mile range ICBM will be tested across the Indian Ocean to Tanzania.

China's diplomatic gain among the Afro-Asian littoral countries of the Indian Ocean became substantial with its identification, albeit self-serving, with the zone-of-peace concept. China tries also to actualize additional diplomatic gain through its help to both governments and antigovernment leftist forces. The convenient differentiation of state-to-state and people-to-people diplomacy provides rationale for Chinese initiatives in opposing quarters. Thus, Peking may actively support a government while helping rebels to oust the same. The enunciated role is said to be that countries want independence, nations want freedom, and people want liberation. [17]

The Chinese leaders also use trade in their politicodiplomatic efforts. With a policy of liberal aid terms and bartering goods produced by the littoral countries for Chinese items that are needed by such countries, for example, rice in exchange for Ceylonese rubber, Peking has created warm relationships. Rice, in fact, has become one of the most effective tools of Chinese diplomacy, doubly so because China manages to obtain enormous quantities of rice for such transactions. [18]

Peking's vision of its role in the Indian Ocean requires a naval capability of great proportions. The emphasis on the need for a powerful navy has been regularly indicated by China's continuing ship construction. The Peoples' Daily wrote a few years ago:

> Whether or not we vigorously strive to develop the ship-building industry and build a powerful maritime navy as well as a powerful maritime fleet is an important issue concerning whether or not we want to consolidate our national defense, strengthen the dictatorship of the proletariat, . . . develop freight business, build socialism, and support world revolution. [19]

Although the Chinese navy has not reached "blue water" capability, China has acquired reasonably adequate strength for its immediate needs in the Indian Ocean, and its submarines can be a potent force there. [20]

China is moving into the ballistic missiles field, and further emphasis on seaborne strategic weaponry can be expected. As naval prowess increases, visible deployments of the Chinese naval units as a show of force also may be expected. China's seizure of the Paracel Islands may be cited in the context.

China will continue to speak and act differently about the U. S. naval buildup in the Indian Ocean. While, for reasons of diplomacy and long-term interests, Peking will continue to be vocal publically against big-power rivalry in the ocean, it will maintain its private support and words of encouragement for Washington's naval buildup

as a necessary counterbalance to the Soviets. With the new accent
on containing the increasing Soviet power, Peking may genuinely
see in the United States a partner in the pursuit of its grandiose plan
for expansion of influence. [21] Washington's silence during the seizure
of the Paracel Islands from South Vietnam—the acknowledged ally of
the United States—may signify the nature of a Washington-Peking
understanding on spheres of influence. It is also plausible that
Washington wants China as a bulwark against a possible resurgent
militarized Japan. [22]

Peking's general outlook toward Washington as an essential ally
seems justifiable in the light of the present American role in Taiwan.
As was observed, U.S. forces in Taiwan are in a sense working for
Mao:

> preventing any Unilateral Declaration of Independence
> by Taiwan under Japanese economic and Soviet politi-
> cal aegis. The purpose of U.S. policy seems similar
> to that of the powers after the Boxer Rebellion of
> 1900—to prop up a weak Chinese government against
> Russia, precisely mirroring Peking's policy of sup-
> porting the declining imperialist force against the
> rising threat of "social imperialist" Russia. [23]

Even though it is difficult to believe that the United States
is preserving the Indian Ocean for China, it is logical to believe that
the U.S. presence in the ocean is beneficial to long-term Chinese
interests. With the effective counterbalancing of the Soviet presence
in the Indian Ocean, the United States is preserving a future opportunity for Chinese visibility in the waters. Peking's support of the
U.S. buildup is thus seen as justified by China's national interests.
In exchange for Chinese acceptance of U.S. policy in the Indian Ocean,
the United States is helping China to preserve its future options for
expansion of influence.

JAPAN

The importance of the Indian Ocean to the Japanese cannot be
exaggerated; it may be said that, of the external powers, Japan alone
can reasonably consider the Indian Ocean as its lifeline. Much more
than the United States, the Soviet Union, or Western Europe, it is
Japan that literally survives by the goods and services that the Indian
Ocean carries for it.

In the light of its overwhelming dependence on the ocean, Japan
was disturbed at the sudden British decision to withdraw from east

of Suez. Uncertainty about the nature of the prospective developments worried Tokyo, and the Japan Times expressed the apprehension that "a dimunition of British influence in the Far East will encourage disruptive and unstable elements in their revolt against steady evolutionary progress in favour of violent and revolutionary courses."[24]

Japan depends on the Indian Ocean for continuing oil supplies. In the sea-lanes carrying the vital raw material, there is a continuous string of oil tankers every 50 miles along the entire route from the Persian Gulf to the Sea of Japan.[25] The United States secures about 8 percent of its oil needs from the Persian Gulf, while Western Europe takes 64 percent. But, for Japan, the gulf is the source of about 80 percent of its oil. Mideast oil holds Japan hostage. The strength of oil as a weapon became evident in the short Arab oil embargo following the 1973 Mideast War. In one stroke, the Arab world forced Japan to kowtow and modify its Mideast policy.[26]

Japan is dependent on Indian Ocean sea-lanes for other raw materials as well. (For the importance of the sea-lanes, see Table 1.1.) Increasingly, Japan imports from western Australia, East Africa, and South Asia such vital raw materials as iron ore, copper, zinc, coal, and uranium. Apart from its imports, the ocean is the way that Japanese goods and services flow to the Afro-Asian market.

Tokyo is highly sensitive to developments that could in some way hamper the freedom of the seas, particularly the Straits of Malacca. The Malacca Straits play a vital role in the survival of Japan. In 1970, for example, over one third of Japan's export-import volume crossed the straits. Nearly 85 percent of its oil imports, 60 percent of mineral fuel and lubricating oil, and over a third of its main export of machinery and transporting systems went through these waterways.* No alternatives to the straits could be developed without exorbitant cost.

When the governments of Malaysia and Indonesia, in the process of extending their territorial waters to a 12-mile limit (1969), declared that the Straits of Malacca and Singapore were national, not international waters, Tokyo opposed the move as one of the most affected parties. Even though the Malaysian and Indonesian governments acknowledged the right of innocent passage through the straits, Tokyo felt that the move was of great danger to its interests. Tokyo has also opposed these countries' moves to restrict and regulate tanker traffic in order to prevent mammoth pollution and similar environmental problems.

---

*The obvious alternatives to the Straits of Malacca are the straits off Indonesia, the Sunda Straits or the Lombak Straits, that lie south of Sumatra. However, while the Sunda poses problems to supertankers for its northern shallow approaches, the Lombak increases the distances by at least three days.

Japan opposes any change in the status of the straits because such a change would make possible curtailment of free passage through the straits. The 1958 Geneva Convention of the Territorial Sea and Contiguous Zone defined an international strait under Article 16(4), and provided that

> there shall be no suspension of the innocent passage
> of foreign ships through straits which are used for
> international navigation between one part of the high
> seas and another part of the high seas or the terri-
> torial sea of a foreign state. [27]

The term "innocent" itself was defined as "not prejudicial to the peace, good order or security of the coastal state. [28]

The prospect of limitations on the freedom of transit through the Malacca Straits has reawakened Japanese interests in the Kra Canal. The Kra involves a canal and a pipeline with exits to the South China Sea. The distance through this route connecting the Indian Ocean with the South China Sea across the narrow isthmus in southern Thailand would be less than through Malacca Straits by hundreds of miles. The plan has been enthusiastically pursued by the Thai government as well as by Japanese industrialists. [29]

Tokyo has consistently supported the Indian Ocean zone-of-peace proposal, although it also continues to favor a strong U.S. presence in the entire Asian region. Tokyo believes that the coastal states should increasingly take over the task of maintaining peace in the area and that the littoral countries should be encouraged to ensure the freedom of the Indian Ocean sea-lanes through mutual cooperation. [30] The Japanese delegate to the U.N. Indian Ocean ad-hoc committee, to which Japan was invited as a representative of the major users of the ocean, thus echoed the desire that peace in the Indian Ocean be strengthened and the right to free and unimpeded free use of the zone by commercial vessels be guaranteed. [31]

Japan's primary concern is to ensure that the ships carrying necessary goods be allowed to travel in the Indian Ocean without impediment. It is therefore natural for Japan to consider its national interests as being enhanced by the zone-of-peace concept. Japan's interests are protected with such an order in the ocean, which would continue to respect the right of innocent passage and keep the sea-lanes from being tampered with by one of the big powers in a potential rivalry.

Japan views the Soviet entry into the ocean as a natural phe-nomenon, and believes that it does not portend danger for its use of the sea-lanes. Tokyo believes that the Soviet Union has come

to attach increasing importance to maritime issues like "freedom
of commerce and navigation, freedom of the high seas, ocean development projects, antipollution measures, and economic aid to developing countries,"[32] and that it poses no threat to freedom of the
seas. In fact, Japan sees the Soviet Union as a potential victim of
any destabilization of the traditional maritime traffic lanes. Because
the USSR is one of the leading maritime powers, Soviet behavior
would be anything but destructive to use of the seas. Thus, Japan
expects that the Soviets will play a constructive role in "ensuring
peace and freedom on the world's oceans."[33]

Japan's concern for a secure and free access to the seas has
led Tokyo to look to its own naval capability. Tokyo sees the possibility of a future need for escorts for its seagoing vessels in the
vital eastern Indian Ocean, particularly in and around the vulnerable
Straits of Malacca. Although the director of the Japanese Defense
Agency, Masumi Esaki, observed that it is inconceivable that
Maritime Self-Defense Force craft can ever operate in any part of
the Indian Ocean, Japanese naval units had made goodwill visits
to the Straits of Malacca and even as far west as the ports of Sri
Lanka.[34] Former U.S. Secretary of Defense Melvin Laird openly
advised the Japanese leaders to increase their naval reach in the
Indian Ocean as indication of their determination to protect Japanese
interests.[35]

There have also been suggestions that the United States had
tried to persuade Japan to take over the task of defending the Malay
Peninsula in the aftermath of the British withdrawal.[36] As early as
1968, the Japanese Defense Agency published its plans to build ships
to escort vital supplies from abroad. In fact, it was predicted that
the sphere of the Maritime Self-Defense Force would be extended to
the Straits of Malacca.[37] A Japanese naval buildup for visibility in
the Indian Ocean was once seen as being in conflict with the restrictions under Article 9 of the Japanese constitution, which forbids
Japanese rearmament.[38] However, the constitutional difficulty for
such a buildup has been successfully overcome.[39]

The Japanese Maritime Self-Defense Force has considerable
potential to extend the Japanese maritime presence in the Indian
Ocean. Japan will significantly increase its maritime force capability under the present Fifth Defense Plan (1976-81), which
allocates approximately $22 billion for force buildup.[40] With its
technological progress in nuclear engineering, expertise in shipbuilding, and success in rocketry and ballistics, Japan can acquire
a maritime forward deployment capability without much delay.[41]

Concern for free and regularly accessible sea-lanes will
continue to shape Japanese response toward U.S. strategy in the
Indian Ocean. Thus, while continuing to advocate for a U.S. military

presence in the Far East, Tokyo remains unfavorably disposed toward a U.S. naval buildup in the Indian Ocean. Tokyo identifies with the littoral opposition to big-power rivalry and welcomes the zone-of-peace ideal as both desirable and feasible. [42]

WESTERN EUROPE

Western Europe responds positively to American strategy in the Indian Ocean. The economic, political and strategic interest of Western Europe are seen as better protected by a visible U.S. presence in the waters. The primary interest of Western Europe in the Indian Ocean region is, of course, oil. It is the Mideast and Persian Gulf oil resources that keep the region running. In spite of recent discoveries of oil in the North Sea and in various other parts of the world, the Persian Gulf oil resources still remain the largest; gulf oil sources are still over half of the entire world's reserves.

For the next several years, Western European dependence on oil will remain considerable, and any disruption in the oil supplies will probably lead to the strangulation of industrial Western Europe. With its economy, transportation systems, and even military apparatus totally dependent on the continued flow of oil from the Persian Gulf-Mideast region, the interests of these nations in the developments in the waters can be well understood. [43]

Western Europe sees it essential that a strong Western presence remain in the Indian Ocean. For a continuing hold over the area, with which Western European countries like Great Britain and France still have some colonial connections, the U.S. recent resolve to enter the ocean is seen as considerably important. The Western European nations, particularly Great Britain and France, opposed the zone-of-peace proposal at the United Nations. They view it as antithetical to the international law concept of freedom of the seas, and they are concerned with any attempt by the Indian Ocean littoral countries to exclude the military presence of the external countries.

NATO has been giving voice to the general Western European feeling of the necessity of an augmented Indian Ocean presence. In this context, there had been talk of extending the southern flank of NATO to the Indian Ocean itself. NATO circles have even referred to the Persian Gulf as the "eastern flank," indicating the desire to have an important presence in the area. The extension of the southern flank into the Indian Ocean is seen as a necessary step toward "preventive intervention." It is being argued that such an extension for the survival of Western Europe has become essential as a result of the Soviet naval buildup in the Indian Ocean.

It is said that NATO can no longer afford to think of the East-West confrontation as a double line of barbed wire from Nordkap to Anatolia since Russian sea power has taken the Cold War out of Europe. [44] A worldwide presence of NATO security forces becomes inevitable in the face of what is perceived as a Soviet threat. [45] A global maritime posture to counter the Soviets is thus seen by Western Europeans as an inescapable requirement for NATO.

The Fifteenth General Assembly of NATO formally acknowledged the fact that the Soviet maritime buildup, not only in the Baltic and Mediterranean but also in the Atlantic, Pacific, and Indian Oceans, now presents serious threats to the northern and southern flanks of the alliance and to the interests of its members in all parts of the world. [46] The 1970 OKEAN exercise of the Soviets, for example, was called a "clenched fist in the face of NATO. "[47]

Great Britain and France have also maintained a presence in the Indian Ocean. London sees its Indian Ocean presence as an historic continuity of its centuries-old association with the region. Former Prime Minister Edward Heath could thus tell the Commonwealth partners in Singapore that while Great Britain looks to the United States for the safety of the Pacific and contributes to NATO for the guarding of the Atlantic, in the Indian Ocean it sees an historic responsibility to lead the efforts for peace and stability. [48]

As a commercial nation, Great Britain also values the sealanes as of utmost importance. In fact, Heath dramatically warned that "the sea lanes of the world are Britain's arteries: choke them and we die. "[49] A military presence in the Indian Ocean is viewed in London as essentially contributing to the country's economic interests "in ways that rub off on U. K. products and profits. "[50] London's exports to the Indian Ocean region run to millions of pounds sterling every year and its investments alone are well over £ 10 billion. By conservative estimate, Great Britain's investments in the Malay Peninsula and the Persian Gulf alone are over £ 7 billion. [51]

In spite of the withdrawal from east of Suez, British presence in the Indian Ocean region remains impressive. Great Britain is the primary contributor to the ANZUK (Australia, New Zealand, United Kingdom) forces under the Five-Power Defence Arrangements, which tie it with Australia, New Zealand, Malaysia, and Singapore. Under ANZUK, Great Britain maintains a permanent naval unit with six destroyers, frigates, Nimrods, and other helicopters with amphibious capability in the area. In the Persian Gulf, the withdrawal ended the substantial military presence, but London remains aligned with the sultanates of Bahrain, Qatar, and the United Arab Emirates, and the Royal Navy and the Royal Air Force continue to make periodic visits to the waters. A small unit of British advisers is still

present in the gulf sultanates as an indication of British interests
and to help the local forces attain a level of sophistication.

The 1973 Statement on the Defence Estimates stated clearly
Great Britain's position and interests in the Indian Ocean. The
White Paper asserted that London will continue to take an active part
in the Five-Power Defence Arrangements for defense in Southeast
Asia. It also stated that "British military vessels will be present
in the Indian Ocean; British forces will visit the Persian Gulf. . . ."[52]
The White Paper spoke of British determination to provide military
assistance in Africa, Asia, and the Mideast in order to maintain
"Britain's worldwide political and trading interests."[53]

Great Britain has closely identified with U.S. Indian Ocean
strategy for over a decade. In fact, Diego Garcia itself is a joint
U.K.-U.S. base, with Great Britain contributing the "real estate"
under "unusually" liberal terms.[54] British concern for a viable
Western presence in the Indian Ocean is also indicated from the
fact that London has risked the anger of the littoral countries, particularly of its Commonwealth partners of the Indian Ocean region,
in promptly ratifying the agreement for the expansion of the Diego
Garcia communications facility into the logistics base.

The French response to the U.S. presence in the Indian Ocean
is indicative of its concern about the Indian Ocean area. French
leaders have always asserted their determination to maintain a military presence in the area, even though they have no more colonies
in the region. The former minister of defense, Michael Debre, once
said that the "Indian Ocean falls squarely within the French strategic
concerns." As part of France's determination to continue its role
as a world power, a French presence in the Indian Ocean is bound
to continue. According to Debre, outside Europe, France would
maintain its ability to intervene so that it could assert itself on its
own accord, or under other conditions in the context of a joint
endeavor.[55]

The French presence in the Indian Ocean is more impressive
than that of the United States or the Soviet Union, and recent steps
have made the French presence even more visible. The French
government has established an Indian Ocean command, headquartered
aboard the 26,000-ton (dead weight tonnage) La Charante located in
the western Indian Ocean.[56] French vessels and patrol frigates have
also been increased, and one patrol frigate has even been equipped
with surface-to-surface missiles.[57] The French naval air and land
forces that had to leave the Malagasy Republic on the request of
General Gabriel Ramanantsoa were assigned to the Le Reunion
Island facility, which has been built up as an impressive station for
French Indian Ocean units.[58]

The French base at strategically located Dijibouti is still one of the best naval facilities in the entire Indian Ocean, with both naval and military personnel as well as legionnaires. Dijibouti attains greater importance in the context of the Mideast situation compelling Western interest in the oil of the region. The strategically located base can ensure a dominant influence on developments in and around the Red Sea-Suez approach as well as in and around the lower gulf. Although the territory of Afars and Issas gained independence in June 1977, Paris had an agreement to retain Dijibouti after independence. [59]

France maintains a force of over 5,000 at Dijibouti alone. [60] The combined French presence in the Indian Ocean region is the largest of all the external powers. The French government also possesses the capability to augment rapidly its Indian Ocean forces, as was made evident in the recent crisis when France increased its overall Indian Ocean strength by two submarines and one logistics vessel and sent three warships to the Red Sea as a show of force against Somalia. [61]

France's policy toward the Indian Ocean and its response toward the U.S. buildup reflect the overall conviction of the need for an independent presence for both visibility and deterrence. In short, French determination to maintain an adequate Indian Ocean presence conforms to the general belief in the efficacy of its own Force de Frappe. However, French collaboration with the United States can be safely expected in the event of necessity. In fact, the possibility of a joint Western European presence in the Indian Ocean has been actively explored. [62] A common basis for such a collaboration already exists in the similarity of approaches in regard to the littoral perspectives toward U.S. strategy in the Indian Ocean.

NOTES

1. Harold Hinton, China's Foreign Policy: Recent Developments, Asian Studies, Occasional Paper Series, no. 8 (Edwardsville: Southern Illinois University, 1973), p. 5.

2. Harold Hinton, The Bear at the Gate: Chinese Policy Making Under Soviet Pressure (Washington, D.C.: American Enterprise Institute for Public Policy Research, 1971). See also Robert S. Elegant, "China, the U.S. and Soviet Expansion," Commentary 61 (February 1976): 39-46; and Parris H. Chang, "China's Foreign Policy Strategy: Washington or Moscow 'Connection'?" Pacific Community 7 (April 1976): 406-22. For a discussion of China's anti-hegemony policy, see Joachim Glaubitz, "Anti-hegemony formulas in Chinese Foreign Policy," Asian Survey 16 (March 1976): 205-15.

3. Hua Chih-Lai, "Understanding the World Situation by Studying Geography," Peking Review, no. 48 (December 1, 1972): 7.

4. Peking Review, no. 26 (June 27, 1969), p. 17.

5. Peking Review, no. 24 (June 13, 1969), p. 38.

6. Ibid.

7. Returning from a private visit to China, former Secretary of Defense James Schlesinger admitted that the U.S.-China strategic relationship involves a "high degree of American dependence" on Peking for maintenance of the military-political equilibrium in the post-Vietnam era. Peter Grose, "Schlesinger Doubts That Peking Will Seek to Heal Rift with Soviet," New York Times, October 27, 1976, p. A-2; see also T. C. Rhee, "Peking and Washington in a New Balance of Power," Orbis, 18 (Spring 1974): 151-78.

8. Chinese leaders believe that such a continued U.S. presence can check the Soviet design for hegemony from the Sea of Japan through the Straits of Malacca to the Indian Ocean. Incidentally, American naval leaders have also made similar suggestions. See New York Times, March 18, 1975, pp. 4-5. For a discussion of the Chinese efforts to gain international support against Moscow, primarily through detente with the United States, see Robert F. Rogers, "China's Policy Options," Military Review 54 (August 1974): 3-11. For a discussion of U.S.-Chinese military ties, see Michael Pillsbury, "U.S.-Chinese Military Ties?" Foreign Policy, no. 20 (Fall 1975): 50-64; Roger Glenn Brown, "Chinese Politics and American Policy: A New Look at the Triangle," Foreign Policy, no. 23 (Summer 1976): 3-23; and David Bonavia, "The Delicate Dance of the Three Big Powers," New York Times, February 10, 1964, p. E4.

9. Chou En-lai, interview with Dara Janekovich, Yugoslavian journalist, cited in Hindusthan Times, August 29, 1971, p. 1.

10. Peking Review, January 4, 1972.

11. United Nations, General Assembly (A/C.1/P.V. 1910), December 5, 1972, pp. 8-12.

12. Ibid. See also J. P. Jain, "The Indian Ocean as a Zone of Peace: An Appraisal of China's Attitude," China Report 10 (May-June 1974): 3-9; and Leslie R. Marchant, "The People's Republic of China and the Indian Ocean Imbroglio: An Indicator of the Need for a Gestalt Approach to the Study of Peking's Foreign Relations," Spectrum 3 (October 1974): 23-41.

13. See Alan Hutchinson, "China in Africa: A Record of Pragmatism and Conservatism," Round Table, no. 259 (July 1975): 263-71; see also "China's Decade in Africa," African Institute Bulletin 11, no. 8 (1973): 295-303.

172   U.S. STRATEGY IN THE INDIAN OCEAN

14. Carol H. Fogarty, "China's Economic Relations with the
Third World," in China: A Reassessment of the Economy: A Compen-
dium of Papers to the Joint Economic Committee, (Washington, D.C.:
Government Printing Office, 1975), pp. 730-37.

15. For a discussion of the Chinese motives for providing such
large quantities of aid to Tanzania, see Martin Bailey, "Tanzania and
China," African Affairs 74 (January 1975): 39-50.

16. United Nations, General Assembly (A/C.159/1), p. 19.
However, the Tanzanian government denied the existence of any such
base (see United Nations, General Assembly [A/C.159/1], p. 1).

17. Peking Review, no. 2 (January 14, 1972): 13-15.

18. U.S., Central Intelligence Agency, People's Republic of
China: International Trade Handbook, Washington, 1975; see also
Alva Lewis Erisman, "China: Agriculture in the 1970's," in China:
A Reassessment, op. cit., pp. 324-49.

19. People's Daily, June 4, 1970, cited in W.A.C. Adie,
Oil, Politics, and Seapower: The Indian Ocean Vortex (New York:
Crane, Russak, 1975), p. 74.

20. Angus Fraser, "Military Capabilities in China," Current
History 69, no. 408 (September 1972): 72-73; and Laurence W. Martin,
The Sea in Modern Strategy (London: Chatto & Windus, 1967),
p. 82. 1974 marked the emergence of China as a potential competitor with maritime superpowers on world trade routes. The Chinese
merchant marine has one of the world's highest growth rates. See
Irwin M. Heine, "Red China: The New Maritime Superpower,"
Sea Power 18 (February 1975): 14-18. For present Chinese naval
strength, see The Military Balance, 1976-77 (London: International
Institute for Strategic Studies, 1976); see also Jane's Fighting Ships,
1976-77 (New York: Franklin Watts, 1976), pp. 100-09.

21. Moscow makes accusations about Peking-Washington com-
plicity; see G. Apalin, "Peking and the 'Third World'," International
Affairs (Moscow), no. 3 (March 1976): 88-97.

22. Nixon-Chou communique expressed Chinese concern about
Japanese militarism. See New York Times, February 28, 1972, p.
14; for the text of the communique, see ibid., p. 14. Washington's
apprehension about a militarized Japan was also apparent from the
fact that Japanese leader Takeo Fakuda had to assure Henry Kissinger
that Japan would not become a military power (New York Times,
June 12, 1972, p. 6).

23. Adie, op. cit., p. 83.

24. Cited by Dick Wilson, "The Indian Ocean Frontier," Far
Eastern Economic Review 57 (September 14, 1967): 520.

25. William Graves, "Iran Desert Miracle," National Geographic, January 1975, p. 35.

26. See New York Times, November 13, 1973, p. 61; November 9, 1973, p. 13; and November 16, p. 12; see also Miyoshi Shuichi, "Oil Shock," Japan Quarterly 21 (April-June 1974): 20-28; and Koji Nakamura, "Oil: Reassessment in Japan," Far Eastern Economic Review 84 (April 1, 1974): 53-54. Extreme vulnerability to the oil crisis forced Japan to intensify its search for other energy sources--see R. P. Sinha, "Japan and the Oil Crisis," World Today 30 (August 1974): 335-44. For a postmorten analysis, see Koji Taira, "Japan after the 'Oil Shock': An International Resource Pauper," Current History 68 (April 1975): 145-48, 179-80, 184; see also Yuan-li Wu, "The Economic, Political and Strategic Implications of Japan's Search for Oil," Spectrum 3 (January 1975): 27-41. The resource problem in Japanese foreign policy is indeed acute and this continues to pose problems in Japan's diplomacy--see Yamamoto Mitsuru, "'Resource Diplomacy' Runs into a Stone Wall," Japan Quarterly 22 (October-December 1975): 301-26; and Charles V. Kincaid, The Energy Crisis and Japan: Future Strategic and Foreign Policy Implications (Washington, D. C.: National War College, Strategic Research Group, 1975).

27. Malta, Department of Information, United Nations Conference on the Law of the Sea, 1st, Geneva, April 29, 1958, Treaty Series no. 50, 1967.

28. Ibid., for a discussion of the juridical status of the Malacca Straits, see K. E. Shaw and George G. Thomson, The Straits of Malacca: In Relation to the Problems of the Indian and Pacific Oceans (Singapore: University Educational Press, 1973).

29. For a discussion of the recent progress on the scheme, see W. F. Libby, "Thailand's Kra Canal: Site for the World's First Nuclear Industrial Zone," ORBIS 19 (Spring 1975): 200-08.

30. Shinsaku Hogen, "The Present State of the Indian Ocean," in The Indian Ocean: Its Political, Economic, and Military Importance, ed. Alvin Cottrell and R. M. Burrell (New York: Praeger, 1972) p. 390.

31. United Nations, Provisional Verbatim Record (A/C.1/P.V. 1910), op. cit. pp. 16-20.

32. Hogen, op. cit., p. 391.

33. Ibid.

34. The United States urged Japan to increase the antisubmarine warfare resources of the Maritime Self-Defense Force. Japan depends solely on the United States for protection of vital seaborne supplies. A Japanese capability for antiwar submarine war effort is necessary because Tokyo is almost completely dependent on oil supplies from the Mideast and there are never fewer than 110 tankers at sea between Japan and the Mideast, with the majority using the

Straits of Malacca. Stoppage of the straits or the alternate Indian Ocean routes would mean disaster for Japan. See New York Times, November 25, 1973, p. 4. For an alternate view, which suggests how Japan could provide for a large part of its naval defense needs without embarking on a military buildup, see David Shilling, "A Reassessment of Japan's Naval Defense Needs," Asian Survey 16 (March 1976): 216-29.

35. New York Times, December 14, 1972, p. 14.

36. Washington Post, February 14, 1976, p. D-9.

37. G. A. Plumer, "The Straits of Malacca," Brassey's Annual, 1973, p. 191.

38. The Japanese District Court in Sapparo, in fact, ruled (September 7, 1973) that the nation's maintenance of military forces was unconstitutional (Ito vs. Minister of Agriculture and Forestry, Hanrai Jiho [No. 212-24, 1973]). Judge S. Fukushima said in his decision that ground, maritime, and air self-defense forces, in light of their size, equipment, and capabilities, came under land, sea, and air forces mentioned in provision 2 of Article 9 and were unconstitutional. See New York Times, September 8, 1973, p. 9. For the text of Article 9, see Japanese constitution, in Amos Jenkins Peaslee, Constitution of Nations, vol. 2 (The Hague: Martinus Nijhoff, 1966), p. 523. For a discussion of the constitutionality question, see Robert L. Seymour, "Japan's Self-Defense: The Naganuma Case and Its Implications," Pacific Affairs 47 (Winter 1974-75): 421-36.

39. The Sapparo High (Appellate) Court on August 5, 1976 overruled the district court verdict. See Asahi Shimbun, August 5, 1976, p. 1.

40. The Nixon doctrine, calling on Asian nations to shoulder major responsibility for self-defense, is seen as having forced Japan into a position of considering seriously the necessity of rearmament. See James H. Buck, "The Japanese Self-Defense Force," Naval War College Review 26 (January-February 1974): 40-54. Indeed, the Japanese armed forces drafted its first military doctrine in 22 years, setting forth fundamental plans for defending Japan in the light of the belief that the Nixon policy was unclear on U.S. commitment to Japan. See New York Times, March 4, 1973, p. 1. For the Japanese desire to make its defense forces worthy of an "independent nation," see Ichiji Sugita, "Japan and Her National Defence," Pacific Community (Tokyo) 5 (July 1974): 495-515; see also John K. Emerson, Arms, Yen and Power: The Japanese Dilemma (Tokyo: Tuttle, 1972).

41. If present efforts are taken along with what has already been accomplished, Japan could attain a first-generation weapon capability as early as 1978. See Jay B. Sorenson, "Nuclear Deterrence and Japan's Defense," Asian Affairs, An American Review 2 (November-December 1974): 55-69.

42. Japan's response reflects the overall attempt to balance its relationships with the three major powers to serve its perceived interests. In the light of the policy of equal relations that Japan is trying to pursue with the Soviet Union and China, a certain balancing of Japan's relations with its (erstwhile) mentor, the United States, is natural. See Bhabani Sen Gupta, "Japanese perceptions of the Soviet Union," Pacific Community (Tokyo) 7 (April 1976): 331-46.

43. Peter R. O'Dell, "Oil and Western European Security," Brassey's Annual, 1972, p. 72.

44. J. M. Palmer, "The Balance of Sea Power in the Seventies," NATO's Fifteen Nations 14, no. 4 (August–September 1969): p. 32.

45. Ibid.

46. The resolution was taken in the meeting in Washington, D.C., cited in Geoffrey Rippon, "The Importance of South Africa," Round Table, July 1970, p. 294.

47. Lawrence Griswold, "The View from Moscow," Sea Power 15 (May 1972): 11. For a discussion of the challenge presented by Soviet naval expansion, see B. B. Schofield, "Problems of NATO 1974, 1, Soviet Maritime Power," World Survey, no. 62 (February 1974): 1-16.

48. Cited in Laurence Martin, "British Policy in the Indian Ocean," in The Indian Ocean, op. cit., p. 413.

49. Ibid., p. 414.

50. Ibid., p. 410.

51. Ibid.

52. United Kingdom, Ministry of Defence, Statement on the Defence Estimates, 1973.

53. Ibid.

54. Ibid.

55. Cited in Jacques Freymond, "Western Europe and the Indian Ocean," in The Indian Ocean, op. cit., p. 430.

56. U.S., Congress, House, Committee on Armed Services, Full Committee Consideration of H.R. 12565, testimony of Admiral Moorer, 93d Cong., 2d sess., March 18, 1974, pp. 16-17.

57. Ibid.

58. "Clouds Loom as Soviet Penetration Grows," Sketch, August 30, 1974, pp. 43-44; United Nations, Report of the Secretary General, op. cit., p. 18.

59. Washington Post, February 6 and 7, 1976, pp. 1 and 6, respectively. France believes that in view of the developments in and around the western Indian Ocean along the shores of East Africa, it (France) must provide a continuing presence in the ocean. For a detailed account of French thinking, see Defense Nationale, pp. 25-177, February 1976, JPRS translation no. 67009, March 23, 1976.

60. Ibid. For the growing strategic importance of Dijibouti, see Thomas A. Marks, "Dijibouti: France's Strategic Toehold in Africa," African Affairs 73 (January 1974): 95-104.

61. Washington Post, February 6 and 7, 1976, op. cit.

62. Ibid.

9

PERSPECTIVES OF THE LITTORAL COUNTRIES

A declaration should be adopted calling upon all States to consider and respect the Indian Ocean as a zone of peace from which great Power rivalries and competition as well as bases conceived in the context of such rivalries and competition, either army, navy, or air force, are excluded. The area should also be free of nuclear weapons.

> Final Communique, Fourth Summit of Heads of the Non-aligned States, Lusaka, Zambia, cited in Review of International Affairs, September 1970, p. 33.

The littoral states, in light of their general aversion to big-power rivalry, show concern about a U.S. buildup in the Indian Ocean. An expanded presence in the area is seen as a certain contribution to heightened power rivalry. The littoral countries fear that an external superpower extension in the waters will place the peaceful Indian Ocean at the center of the kind of power play that the Atlantic and the Mediterranean have come to witness in the recent years. Indeed, the two crises of the recent years—the Indo-Pakistani War of 1971 and the Mideast War of 1973—witnessed naval displays that attempted to influence events in particular directions. There were, for example, as many as 40 ships of the two superpowers in Indian Ocean waters during the Indo-Pakistani War of 1971.[1]

The littoral countries increasingly find themselves confronted with developments that considerably limit their freedom of action.

The superpowers have built and augmented their naval presence as
a show of force, while the lesser superpowers strive for ways and
means to secure access to the resources and the markets of the area.
While the United States ignores the littoral countries' concern and
continues to build its naval presence in the ocean to preserve its own
vital interests, as well as to counter the Soviets, the Soviets also
increase their presence and ability to maneuver in order to neutralize any U. S. attempt at gunboat diplomacy and to check alleged
Chinese expansion.

The lesser superpowers have their own strategy. The Chinese
offer to mobilize the small nations of the area against superpower
hegemony, particularly against Soviet socialist imperialism while
Western Europe and Japan try to maintain their hold over the markets
and the resources of the area.

The littoral countries see these developments, particularly the
action-reaction process between the two superpowers, as potentially
creating a situation that would be detrimental to their independence.
Srimavo Bandaranaike, Sri Lankan prime minister, echoed the
despair at such developments when she deplored the Indian Ocean
becoming a launching and target area for nuclear systems. [2]

The transformation of the area into a potential zone for superpower rivalry attains greater significance in the light of the fact that
sea warfare is increasingly viewed as the threat of the coming years,
as land wars are more dangerous because of their potential for escalation into total wars. [3] The possibility of naval warfare in the region
is also increased by the stated intention of the superpowers, particularly the United States, to intervene militarily in situations where
vital interests are at stake. Military intervention remains an
announced part of U. S. policy, and talk of military intervention in
the event of another oil embargo is still in the air. [4] At the official
level, Washington has espoused the possibility of intervention as
one of the courses of action that it might take in a time of need.
Secretary of Defense James Schlesinger talked of using the might of
the Western world to bring the third world into line. [5]

The absence of any regional unity and oneness of purpose stands
in the way of the littoral countries providing a united front that could
defeat the designs of the outside powers. [6] No littoral country has
ever exercised control over the entire area, and there seems to be
little likelihood for the regional powers to unite for such a purpose.
Any attempt by a regional power at self-assertion will lead its relatively smaller and weaker neighbors to invite outside powers to provide a counterbalance. The area is thus ideal for penetration by outside powers, and the intensity of the big-power rivalry has increased
in the recent years. [7]

With many unresolved disputes, the area may be said to be a vacuum to be filled by outside powers. [8] The theory of a vacuum is, however, not a proper indication of the post-British Indian Ocean. The vacuum theory presupposes two things: one, that the area cannot be left "powerless," but must be "powered," dominated by a major power; and two, that there had been a major British presence that kept the area "filled," but now that British forces had been withdrawn, the area has become vacant. [9]

The littoral countries do not subscribe to these assumptions, and they see the vacuum concept as being rooted in prejudice. These countries had to fight for their independence, and in their view British withdrawal was caused by British inability to withstand the forces of nationalism; it is contended that replacement of the British by independent nations did not in any way lead to a vacuum. Indira Gandhi, prime minister of India, reflected the accepted view of the area countries that

> There has been no dearth of theories to justify a
> military presence. One of the most inane of them is
> the theory of power vacuum. The colonial Powers
> were compelled to leave because of an opposite poli-
> tical force—the upsurge of nationalism. There can
> be no question of a vacuum if we make our economies
> viable and our societies stable. Our common resolve
> to strengthen our independence rejects the orthdox
> power theory. [10]

The apprehensions that shape the reaction of the littoral countries toward the proposed U.S. naval buildup in the ocean are based on their concern about the impact of the proposed buildup. The area has seen itself transformed into an unwilling partner of European power rivalries for long periods in the past, and their apprehension is understandable. In the formative years of these newly independent countries' struggle for economic and sociopolitical developments, any diversion of their economic resources and attention to ward off the impact of the ongoing big-power rivalry is naturally seen as painful waste.

To some, the term "Afro-Asian Ocean" signifies the littoral nations' feelings of increasing determination to shape their own destiny. It signifies their desire to see a reduction of outside presence. [11] The historic reality of the past centuries, that is, the predominance of external powers in the vital ocean, has naturally prompted these countries to propose that the ocean be left as a zone of peace free from big-power rivalry. The Indian Ocean countries

were profoundly affected by the developments in the ocean. Great
Britain established its empire over the region by controlling the
ocean. A formidable naval presence in the waters enables an
external power to establish leverage over the region, and the realization prompts the littoral nations to oppose any such external presence.

The apprehension of the littoral countries about the external
naval buildups in the ocean has been repeatedly expressed at both
international and regional levels. In fact, as early as 1964, the
littoral nations expressed their apprehension about the possible
naval buildup by the United States. The heads of the nonaligned
states at their conference in Cairo (1964) deplored the move as a
calculated attempt to intimidate the emerging countries of Africa
and Asia and as an unwarranted extension of neocolonialism and
imperialism. [12] Rhetoric aside, the feeling expressed was genuine.
The countries of the region, with their past experience of colonialism and subjugation, naturally value their newly won independence.
The policy of nonalignment—not to join either bloc in the Cold War,
but to judge each issue on its merits—is, in itself, a manifestation
of their desire to be left out of the imbroglio of big-power rivalry.
The fate of the Atlantic and the Pacific led them to wish sincerely
that the Indian Ocean, the only ocean that had remained outside
intensive Cold War rivalry, be left alone.

The Lusaka Conference of the nonaligned nations (1970) articu-
lated the littorals' feelings on the issue of the impending big-power
buildup in the Indian Ocean. The fourth summit of heads of the nonaligned states called for the adoption of a declaration in its final communique designating the Indian Ocean as a zone of peace free from
big-power rivalry as well as from nuclear weapons. [13]

The major effort of the littoral countries to ward off an ever-
escalating arms race in the ocean centered in the United Nations.
The twenty-sixth session of the General Assembly of the United
Nations, at the request of Sri Lanka, later joined by the United
Republic of Tanzania, took up the issue of the potential arms race
in the Indian Ocean. The General Assembly declared that the
Indian Ocean, within limits to be determined, was designated for
all time as a zone of peace, and called upon the great powers, the
littoral and hinterland states, and other maritime users of the Indian
Ocean to enter into consultations with each other with a view to
realizing the aims of the declaration. [14] The 1971 resolution also
requested the secretary general to report to the General Assembly
"at its twenty-seventh session of the progress that has been made
with regard to the implementation of the Declaration." [15] The General

Assembly also decided to discuss the declaration of the Indian Ocean as a zone of peace in the next (twenty-seventh) session.[16]

Resolution 2832 (XXVI) of the UN General Assembly was in many ways unique. The Sri Lankan- and Tanzanian-sponsored resolution asked for the exclusion of both defensive and offensive military installations and that the existing installations be removed in consultation with the littoral and hinterland countries. It also expressed the hope that naval and air units of an external power or its ally in the region would not use the ocean for any threat "or use of force against the sovereignty, territorial integrity, or independence of any littoral or hinterland State" in contravention of the purposes and the principles of the UN Charter.[17] While the right to free and unimpeded use of the ocean by vessels of all nations and countries as guaranteed under international law was acknowledged as unabridged, access to littoral ports and facilities of the area was restricted to only emergency and humanitarian purposes. It was also hoped that there would be no manifestation of naval and air forces in the form of maneuvers or exercises in the ocean.

The concept of the zone of peace was wider and more extensive than similar resolutions. Compared to it, the Treaty of Tlateloco, prohibiting nuclear weapons in Latin America, or the Organization of the African Unity (OAU) declaration for a nuclear-free zone for Africa seems to be more restricted in scope and intent.[18] The resolution tried to establish a totally demilitarized zone covering both nuclear and conventional offensive weapons.[19]

The resolution did not have an easy passage in the General Assembly. In the discussions at the First Committee of the General Assembly, the resolution was considered too radical in nature. The sponsors had to modify the original version to make it acceptable to the maximum number of nations. The draft was, however, billed as an attempt to erect "some signpost in the direction of peace in what is a tropical jungle."[20]

Although 11 more states joined Tanzania and Sri Lanka as sponsors of the revised resolution, the major external powers concontinued to express their general disapproval of the declaration as an attempt to abridge the freedom that the high seas offer. The four countries with major interests in the Indian Ocean—the United States, the Soviet Union, the United Kingdom, and France—finally abstained from voting on the resolution. While the United States noted its opposition to the resolution as setting "a dangerous precedent," the Soviet Union objected to the resolution on the grounds that the declaration "must not lead to undermining or weakening existing generally recognized principles of international law."[21] Among the major powers, only the People's Republic of China endorsed the declaration as reflecting the desire of Afro-Asia to safeguard its national freedom, and a just "demand to oppose the superpowers' contention for hegemony and division of spheres of influence in the Indian Ocean."[22]   The UN General Assembly accepted the resolution on December 16, 1971 (during the height of Indo-Pakistani War and the U.S.-Soviet naval buildup in the Indian Ocean) with a 61 to 0 vote and 55 abstentions.

The 1972 General Assembly duly took up the matter as part of its agenda, although there was no consultation among the littoral countries as called for under the 1971 resolution. After a few weeks of deliberation, a resolution cosponsored by 21 states was introduced and was passed in the General Assembly with a vote of 95 in favor, 0 against, and 35 abstentions. The littoral countries supported the proposal in unison; Thailand, the lone dissenter, later changed from abstaining to voting in favor of the measure. The major powers, as expected, continued their opposition to the measure.

The important operative clause of the 1972 resolution asked for the establishment of an ad hoc committee of 15 members. The ad hoc committee included two external countries, China and Japan, which had supported the resolution from the beginning, and 13 members from the littoral and hinterland area. The committee started working on the ways and means for implementation of the peace zone proposal.

In pursuance of paragraph 6 of the 1972 resolution, the General Assembly took up the matter in its 1973 session. In the resolution that the assembly adopted, the secretary general was called upon to prepare a factual statement of the great powers' military presence in all its aspects in the Indian Ocean, with special reference to their naval deployments, conceived in the context of great power rivalry.

The secretary general accordingly appointed three qualified experts who submitted their report on May 3, 1974.[23] The report considered the military and the naval presence of the five permanent members of the Security Council. As the parent resolution did not consider the impact of military alliance on the course of rivalry, the experts only dealt with the stated manifestations of the great powers' military presence.[24] The visible elements of military and naval presence were taken to consist of naval deployments of both surface ships and submarines, the maintenance of naval and military establishments in the area, the military use of communications facilities, the use of military staging facilities, the military use of airfields, the naval use of mooring buoys in the ocean and fueling facilities as well as the harbors and ports of littoral states, and the general use of bases and other military facilities in the area.[25] The authors of the report, however, acknowledged that the report included items that in reality would not be actual bases or "full naval facilities."[26]

The report generated criticism from the countries that it listed either as hosts or users of bases and facilities in the region. In detailing the external power presence in the region, the experts were highly critical of the Diego Garcia expansion. It characterized the building of a strategic base by the United States as paving the way for an intensified arms rivalry in the future. In the face of the criticism, the secretary general felt it essential to have the original report reviewed by William Epstein, head of the United Nations Disarmament Division, participating as special consultant. [27] A revised report was submitted July 11, 1974, which replaced the previous report in its entirety.

The ad hoc committee, which received the expert report, submitted a report of its own. [28] Among other provisions, the committee suggested that it be transformed into a negotiation forum so that it could start consultations with the four permanent members of the Security Council who are not members of the committee (the United States, the USSR, the United Kingdom, and France) with a view toward lessening the arms rivalry in the Indian Ocean. [29] The committee report also suggested a conference of the littoral and hinterland states of the Indian Ocean to further the cause of the zone of peace as stipulated in the previous General Assembly resolutions.

The General Assembly approved and adopted the recommendations. In its resolution of December 9, 1974 (3259), the General Assembly, with a vote of 103 to 0, with 26 abstentions, called upon "the great Powers to refrain from increasing and strengthening their military presence in the region of the Indian Ocean as an essential first step towards the relaxation of tension and the promotion of peace and security in the area." [30] The assembly also requested the littoral and hinterland states to enter into necessary consultations with a view to convening the stated conference on the Indian Ocean. [31] The consultations resulted in an agreement in principle on the issue, and the General Assembly in its Resolution 3468 (XXX), title "Implementation of the Declaration of the Indian Ocean as a Zone of Peace," requested the littoral and hinterland states to continue finalizing the issues relating to the date and duration, venue, agenda, and the level of participation for the conference. The resolution, adopted with a vote of 106 to 0, with 25 abstentions, also requested the ad hoc committee "to continue its work and consultations with its mandate" and to submit a report of its achievements to the General Assembly at the 31st session.

In addition to the United Nations, the nonaligned conferences and the Commonwealth prime ministers' conferences have regularly taken up the matter of arms rivalry in the Indian Ocean. The littoral countries participating in these organizations have persistently

voiced their apprehension about the dangers from an intensified naval
arms race in the vital ocean. The U.S. decision to ignore the littoral
countries' objections to the Diego Garcia expansion has generated
consistent criticism from the area countries. The opening day of the
Commonwealth Parliamentary Conference in New Delhi (October 1975),
for example, devoted all its working sessions to discussing the consequences of the U.S. expansion of its base facility at Diego Garcia.[32]

The littoral nations have not been successful in reducing power
rivalry and naval buildup in the ocean. The superpowers did not
support the idea of the peace zone at its inception in 1971, and their
respective naval presences have increased considerably since then.
In spite of littoral concerns, the United States continues to refute
the idea that naval buildups in the Indian Ocean contribute to an arms
race in the area. Both superpowers as well as France and the United
Kingdom continue to oppose the very idea of a peace zone organized
by the littoral states. To them, the littoral states have no "special
right to limit or control the use of the high seas by others," and the
United States, in particular, continues to assert that "there must be
unimpaired access to the high seas."[33] Washington even has refused
to participate in any deliberation aimed at reduction of the potential
for the arms tension as part of the zone-of-peace efforts on the grounds
that no country has the right to establish any system that contravenes
the traditional freedom of the high seas.[34] The U.S. ACDA (Arms
Control and Disarmament Agency) believes that any arms control for
the Indian Ocean region must be based on the "considered agreement
of the powers directly concerned," and the agency has characterized
the attempt to impose military limitations on the big powers "without
their consent" as both "unrealistic and undesirable."[35]

The littoral and hinterland states are themselves responsible
for much of the failure to bring about a lessening of the arms race
in the ocean. These countries, most of whom remain pawns of the
big powers, in spite of their vocal support for the generalities of the
concept of the zone of peace, have not gone beyond the rudiments of
the concept. The countries represented in the UN ad hoc committee
have yet to agree on the definitions of terms used in the resolutions
(2832, 2992, 3080, 3259, and 3468) of the General Assembly. Military alliances with external powers are still maintained by many of
these Indian Ocean littoral countries. Some smaller states in the
area find it to their advantage that external power presence in the
area is maintained because it ensures them greater flexibility in
dealings with their more powerful neighbors.

The expanded facility at Diego Garcia is an indication of
U.S. determination to be strongly present in the area. The nature
and the extent of the privileges that the United States enjoys in rela-

tion to the use and expansion of the Diego Garcia atoll for its needs, and the flexibility that the "depopulated" nature of the atoll ensures, add to the danger that some of the littoral countries perceive. The presence of such a powerful state would naturally be viewed as a threat by the less powerful littoral nations. In fact, a powerful state is defined as one that is "able, by the manipulation of the diplomatic, economic, military or subversive instruments at its disposal, to influence the behaviour of foreign governments in a desired direction."[36] A weak state, then, is one that is "susceptible to such influence."[37]

The United States seems to desire to provide a deterrent influence in the area or to act as the policeman on the beat against recalcitrant littorals and against developments adversely affecting U.S. interests. In the light of past instances of U.S. gunboat diplomacy in Latin America and in the Mediterranean, and the recent show of naval force in the Indian Ocean area in 1971 and 1973, the U.S. base at the atoll acquires a dangerous importance.*

The United States, probably like other powers, does not rule out armed intervention as part of its foreign policy options.[38] The use, or the threat to use, limited naval force "otherwise than as an act of war, in order to secure an advantage, or to avert loss" is still an important part of U.S. strategy.[39] Although the strategic parity between the two superpowers has lessened the impunity with which such gunboat diplomacy can be resorted to, the possibilities of amphibious landings or show of force by other forms of naval augmentation still exist. The sea still provides a "neutral place d'armes open to all, where forces may be assembled, ready for intervention."[40]

The significance of the strategic atoll facility, in the light of general superpower politics, is vast indeed. The base at Diego Garcia enables the United States to project its forces (both sea and air) throughout the entire Indian Ocean region. Although technological advances in ballistics and weapons have increased the capability for distant deployment, the proximity of Diego Garcia to the littoral countries adds to its importance strategically in the light of the George Kennan theory that "the effectiveness of the power radiated from any national center decreases in proportion to the distance involved."[41] The location of the atoll was, in fact, one

---

*Instances of such intervention are the Dominican Republic in 1965, Lebanon in 1958, and the steaming of the carrier task forces during the 1971 Indo-Pakistani War and the 1973 Mideast War.

of the primary reasons for its selection for the base facility in the ocean. [42]

The economic and political reasons that are advanced in support of the U.S. presence in the area also worry the area's countries. The area has become vital to the survival of the Western industrial system, and U.S. moves are seen as designed to protect its stake. The British announcement of withdrawal from east of Suez dismayed Washington, as the latter had always assumed that "Great Britain could be counted upon to protect America's western flank in Asia."[43] With the British withdrawal, the United States felt it had to move in to ensure the presence of a policeman. Thus, the U.S. presence in the ocean may be seen as a threat to the liberation struggle of the Afro-Asian region, which would naturally disrupt the status quo. Attempts on the part of the raw-materials-rich countries of the area to form cartels, or any moves on their part to assert their rights at the cost of the Western world, will probably invite a show of U.S. force. *

However, the current primary apprehension of the littoral countries is of a different nature. These countries are more afraid that the U.S. buildup in the ocean is another move toward the increasing arms race. The base facility at the atoll, it seems, would legitimatize similar efforts on the part of the Soviet Union and possibly on the part of the People's Republic of China. [44] With the U.S. move for a buildup, appropriate countermoves by the other principals in the international scene are expected as a matter of course.

In spite of the concern of the littoral states about the increasing pace of the superpower arms buildup in the ocean, nothing significant has been achieved in stopping naval rivalry in the waters. The littoral countries, especially the regional powers of the area, are consciously trying to increase their force and flexibility in relation to the increasing external power buildup in the ocean. The four regional powers—South Africa[†] in the African region, Iran in the Persian Gulf, India in South Asia, and Australia in the Southeast Asia region—are responding to the developments in the Indian Ocean, in particular to U.S. moves, in their own manner.

----

*Threats of show of force had already been made in the case of the OPEC cartel.

[†] The UN General Assembly does not recognize South Africa as an Indian Ocean littoral country, as Pretoria primarily abuts on the Atlantic. However, South Africa is recognized as a littoral country for the purpose of this dissertation.

SOUTH AFRICA

South Africa, more than any of the littoral countries, has perceived the growing Soviet presence in the area with concern. It views the Communist penetration of the vital waters as a danger to the free world, of which it sees itself a member. This is exacerbated by recent developments in Angola and southern Africa. In terms of defense capability, South Africa is the strongest power in the subregion of southern and East Africa. Nearly self-sufficient in defense, the regime in Pretoria, in fact, exports arms to other countries. The conventional might of South Africa excels the combined strength of the rest of Africa taken together.

The South African strategy in the Indian Ocean is to encourage active Western participation in order to provide a counterpresence to the Soviet buildup. In that light, Pretoria welcomes an effective U.S. buildup in the ocean. With its military wherewithal and strategic location, South Africa desires to play a major role in the western Indian Ocean buildup. Richly endowed in raw materials and equipped with the strategically important Simonstown base, * South Africa has already attracted the attention of Western defense analysts, who have advocated the extension of the strategic perimeter to include Pretoria as a vital link in the overall Western security. [45] With the increase of Soviet-Chinese influence in Africa, Pretoria is successfully portraying itself, with Australia, as comprising the "great defence circle" of the West. [46] South Africa openly acknowledges that, in the event of a global clash between the free world and communism, "the Communists would regard gaining control of the Cape Sea route as a valuable prize." [47] Pretoria notes with satisfaction that NATO recently had suggested an extension of its area of operations to south of the Tropic of Cancer. [48]

The South African program to bring the West closer started in the post-World War II years. In 1948, Pretoria proposed a Western Indian Ocean Treaty along the lines of NATO. Although countries like Portugal, France, Belgium, and a few others showed interest in a joint agreement, eventually Great Britain alone entered into a bilateral agreement with South Africa. In the agreement, which is known as the Simonstown Agreement, Great Britain and South Africa

---

*Great Britain acknowledged the importance of the Simonstown base and entered into the Simonstown Agreement (June 1955) in spite of opposition from other African countries. The importance of the base increases in the light of the increase in the Indian Ocean trade, particularly with tankers that carry Persian Gulf oil to the West.

recognized the "importance of sea communications to the well being of their respective countries in peace and to their common security in the event of aggression."[49] The Simonstown base has featured prominently in the joint naval exercises involving the navies of the United States, the United Kingdom, South Africa, and other Western nations on an annual basis.[50]

The United States itself has come to view a strong South Africa essential for the protection of the Indian Ocean sea-lanes through the Cape of Good Hope.[51] The reluctance of the United States to be openly associated with the South African regime in terms of availing the South African offer of base and related facilities to the United States Navy has led to criticism of the Washington posture. It is being said that:

> In ignoring the contribution that South Africa can make
> to the Western—especially U.S.—cause to keep the Soviets
> at check, the West and the U.S. are basing their foreign
> policies on the ideological preferences that have no rela-
> tion to the real needs and interests of the Western
> powers.[52]

However, covert relationships between the military services of the two countries do exist.[53] In fact, South Africa, "the Gibraltar of the Southern Hemisphere," is closely linked with the overall U.S. military reconnaissance network in the Indian Ocean region. A super-secret communications station sunk into a mountain in Silvermine scans Indian Ocean shipping to the farthest shores of the Bay of Bengal for the Pentagon.[54]

IRAN

Iran, the predominant power in the Persian Gulf, occupies a central position in U.S. Indian Ocean strategy. The United States looks toward Iran and Saudi Arabia, the two leading states in the area, to ensure regional peace and stability.[55] The shah recognizes his importance and his response to U.S. strategy is greatly influenced by this realization. Iran wants a dominant role in the Indian Ocean, particularly in and around the Persian Gulf. The shah, although desiring the ultimate withdrawal of all outside powers from the gulf, continues to look to the United States for support to establish his predominance in the region. Because U.S. policy is in support of the status quo in the region, Washington is the external power to which Iran would turn in the event of a threat from outside or local powers.

Iran feels itself to be threatened both internally and externally. The danger to Iran from an external power is from the Soviet Union. The shah sees two possible courses of Soviet action. One is a direct Soviet move against Iran and possible occupation of its territory or forced partition under puppet regimes on the lines tried by the Soviets after World War II in Azerbaijan; also, he sees dangers of aggression from Soviet-inspired terrorist groups both from within Iran or from nearby Arab countries. The shah talks of the threat from the Soviet Union in the context of Russia's historic pursuit of a warm-water port in the Indian Ocean.[56] The shah has told Oriana Fallaci, an Italian journalist, that the Soviet Union is engaged in a pincer movement in pursuit of its dream of reaching the Indian Ocean through the Persian Gulf. The 1,200-mile frontier remains quiet, although the Azerbaijan crisis keeps the shah from trusting his neighbors to the north.[57]

In spite of the growing economic and trade relationships with Moscow, Teheran views the former with suspicion. Iran views Soviet relations with its (Iran's) potential rival Iraq with suspicion. Particularly the Fifteen-Year Treaty of Cooperation and Friendship that Moscow signed with Iraq in April 1972 providing for deliberations for mutual defense under clauses 8 and 9 has generated apprehension in Iran about possible Iraqi-Soviet designs in the region.

The threat from leftist subnationalist elements is also a source of concern for the shah. The shah therefore supports a U.S. presence in the area as a counter to any radical developments—a natural corollary to Iran's desire for survival. It may be said that the shah, like the other monarchs of the area, sees his self-preservation guaranteed by plans and programs to keep his subjects materially satisfied and happy, but politically conservative.[58] The creation of an excessive fear of revolutionaries or radical elements is as much a part of this calculated plan as the other measures designed to depoliticize the intellectuals, that is, the ruthlessly efficient security operations and the Machiavellian spreading of fear and suspicion among the populace.

The West, especially the United States, provides the market for Iran's oil and ensures a continued flow of the dollars needed to finance the shah's grandiose "white revolution." Additionally, the wide range of goods and services that the shah is purchasing in pursuit of his developmental plans can be secured only from the Western countries, particularly the United States. Neither the Soviet Union nor any of the developing countries can offer the shah the market for his oil or the wide-ranging goods and services, nor does the shah see these countries as trustworthy in restraining their zeal for revolutionary causes.[59] The assistance of the United States in the creation of an efficient police state is an important reason for the continued Irani support for U.S. strategy in the Indian Ocean.

Iran prefers a strong, visible Western presence in the Indian Ocean, and has advocated a rejuvenated CENTO with more active British participation to bolster its sense of security. However, Iran has made it clear that it would like the Persian Gulf to be free of any external power. The shah, for example, spoke bluntly against any revision of the British decision to withdraw from the area as was suggested by the Tory opposition. The shah, while visiting Helsinki (1971), stated that the era of colonialism was over and that Iran would oppose any British desire to continue a presence in the Persian Gulf. [60]

The shah proposed a Gulf Security System. In this system the states of the Persian Gulf would "form some type of mutual defense link similar to NATO without the big powers." [61] The shah believes that, in the absence of such a system, the gulf area with its weak sultanates, rising wealth, and small population will remain "havens" for subversion and disorder. [62] In proposing the pact, the shah suggested that if the countries of the area agree to the Irani proposal, Iran would initiate the defense system and would seek to represent a profile of power, reason, and humanitarian aims in fulfilling its responsibilities in the region. [63] The Gulf Security System has, however, not yet materialized. Although the United States favors such an idea, the Arab countries in the area have shown no enthusiasm toward an Iran-dominated security system. [64]

In spite of the cool reception to the Gulf Security System, Iran has made itself the dominant power in the region. The shah has unilaterally abrogated the Shatt-al-Arab treaty with Iraq that regulated the use of that river since 1937. [65] The unilateral abrogation in 1969 gave Iran almost all the advantages that Iraq once enjoyed under the treaty. The acquisition of the strategically located approach to the port and refinery facilities at Shatt-al-Arab was followed by the Irani seizure of the two strategically located islands of Musa and Abu in December 1971, barely a month before the British withdrew from the area. The possession of these two islands gives the shah complete control over the Gulf of Hormuz. The shah has already begun policing the trouble-ridden lower gulf and has played the most important role in reducing the danger of the Dhofari rebellion in the nearby sultanate of Oman.

The shah openly acknowledges his desire to make Iran the most powerful Indian Ocean littoral power before the end of the century. He expresses his intention to extend the Irani defense perimeter southward to include a sizable part of the Indian Ocean. He defines the Irani defense perimeter as "extending ten degrees south of the equator, and covering most of the Indian Ocean." [66] The shah's desire to play an important role in the Indian Ocean is evident from the naval buildup of recent years; the Royal Irani Navy is the most sophisticated in the entire Indian Ocean area. Iran has also entered into agreement with Mauritius for port access as part of the plans for outward deployment of the Irani navy.

The Irani plans for the area are endorsed by the United States, as evidenced by U.S. readiness to help modernize the Irani armed forces with billions of dollars for sophisticated weaponery. Unwaivering administration support for the Irani arms buildup continues, although many leaders both in and out of the U.S. Congress view the continued close cooperation with the shah as detrimental to U.S. long-term interests in the Persian Gulf and Indian Ocean region.[67] The support of the ambitious Irani plans for dominance of the gulf region raises the ire of the Arabs of the area. The shah has already spoken of the Persian Gulf as his lake and has asserted his determination to intervene unilaterally in the gulf region to ward off any change that he regards as adverse to Iran and to his dynasty.[68]

Irani reaction to U.S. strategy reflects the dual nature of the shah's thinking. While, on the one hand, the shah privately encourages the United States to build up its presence in the Indian Ocean, at the same time he is frantically building his own forces to establish Indian Ocean dominance.[69] Teheran occupies an important position in the overall U.S. Indian Ocean military reconnaissance operations, and Diego-Garcia-based U.S. P-3 Orions regularly use the Irani airfields facilities during their reconnaissance sorties. The shah has also allowed the U.S. to set up an electronic listening post in the strategically located Abu Musa Island (which overlooks the Strait of Hormuz). Iran is building a chain of military bases along its entire coastline that will be available for American use. The U.S. Navy, in particular, is looking forward to the naval-cum-air complex at Chah Bahar, which is under construction with American know-how and assistance. The $1.6 billion base will be the largest facility of its kind in the entire Indian Ocean region, and the U.S. Navy will look toward major access to its facilities if U.S. carrier task forces are committed in the ocean.[70] Although South Africa, Iran, Australia, and Indonesia are often called the four pillars of the U.S. Indian Ocean strategy, it is Iran that is characterized as the linchpin of the strategy.[71]

As the shah moves into the Indian Ocean, his ties with South Africa and Australia are expected to become stronger. In fact, the shah has already proposed a trilateral security force comprising Iran, South Africa, and Australia, with Iran as the cornerstone, to protect the sea-lanes in the Indian Ocean.[72]

The public identification of the shah with the zone-of-peace proposal and his vocal opposition to external big-power presence in the
gulf reflect his sense of insecurity with buildups, including that of
the United States. In spite of their close assocation, the shah does
not trust Washington, while Washington itself views the shah with
suspicion. Indeed, a psychological profile of the shah prepared by
the CIA finds the shah "a dangerous megalomaniac, who is likely to
pursue his own aims in disregard of U.S. interests."[73] The shah is
aware of the implications of the publicly stated U.S. warning against
any OPEC attempt to disrupt the oil flow to the West. The Irani
leader is also aware of the possibility that the United States is developing "alternative options" against a "recalcitrant shah" in the armed
forces of Iran as it did "in Pakistan, South Vietnam, Cambodia, Laos,
and Greece."[74] The shah reflected the sense of insecurity in his
assertion that "I take absolutely no chance. I must not depend on
anyone. . . ."[75] In spite of possible reservations about the eventual
outcome of the U.S. naval buildups in the ocean, the shah is still seen
by many as an agent of the United States for the execution of American
interests in the area.[76]

INDIA

In spite of size, population and importance, India's perspective
on the Indian Ocean question has hardly been an influencing factor on
U.S. strategy. India itself realized too late the importance of the
Indian Ocean (with India's over 3,000-mile coastline and the sea-
lanes still remaining its lifeline to the outside world). It was even
widely spoken out that "whoever controls the Indian Ocean has India
at its mercy."[77] However, the apparent tranquility and the distance
of the ocean from the big-powers' rivalry kept the strategic import
of the waters out of the consideration of the Indian defense planners.
The country's preoccupation with the socioeconomic and the political
problems that beset it had kept its attention inward. Land-based
aggression against India, which started soon after the independence,
still clouds Indian strategic thinking. The four major incursions from
Pakistan and the People's Republic of China in the northern part of
its territory and the continued threat from the same quarters force
India to put considerable emphasis on the land forces.

The apparent disregard of sea-based danger is ironic in view of
the fact that it was the sea that carried the forces that subjugated and
occupied India for over two centuries. It was also apparent from
World War II that the ocean would play an increasingly vital role in
overall world security and that of the subcontinent in particular.
The advancing Japanese made the strategic value of the ocean appar-

ent to the students of Indian security who suggested a regional
arrangement both for security and economic purposes soon after the
Japanese were defeated. [78]

The noted student of strategy, K. M. Panikkar, pointed out
the fact that India is a maritime state with a predominant interest
in the sea. [79] Panikkar also pointed out that, for security interests,
India should capitalize on its importance in the maritime context.
Only by this did Panikkar see the possibility for India to be a great
power. [80] Dominance of the Indian Ocean was seen as an imperative
for India's independence and security. To keep the Indian Ocean
truly Indian Panikkar suggested a maritime policy for India that would
put the Indian defense perimeters as far as Mauritius, Socotra, Aden,
and Singapore. [81] In the light of the apparent Indian inability for such
a deployment, it was suggested that India enter an Indo-British naval
defense arrangement that would put the British naval might behind
Indian maritime dominance over the Indian Ocean. [82]

K. B. Vaidya, another student of strategy, also believed that
India must dominate the Indian Ocean to ensure its security in the
future. He said that "even if we do not rule the waves of all the five
oceans of the world, we must at least rule the waves of the Indian
Ocean." [83] Vaidya advocated turning the Indian Ocean into an Indian
lake. [84]

The Indian Council of World Affairs also studied the implications of the ocean in the context of the defense and security of the
area and concluded that only an effective naval force from the subcontinent could stop the waters from being controlled by an external
power. [85]

After independence, India worked consistently to keep the Indian
Ocean area free from external power rivalry. Knowledge of past
events, particularly the awareness that the extension of European
naval rivalry during the later eighteenth and early nineteenth centuries, coupled with the squabbles and disputes of the countries and
principalities of the region, ultimately led to colonization of much
of the Indian Ocean region and persuaded the Indian leaders to mini-
mize the possibilities of any extension of the big-power rivalry into
the area in general. India's policy of nonalignment and its emphasis
on peaceful coexistence could be cited as being specifically tailored
by this historic awareness of the pitfalls of any extension of European power rivalry into the Indian Ocean.

The Chinese aggression (October 1962), however, marked a
change in the tone of India's opposition toward a Western, albeit
U.S., presence in the Indian Ocean. The proposed U.S. entry into
the Indian Ocean was accepted as a simple act of "familiarization,"
and the long-term consequences of the act itself were seen as minimal. Thus, Prime Minister Jawaharlal Nehru denied the possibility

that U.S. entry into Indian Ocean would pave the way for an arms rivalry jeopardizing India's security. Nehru not only asserted that U.S. entry into those waters would not act as an invitation to other powers (particularly powers antagonistic to India) to do likewise but saw no other power as having the capability to send "a considerable number of ships roundabout here."[86]

The first visit of the U.S. carrier task force did not create any furor, and when asked, the Indian prime minister assured Parliament that "It would be quite wrong to suggest that a cruise by a few U.S. naval vessels in the Indian Ocean either threatens our freedom, or imperils our policy of non-alignment."[87] The visit of General Maxwell Taylor, U.S. Joint Chief of Staff, and his meeting with Nehru (December 17, 1963) two days before the first unit of the Seventh Fleet entered the Indian Ocean was seen as tacit support by India of U.S. involvement in the Indian Ocean.[88] In conjunction with the much talked about "air umbrella" that the United States proposed as part of India's defense against a Chinese advance, there was speculation that the U.S. Seventh Fleet in the Indian Ocean was part of an overall U.S. strategy against any Chinese advance southward. The initial response of New Delhi toward the sequence of developments, starting with the creation of the British Indian Ocean Territory to the establishment of the communications station on Diego Garcia, was mild and low-key.[89] New Delhi became vocal only after the pitfalls of the increasing big-power activity became apparent during the late 1960s and early 1970s.

India actively supported moves aimed at keeping the Indian Ocean free from big-power rivalries. In the conferences of the Commonwealth prime ministers, of the nonaligned nations and in the UN General Assembly, India lent valuable support to the efforts aimed at establishing a zone of peace in the Indian Ocean. India's opposition to the developments leading to an intensified power rivalry in the Indian Ocean is a natural expression of its conviction that big-power rivalry is detrimental to the interests and the well-being of the area's countries. It views the extension of the big-power rivalry into the Indian Ocean as dangerous because such an extension of the Western military systems into the ocean would lead to future Chinese attempts to expand southward as well as to the establishment of Western influence in West, South, and Southeast Asia.[90] In fact, New Delhi believed that the Afro-Asian littoral countries would be able to look after their own interests without the presence of outside contentious powers. India welcomed the process of the British withdrawal from the region as part of its (India's) advocacy and support for decolonization, and expressed continued faith in the littoral countries' capability "to meet the challenges that come with a measure of self-respect, dignity and self-reliance without looking to Washington or Moscow."[91]

India strongly opposed the establishment of the base at Diego
Garcia in line with its strong opposition to any kind of military base
in the region. In the present context, it holds the two superpowers
ultimately responsible for restoring the peace in the ocean. As
Indian External Affairs Minister Y. B. Chavan says:

> Taking into account the political and military realities,
> the onus for taking concrete action towards establishment
> of the Indian Ocean as a zone of peace lies clearly with
> the great Powers; for it's they who have to curb their
> military presence and activity in the Indian Ocean and
> to eliminate existing bases and to refrain from setting
> up new bases. [92]

New Delhi had hoped that with detente and a lessening of tension the
Indian Ocean would not see an increased arms buildup. India sees
the expansion of Diego Garcia as reminiscent of gunboat diplomacy. [93]

In spite of its support of the peace zone and its genuine desire
to see the Indian Ocean free of big-power arms rivalry, India realizes
that the possiblity is remote. Confronted by the fact of the immense
importance of the ocean in its security and survival, India is taking
a close look at the arms buildup. While attempting through diplomatic channels to restrain the big powers from making the ocean a
central part of the arms rivalry, New Delhi is also trying to increase
its capability to respond to the developments in the area.

Although the largest of the littoral countries and the most highly
exposed to the developments in the waters, India finds itself constrained in terms of economic flexibility and the necessary wherewithal for a successful offensive on this score. Even with an industrial base that ranks among the ten largest in the world and that sets
it apart from other Indian Ocean littoral countries, India has not been
able to overcome the impact of the population-development cycle.
Constrained by its lack of resources to confront unexpected realities
in the ocean, India has a sense of claustrophobia and an apprehension
that it is at the receiving end of events in the vital area.

India opposes the U.S. naval buildup in the Indian Ocean both
privately and publicly. The onset of the big-power rivalry in the
ocean is seen as detrimental to its aspirations for peace and progress
as smaller neighbors become involved in continuing squabbles and
disputes. By being manipulated by the big powers to act as their
proxies or by manipulating the big powers, the contentious small
states of the region can create a dangerous disequilibrium in the area.
India views the U.S. strategy of naval augmentation with dissatisfaction. It believes that the U.S. naval augmentation would invite a

Soviet counterpresence leading to a dangerous show of arms too close
to India. The ensuing arms rivalry between the contending superpowers, New Delhi fears, will force India to use its scarce resources
for necessary security buildups to insulate it from the possible spillover of the rivalry.

The Indian attitude toward the U.S. Indian Ocean strategy is
also influenced by New Delhi's perception that Washington does not
accord India its due recognition. [94] Over the years, India has seen
constant attempts by Washington to neutralize its importance and
legitimate standing. New Delhi continues to see a Washington attempt
to establish an artificial balance in South Asia to frustrate its legitimate aspirations. In the post-1971 scene, India's attitude toward
the United States was also affected by the Washington-Peking rapprochement. Indian strategic planners remain apprehensive about
the possibility that with the recognition of Peking by Washington as
the third power center of the world, China might have been given a
freer hand to expand its influence over South and Southeast Asia. The
"Nixon shock" indeed hit New Delhi hard, probably harder even
than Tokyo. [95] The Washington overtures toward Peking were seen as
profoundly detrimental to India as a "medium Asian power. "[96] It was
candidly observed that in the event of India's failure to enact prompt
and effective countermeasures, New Delhi might find itself a pawn
in the Peking-Washington power play.

India's apprehension heightened after Kissinger's warning to
Sri L. K. Jhan, the Indian ambassador to the United States in 1971.
Kissinger made it clear that in case of a war between India and Pakistan over East Pakistan (later the Bangladesh issue), China would
not remain aloof, and that in case of any Chinese intervention India
should not expect U.S. support as it did in 1962. [97] Realizing its
vulnerability to big-power play, particularly from a Peking-Washington axis, India later signed the Treaty of Peace and Friendship with
the Soviet Union and decided to develop the nuclear option.

The realization that New Delhi could not stay out of the power
game became evident from the signing of the treaty. [98] However,
the treaty is in no way an endorsement of any Soviet plan for an Indian
Ocean buildup. The Indian opposition to big-power rivalry of any
sort is unqualified, and a unilateral Soviet move into the waters will
be opposed by India.

Indian displeasure at the U.S. move in the Indian Ocean evokes
in Washington a strong suggestion of a pro-Moscow bias in New Delhi.
Admiral Elmo Zumwalt even suggested that the Soviets enjoy special
base and home-port facilities in India that are unavailable to the
United States. [99] It is the policy of India not to grant any base or
facility to any external power. New Delhi's relationship with Moscow
under the Treaty of Peace, Friendship and Cooperation "means exactly

what the title suggests."[100] As Mrs. Gandhi told the Australian
Broadcasting Commission during the course of an interview:

> It is true we are friends with the Soviet Union. They
> have helped us economically and for many years, it
> was the only country which supported our industrial
> development in the public sector which we think is very
> important for our progress and stability. We formalised
> this friendship in the shape of a treaty but it is not at
> all a military treaty, nor does it come in the way of
> friendship with any other country. I think the whole
> policies of spheres of influence and balance of
> power—this is what creates tension and if one coun-
> try feels that others are doing it, then, they also try
> to do it. But India has always kept out of all this and
> as you know we have not given and we do not intend to
> give any bases to any foreign force, including the Sovi-
> ets.[101]

Mrs. Gandhi also emphasized that India has followed an evenhanded
policy against big-power rivalry. [102]

Washington has remained sensitive to the possibility of closer
ties between India and the Soviet Union. Nixon warned that the United
States would not tolerate India's becoming totally aligned with the
Soviets or acting in concert with Moscow against any area that the
United States designates as important.[103] Washington's desire to
contain Moscow, as evidenced in the warmer U.S.-Peking relationship,
influences the American perception of the Indo-Soviet relationship.

Some supporters of a strong U.S. presence in the Indian Ocean
see the Indian apprehension about big-power rivalry as motivated by
New Delhi's desire to carve out a domain of its own. The Indian
entry (in 1974) into the Nuclear Club was seen as a concrete indication of the Indian plan for hegemony. It is felt that a U.S. presence
in the waters would act to restrain India and ensure the smaller
neighbors their security and territorial integrity. India's nuclear
explosion has even been characterized as a threat to the U.S. itself.[104]

New Delhi continues to believe that in spite of Kissinger's
statement that the United States recognizes the post-Bangladesh realities of South Asia, the United States is still trying to shore up an
artificial balance in the region to the detriment of India. New Delhi
believes that Washington, while pursuing its policy of trilateral
detente, totally ignores India and its aspirations. * The Nixon

---

*Trilateral detente (Washington-Moscow-Peking) and the temp-
tation to sustain equilibrium at the cost of third parties genuinely
worry India.

statement of "Asian hands must shape the Asian future" notwith-
standing, India perceives that Washington still pursues the old
Machiavellian policy of divide et impera (divide and rule) toward
Asian nations. Washington's policy in South Asia in particular is
seen as subject to U.S. configurations with Peking. India also
realizes that U.S. hostility toward India and the attempt to shore up
Pakistan at India's cost will continue so long as Washington favors
improving its relations with Peking. It is believed that the United
States recognizes the fact that Peking considers an anti-India Pakistan as an essential part of its South Asia strategy, and the United
States is very willing to play along for the sake of Chinese friendship. [105]

The U.S. decision to expand the Diego Garcia communications
station into a logistics base is also seen in New Delhi as reneging
on a Washington assurance that there would be no expansion of the
atoll facility to enable the stationing of troops. [106] The U.S. expansion of the base facility is seen as an indication of a continued external interest in keeping the area infested with power politics and the
game of balancing that have stood in the way of regional cooperation
and understanding among the littoral countries.

Despite its stated interest in seeing the Indian Ocean as a
zone of peace, India shows no determination to play a leading role in
formulating any viable alternative that could dissuade the external
powers from an arms buildup in the area. [107] India refused to talk
of an association with Australia, for example, to provide a modicum
of regional collaboration to supplement the withdrawing British. [108]
The Indian external affairs minister categorically rejected the idea
of a New Delhi-Canberra-Tokyo alignment to shoulder the post-
British withdrawal responsibilities in the region. [109] New Delhi's
preference for an Afro-Asian littoral country arrangement to keep
the Indian Ocean free from external power rivalry leads many observers to believe that India might support the Brezhnev idea of collective security in the years to come. So far, New Delhi has refused
to endorse the idea, but an intensification of big-power politics in
the ocean may lead to a reversal of the accepted Indian position.

In contrast to the Nixon doctrine, Brezhnev's collective security is probably more satisfactory to the area countries. While Nixon
wanted to establish a "generation of peace" and an Asian order based
on cooperation among the United States, the USSR, China, and Japan,
the collective security system tries to associate all the area countries
in the management of their own problems. [110] New Delhi's sense of
importance, which it has justifiably maintained all these years, is
catered to by the collective security system, whereas the Nixon doctrine leaves India and other regional powers out. The U.S. plan aims

at the working alliance of the four major powers for an imposed order, while the Brezhnev system provides for regional participation to take care of regional problems. [111] India's strategic thinking falls in line with the Soviet desire to contain China, and the identity of strategic and security concerns with Moscow puts India on the opposite side of the Washington policies and its desire to identify with Peking's aspirations. New Delhi also falls squarely within the strategic considerations of Moscow, while remaining on the periphery of Washington's strategic thinking for the region. [112]

The zone of peace—a free ocean freely navigable by all—still remains the central aspect of India's policy toward the Indian Ocean. It remains both publicly and privately opposed to U.S. moves for expanded military activities. However, the failure of the littoral countries to reduce the arms rivalry in the ocean forces India to look for additional options to insulate itself from developments in the waters.

A determined attempt to acquire a potent military capability is one option that the Indian leaders are pursuing in the context of Indian Ocean developments. In the presence of increased naval activity by external powers, a credible military force becomes essential even for India's relationships with its neighbors. Stung by its past experience of hostility from a neighbor who was armed and equipped by external powers, New Delhi sees great dangers from weakness or perceived weakness. It also realizes that to ward off external interference in its domestic affairs, which China has engaged in since the Indian military weakness became apparent in 1962, India needs to be strong militarily. The need to build a credible power potential is also seen as essential for the huge, pluralistic nation-state, which is under pressure from a bigger, more homogeneous, and more powerful China. A U.S. naval buildup in the Indian Ocean is seen, in this context, as a positive contribution to an increased Chinese leverage over New Delhi, since such a U.S. presence neutralizes the Soviet deterrent capability against China. [113]

India's perspective toward U.S. strategy in the Indian Ocean will continue to be affected by its realization that, despite size, population, and potential, it stands vulnerable to developments that could tip the scales of South Asian politics to New Delhi's disadvantage. [114] Thus, India can be expected to pursue an astute policy of championing the zone-of-peace concept to prevent the big-power naval buildups in the ocean, while it tries to realize its potential to play a significant role in the region.

AUSTRALIA

The Australian perspective of U.S. Indian Ocean strategy has witnessed a dramatic reversal with the change in government. The present Liberal-Country party government of Malcolm Fraser has reversed the Labour policy of Gough Whitlam, and Canberra now strongly supports the U.S. naval buildup in the Indian Ocean. The Indian Ocean plays a vital role in Australian security and prosperity, and in spite of the differences between the two parties on essential tactics, there is general agreement on the need to safeguard and further Australian interests in these waters. With a population concentrated in eastern parts of the country, traditionally Australian attention has been to events in and around the Pacific. This was also due to the fact that after the Japanese successes in Southeast Asia during World War II, Canberra saw potential threats to the country essentially coming from that region. Cushioned by the British presence in the area east of Suez, Australia never felt the need to view Indian Ocean developments in their entirety. Thus Canberra regionalized its concern with the waters and people in the proximity of its eastern sectors, and a western-Australia-oriented defense was unheard of. It was the British withdrawal and the following developments that have forced Australia to view the Indian Ocean in its entirety and to formulate a perspective accordingly. [115]

Australian perception of U.S. strategy in the Indian Ocean is naturally influenced by its perception of the threat from communism in general and from Soviet and Chinese activities in particular. The Soviet entry into the Indian Ocean—long a Western preserve as a British lake—was thus seen as having grave implications. Popular opinion was so strongly against the Soviet presence that Gordon Freeth, the Liberal party minister for external affairs, lost his seat as a result of having asked Australians not to panic at the sight of the Soviets in the Indian Ocean. [116]

Canberra is suspicious of Chinese military buildup and attempts to expand influence among the Indian Ocean littoral countries. Australia remembers Chou En-lai's characterization of it as the "gateway to the south," implying a Chinese desire to use Australia as a route to the Indian Ocean. The Australian outlook also had been influenced by the belief that Southeast Asia, where Australia has defense and economic interests, might still be caught between "the Mao-Ho hammer and Sukarno-Mao anvil!"[117]

The Indian Ocean borders 9,000 of the 12,000 miles of Australia's coastline. The necessity for Australia to change its orientation toward the Pacific and give the Indian Ocean proper attention has been felt for some time. Particularly the World War II experience with Japanese ascendancy over parts of the Indian Ocean caused some Australian security planners to call for a reappraisal of the traditional Australian ignorance of the potential security problems from the Indian Ocean. A turn toward the Indian Ocean was advocated.[118] However, the continued protection from the British Royal Navy, under whose shadow Australia has lived since the day the first fleet arrived at Botany Bay nearly 200 years ago, enabled Canberra to continue its low-key defense posture. With an opening toward the United States, Australia found itself in the privileged position of being "protected on the one side by the British lion and on the other by the American eagle from the dimly perceived but acutely feared threat to the north."[119]

Although Australia came to look toward the United States for the greater part of its security requirements, it always kept its defense association with Great Britain. A continued British presence in the region was seen as essential for Australia's own security. Australia entered joint defense projects with Great Britain for the region and provided material support to the British defense policies in the Malay Peninsula.[120] British withdrawal from the ocean was a blow to the comfortable feeling of security that Australia had enjoyed from the formidable Western presence in the ocean.

Australia's response to British withdrawal from east of Suez has been heavily influenced by its association with the United States. Since World War II, the United States in fact has occupied a central role in the Australian public consciousness. It was observed that "Loyalty to the American alliance has had a powerful electoral appeal, and major Asian policies have been shaped not in terms of Australia's direct interests in the area but in terms of buttressing that alliance."[121] Australia followed the "Lafayette syndrome" in its relationships with the United States.[122] In expecting security from the United States, Canberra came to believe that both political and moral support in peacetime and troop deployment in wartime were essential ingredients of an "insurance policy" it needed to pursue.[123] Under the concept, it was Australia's obligation to keep its premiums "paid up" so that in the event of need the insurer "could be counted upon to provide tangible assurances of security, [meaning] of course, naval and armed forces support."[124] Australian troops dispatched to Vietnam were viewed as such a premium. In spite of its concern to keep the United States happy with Australian support and backing, Canberra opposed a suggestion from Walter Lippmann that America withdraw from other Asian bases to Australia and New Zealand.[125]

Australia viewed the U.S. presence in Asia as an essential condition for its own security. When the British withdrew from east of Suez, Australia tried to cling to the United States.[126] Its dependence on the United States was such that Washington could take Australia for granted. Thus, in the Battle-Barwick Agreement of 1963, under which Australia allowed the United States to have a communications base in the North West Cape, Canberra was barred from any access and control over the facility and the area used for the base.[127]

Australian support for U.S. naval presence in the Indian Ocean was directly linked to the British decision to withdraw from the area. The British decision was seen as drastically altering previous arrangements as to the continuing availability of British forces in the region.[128] In the absence of the British forces, Australia had to look for a positive and continuing assurance from Washington to come to its rescue in the event of an emergency. With such a dependence, Canberra's support for U.S. plans to enter the Indian Ocean on a regular basis can be well understood. In fact, one Australian observer even suggested that Australia take over the British Indian Ocean Territory for joint American-Australian defense purposes.[129]

Australia maintained its support for U.S. policies in the Indian Ocean in spite of the shocks it suffered from the Nixon openings with Peking.[130] In fact, the Nixon visits to Peking and the Nixon doctrine caused apprehension in Canberra as harbingers of a lessening U.S. involvement and interest in Asia. Strong support of U.S. policies in the Indian Ocean could have appeared in Canberra as a timely gesture of support and inducement for a continued U.S. visibility in the area.

The change of government in 1972 after 23 years of Liberal-Country party rule brought opportunities to change the trend of Australian foreign policy. Labour party leader Gough Whitlam, who was his own foreign minister, openly said that his policies would be different from his predecessors, which he thought had given Australia "a racist and military image."[131] The Labour government took an unusually active interest in Australian foreign policy, and Whitlam tried to develop "for the first time a systematic national-interest orientation" on the lines of other regional or smaller countries of the area.[132] The Labour government modified the traditional Australian strategic thinking rather considerably with its own conception of Australia as an Asian power. The traditional habit of Australia to view itself as an appendage of the British Empire and of the United States was replaced by a sense of independent Australian identity in foreign affairs. The change in Australian foreign policy orientation successfully lessened this image.

Australian identification with Asia, to which it geographically belongs, also brought about a change in the Australian attitude toward Asians. With the increased realization that Australia would have to live with Asia, Asians came to be viewed as nations, peoples, and

leaders with whom Australians had to become familiar.[133] The
Labour government effectively made certain of Australia's Asian
identification. In the growing Asian regionalism, the Australian
Labour party saw a healthy respite from excessive dependence on
the United States. As part of the Labour party's efforts to make
Australia more independent of its U.S. and European allies, Whitlam
recognized China, discontinued military aid to South Vietnam and
Cambodia, and started the process of judging foreign policy issues
on their merits. In January 1973, Whitlam even reproached Nixon
for the bombings of North Vietnam, signaling the end of the auto-
matic toeing of U.S. policies by Australia.[134] The popular support
for the Labour party's policy of an independent Australian policy
marked a contrast from the traditional Australian political behavior.

The Labour party voiced opposition to the U.S. plan for a naval
buildup in the Indian Ocean. Canberra believed that such a move
would induce a naval arms race in the ocean to the detriment of the
littoral countries, including Australia. The Labour government identified strongly with the UN declaration of the Indian Ocean as a zone
of peace and took an active part in the ad hoc committee. The Australian prime minister echoed the littoral countries' view that Diego
Garcia expansion was not welcome. He reiterated the total opposition
of the littoral countries against the proposed expansion of the atoll
facility.[135] The Labour party's opposition to the U.S. buildup was
on a par with the opposition of other important littoral countries,
such as India. It was an opposition against the big-power rivalry in
general, which was viewed as dangerous by the countries of the
region.

The change in government in early 1976 brought a change in
the Australian attitude toward the U.S. strategy in the Indian Ocean.
The newly elected Liberal leader Malcolm Fraser reversed the Australian policy of opposition to U.S. expansion of the Diego Garcia
atoll and welcomed the U.S. policy of a buildup in the Indian Ocean.
In keeping with the Liberal party tradition of viewing any Soviet
advance in the vital Indian Ocean region as a danger to Australia,
Fraser exhorted the United States for a "matching" Indian Ocean
presence to counterbalance the Soviet navy. The new government
has also removed the restrictions that the Labour government placed
on U.S. nuclear-weapon-carrying naval units from making calls on
the Australian ports.

Even though the change in the Australian perspective toward the
U.S. Indian Ocean policy appears as radical departure from the
Labour era, in reality Labour's distaste for the U.S. naval buildup
did not affect the U.S.-Australian close naval cooperation. Australia
continued to be a link in the overall U.S. Indian Ocean strategy.[136]

Australia, along with Indonesia, remained the primary pillar guarding the East in the purported U. S. southern hemisphere strategy aimed at acquiring predominant control over the raw-materials-rich Afro-Asian littorals of the Indian Ocean through the control of the Indian Ocean sea-lanes of communication.[137]

NOTES

1. United Nations, General Assembly, Report of the Secretary General (A/C.159/1), p. 9.

2. Cited in Peking Review, no. 6 (February 5, 1971): 21.

3. For a discussion on the subject, see Desmond P. Wilson and Nicholas Brown, Warfare at Sea: Threat of the Seventies, Professional Paper no. 79 (Arlington, Va.: Center for Naval Analyses, 1971).

4. See Robert W. Tucker, A New Isolation: Threat or Promise? (New York: Universe Books, 1972).

5. Cited in Dezil Peiris, "Indian Ocean: The Strategy of Brinkmanship," Far Eastern Economic Review (May 6, 1974): 30.

6. K. P. Misra, "International Politics and Security of the Indian Ocean Area," International Studies 12 (January-March 1973): 141. For an informed analysis on the issue of prospective regionalism in the Indian Ocean region, see G. Bhagat, "Retrenchment of American Power and Regionalism in Asia," Indian Political Science Review (Delhi) 8, no. 2 (July 1974): 129-50.

7. Misra, op. cit., p. 148.

8. A. J. Cottrell, "Indian: Ocean of Tomorrow," Navy/Sea Power 14, no. 3 (March 1971): 11.

9. D. K. Palit, "An Alibi in the Indian Ocean," Overseas Hindusthan Times, May 2, 1974, p. 7.

10. Indira Gandhi, Colombo address, reported in Times of India, April 29, 1973, p. 1.

11. Misra, op. cit., p. 148.

12. Conference of Heads of State and Governments of Nonaligned Countries, Cairo, October 5-10, 1964, A Ministry of National Guidance Publication, pp. 350-52.

13. Review of International Affairs 21, no. 491 (September 1970): 33.

14. United Nations, General Assembly, Resolution 2832 (XXVI).

15. Ibid.

16. Ibid.

17. Ibid.

18. SIPRI Yearbook, 1975, p. 61.

19. Ibid.

20. Statement of Hamilton S. Amerasingha, Sri Lanka ambassador, cited in Homer A. Jack, The Indian Ocean as a Zone of Peace, Disarmament Report, no. 26 (New York: World Conference of Religion for Peace, 1973), p. 3.

21. United Nations, General Assembly, First Committee Provisional Record of the Nineteen Hundred and Eleventh Meeting, 27th sess. (A/C.1/P.V.1011), December 5, 1972.

22. Ibid.

23. United Nations, A/AC.159/1, op. cit.

24. Ibid., p. 4.

25. Ibid., p. 5.

26. Ibid., p. 6.

27. United Nations, Statement pursuant to paragraphs 6 and 7 of General Assembly Resolution 3080 (XXVIII), A/AC.159/1, Rev. 1, July 11, 1974.

28. United Nations, Ad Hoc Committee on the Indian Ocean, Official Records, 29th sess., Supplement No. 29 A/9629.

29. Cited in SIPRI Yearbook, 1975, p. 437.

30. For the text of the resolution, see United Nations, General Assembly, Resolution 3259 (XXIX).

31. Ibid., paragraph 4.

32. U.S., Congress, House, Committee on International Relations, Diego Garcia: The Debate Over the Base and the Island's Former Inhabitants, testimony of John C. Culver, 94th Cong., 1st sess., 1975, p. 39.

33. U.S., Congress, House, Diego Garcia: The Debate, op. cit., p. 5.

34. Interview with George T. Churchill, director, Office of International Security Operations, Department of State, March 1976. American feeling on the issue of the freedom of the seas is very strong. For a discussion of the issue, see Francis Wrigley Hirst, "What the Americans Mean by Freedom of the Seas," in Grotius Society, Problems of the War, vol. 4 (London: 1916-1919), pp. 26-34; Chandler Parsons Anderson, Freedom of the Seas, American Academy of Political and Social Science Publication, no. 1137, (1917); Earl Willis Crecraft, Freedom of the Seas (Freeport, N.Y.: Books for Libraries Press, 1969).

35. U.S., Congress, House, Subcommittee on the Near East and South Asia, Committee on Foreign Affairs, Proposed Expansion of U.S. Military Facilities in the Indian Ocean, 93d Cong., 2d sess., 1974, p. 5.

36. David Vital, The Making of British Foreign Policy, (New York: Praeger, 1968), pp. 104-05.

37. Ibid.

38. For a discussion, see Hans J. Morgenthau, "Imperialism and Intervention: The Dynamism of the Strong," in At Issue: Politics in the World Arena, ed. Steven L. Spiegel (New York: St. Martin's Press, 1973), pp. 61-70.

39. Ibid.

40. James Cable, Gunboat Diplomacy: Political Applications of Limited Naval Force (New York: Praeger, 1971), p. 21.

41. Cited in Albert Wohlstetter, Strength, Interest and New Technologies, Adelphi Paper no. 46, March 1968, p. 7.

42. Interview with Admiral (Ret.) John C. McCain, March 1976.

43. Michael T. Klare, War Without End: American Planning for the Next Vietnams (New York: Knopf, 1972), p. 314.

44. Interview with T. N. Kaul, ambassador of India to the United States, March 1976.

45. See, for example, "The Security of the Southern Oceans: Southern Africa the Key," report of a seminar held at the Royal United Services Institute for Defence Studies, February 16, 1972, London, Royal United Services Institute for Defence Studies, 1972. See also Tad Szulc, "Why Are We in Johannesburg?" Esquire, October 1974, pp. 48, 50, 56, 58, 60; and Wesley A. Groesbeck, "The Transkei—Key to U.S. Naval Strategy in the Indian Ocean," Military Review 56 (June 1976): 18-24.

46. Pieter W. Botha, South Africa defense minister, cited in Paul Giniewski, "South Africa and the Defence of the Cape Route," NATO's Fifteen Nations 17, no. 2 (April-May 1972): 26.

47. "Indian Ocean, Why the West Needs South Africa," Africa Report 20, no. 1 (January-February 1975): 20.

48. Ibid.

49. See United Kingdom, Exchanges of Letters of Defence Matters Between the Government of the United Kingdom and the Union of South Africa, June 1955, Cmd. 9520; for a detailed discussion of the purported strategic significance of South Africa, see John Edward Spence, The Strategic Significance of Southern Africa (London: Royal United Services Institution, 1970).

50. E. S. Virpsha, "Strategic Importance of South Africa," NATO's Fifteen Nations 12, no. 1 (February-March 1969): 42.

51. For a detailed discussion, Maxine Isaacs Burns, "Tilting Toward South Africa," Africa Report 21, no. 2 (March-April 1976): 7-8, 10-11.

52. J. F. Spence, "South Africa and the Defence of the West," Round Table 61, no. 241 (January 1971): 19.

53. The United States identified itself closely with South Africa during the Angolan crisis. See Anthony Lewis, New York Times, January 15, 1971, p. 33. In the aftermath of Angola, Secretary of State Kissinger is reported to have ordered a U.S. administrative study to review Washington's relationships with Pretoria and to suggest possible changes. For details of this study (January 29, 1976), see New York Times, January 31, 1976, p. 2. Kissinger also met with Prime Minister John Vorester in both Zurich and Pretoria during September. For details, see New York Times, September 5, 6, and 7, 1976. The Angolan affair lent strength to the demand for a closer Washington-Pretoria military connection. See Sean Gervase, "Under the NATO Umbrella," Africa Report 21, no. 5 (September-October 1976): 12-16.

54. Tom Engelhardt, 'New U.S. Alliance in the Indian Ocean," Pacific News Service, 1974; Alan Hutchinson, "Indian Ocean: The Island Viewpoint," Africa Report 20, no. 1 (January-February 1975): 52.

55. U.S., Congress, House, Committee on Foreign Affairs, New Perspectives on the Persian Gulf, 93d Cong., 1st sess., 1973, p. 39.

56. "Interview with the Shah," New Republic, December 1, 1974, p. 20.

57. The Azerbaijan incident, though often overlooked, played an important role in the beginnings of the U.S.-Soviet Cold War; see Gary R. Hess, "The Iranian Crisis of 1945-46 and the Cold War," Political Science Quarterly 89 (March 1974): 117-46; and William R. Andrews, "The Azerbaijan Incident: The Soviet Union in Iran, 1941-46," Military Review 54 (August 1974): 74-85.

58. Marcus Franda, "The Indian Ocean: A Delhi Perspective," American Universities Fieldstaff Reports, vol. 19, no. 1, Southeast Asia Series, 1975, pp. 3-5.

59. Ibid.

60. R. M. Burrell, "The Indian Ocean: An Iranian Evaluation," The Indian Ocean: Its Political, Economic, and Military Importance, in ed. Alvin Cottrell and R. M. Burrell (New York: Praeger, 1972), p. 96.

61. U.S., Congress, House, New Perspectives on the Persian Gulf, op. cit., p. 61. See also Rouhollah K. Ramazani, The Persian Gulf: Iran's role (Charlottesville: University Press of Virginia, 1972).

62. Internal developments can propel decisive changes in the area; see William E. Griffith, "The Great Powers, the Indian Ocean and the Persian Gulf," Jerusalem Journal of International Relations 1 (Winter 1975): 5-19.

63. "The Shah on the Persian Gulf," in Iran's Foreign Policy, ed. Ardeshir Zahedi (Teheran: Ministry of Foreign Affairs), p. 92.

64. The Arab countries are apprehensive about the Iranian military buildup. In fact, the Saudi buildup is said to be mainly against Iran. See John W. Finney, "U.S. Discourages the Saudis from Buying Advanced Weapons," New York Times, July 8, 1976, p. 6. The close Irani relationships with Israel naturally contributes to the Arab coolness toward the shah. For a discussion on the Israeli-Irani relationships, see Robert B. Reppa, Israel and Iran: Bilateral Relationships and Effect on the Indian Ocean Basin (New York: Praeger, 1974); see also Simon Head, "The Monarchs of the Persian Gulf," New York Times Review of Books March 21, 1974, pp. 29-36.

65. For a discussion of the Shatt Al-Arab River dispute, see Khalid Yahya al-Izzi, The Shatt Al-Arab Dispute (Groningen: State University, 1971).

66. U.S., Congress, House, Committee on Foreign Affairs, The Persian Gulf, 1974: Money, Politics, Arms, and Power, 93d Cong., 2d sess., 1975, cites Robert P. Berman, Appendix 8, p. 249. For an examination of the political and practical limits to the shah's desire to play an active role in the Indian Ocean, see Alexander Macleod, "Shah of the Indian Ocean?" Pacific Community 7 (April 1976): 423-32; see also Ehsan Yar-Shater, ed., Iran Faces the Seventies (New York: Praeger, 1971).

67. For a gist of the misgivings of a continued close relationship with the shah as perceived by these leaders, see U.S., Congress, House, Hearings, New Perspectives on the Persian Gulf, op. cit.; The Persian Gulf, 1974, op. cit.

68. Cited in U.S., Congress, House, New Perspectives on the Persian Gulf, op. cit., p. vi. For a discussion of the prospects for stability in the Persian Gulf, see J. C. Hurewitz, The Persian Gulf, Headline Series, no. 220 (New York: Foreign Policy Association, 1974).

69. In public, however, the shah is committed to the Indian Ocean zone-of-peace concept. Iran has voted in favor of the proposal in the United Nations, and the shah reiterates Iran's support in state visits to other littoral countries. For example, see the text of the joint communique on the shah's visit to India as reported in FBIS-MEA-74-195, October 7, 1974, p. U1.

70. Engelhardt, op. cit.

71. Ibid.

72. Richard Burt, "Iranian Navy Growing as an Indian Ocean Power," Christian Science Monitor, August 22, 1975.

73. Jack Anderson and Les Whitten, "CIA Study Finds Shah Insecure," Washington Post, July 11, 1975, p. D15.

74. K. Subrahmanyam, "India and the Arms Buildup in West Asia," India and Foreign Review 10, no. 21 (August 15, 1973): 16-17.

75. Interview with the shah, Spiegel magazine, January 4, 1974, pp. 8-9.

76. U.S., Congress, House, New Perspectives on the Persian Gulf, op. cit., pp. 65-70.

77. K. M. Panikkar, cited in Anthony Harrigan, "India's Maritime Posture," Military Review 49 (April 1969): 30.

78. See "Notes and Memoranda," India Quarterly 2, no. 3 (July-September 1946): 288-89; G. N. Molesworth, "Some Problems of Future Security in the Indian Ocean Area," Asiatic Review 42 (January 1946): 25-28.

79. K. M. Panikkar, "The Basis of an Indo-British Treaty," Asiatic Review 42 (October 1946): 357-59.

80. Ibid.

81. K. M. Panikkar, India and the Indian Ocean (London: Allen & Unwin, 1945), p. 90.

82. Ibid.

83. K. B. Vaidya, The Naval Defence of India (Bombay: Thacker and Co., 1949), p. 91.

84. Ibid., p. 101.

85. Indian Council of World Affairs, Defence and Security in the Indian Ocean Area (New York: Asia Publishing House, 1958), p. 30.

86. For the Lok Sabha (House of the People) debate on U.S. entry, see India, Parliament, Lok Sabha Debates, ser. 3, vol. 24, December 19, 1963, cols. 5667-775.

87. Nehru's statement on the floor of the Rajya Sabha (Council of States), December 21, 1963, cited in Devender Kaushik, The Indian Ocean: Towards a Peace Zone (Delhi: Vikas Publications, 1972), p. 111.

88. For a detailed account of the parliamentary debates, including the expression of the stated suspicion, see India, Parliament, Lok Sabha Debates, ser. 3, vol. 24, op. cit.

89. See India, Parliament, Rajya Sabha Debates, vol. 54, Pt. I, November 18, 1965, cols. 1815-822; Lok Sabha Debates, ser. 4, vol. 2, April 6, 1967, cols. 3207-223.

90. K. Subrahmanyam, "The Challenge of the Seventies to India's Security," India Quarterly 27, no. 2 (April-June 1970): 139.

91. Dinesh Singh, minister of external affairs, cited in Kaushik, op. cit., p. 110.

92. Y. V. Chavan, "Expansion of Diego Garcia Will Aggravate Tension" (Paper delivered at the International Conference on the Indian

Ocean, World Peace Council, New Delhi, November 23, 1974), reported in FBIS-NEA-74-222 5, no. 222 (November 15, 1974): U2-U3.

93. Ibid.

94. Baldev Raj Nayar, "Treat India Seriously," Foreign Policy, no. 18 (Spring 1975): 133-54; for Mrs. Gandhi's charge to that effect, see New York Times, October 19, 1971, p. 6. See also Inder Malhotra, "Power Game Worries in India," Guardian, July 19, 1971. p. 2.

95. Malhotra, ibid.

96. Ibid.

97. Interview with T. N. Kaul, Indian ambassador to the United States; see also Max Frankel, "To India the U.S. Is a Bitter Disappointment," New York Times, November 30, 1971, p. 2. The United States indeed remained aloof while China was threatening physical intervention against India. Throughout the Bangladesh crisis, culminating in the short Indo-Pakistani War of December 1971, the Nixon administration, in spite of its professed "strict neutrality," tilted heavily toward Pakistan. For a detailed account, see Vinod Gupta, Anderson Papers: A Study of Nixon's Blackmail of India (New Delhi: Indian School Supply Depot, Publication Division, 1972). The U.S. posture put a deep scar on Indo-U.S. relations. See T. V. Kunhi Krishnan, The Unfriendly Friends, India and America (Thompson, Conn.: Interculture Associates, 1974).

98. Sisir Gupta, "Not Outside the Contest," Hindusthan Times, Sunday World, August 22, 1971, p. 1.

99. See U.S., Congress, Senate, Committee on Appropriations, Second Supplemental Appropriations, FY 1974, 93d Cong., 2d sess., 1975, Zumwalt testimony, p. 2145. For a strong rebuttal of the implication, see U.S., Congress, Senate, Committee on Appropriations, Military Construction Appropriations, FY 1975, 93d Cong., 2d sess., 1976, Pell testimony, p. 416; see also Marcus F. Franda, "India and the Soviets: 1975," American Universities Fieldstaff Reports, vol. 18, no. 5, Southeast Asia Series, 1975.

100. Easwar Sagar, "India and the Two Won'ts," Sea Power 16 (March 1973): 32.

101. Cited in "Indian Ocean as a Zone of Peace," Indian and Foreign Review 10, no. 17, (June 15, 1973): 7. Original interview to ABC was on May 26, 1973 in New Delhi.

102. Ibid.

103. U.S., Congress, Congressional Research Services, Foreign Affairs Division, U.S. Foreign Policy for the 1970s, prepared for the Committee on Foreigns Affairs, House, 93d Cong., 1st sess., 1973, p. 66.

104. Cited by Representative Charles Vanik, Congressional Record, 93d Cong., 2d sess., November 26, 1974, 120: H1117.

For a discussion of the impact of the bomb on Indo-U.S. relations, see Shelton L. Williams, The U.S., India, and the Bomb, Washington Center of Foreign Policy Research, Studies in International Affairs, no. 12 (Baltimore: Johns Hopkins University Press, 1969); see also Wayne Ayres Wilcox, Nuclear Weapon Options and the Strategic Environment in South Asia: Arms Control Implications for India (Santa Monica: Southern California Arms Control and Foreign Policy Seminar, 1972).

105. See Marcus F. Franda, "America and Pakistan: The View from India," American Universities Fieldstaff Reports, vol. 19, no. 3, Southeast Asia Series, 1975; see also Harish Kapur, The Embattled Triangle, Moscow—Peking—New Delhi (New York: Humanities Press, 1973).

106. A. P. S. Bindra, "The Indian Ocean: As Seen by an Indian," U.S. Naval Institute Proceedings 96 (May 1970): 187.

107. For a discussion of India's disinterestedness in playing a leading role, see Wayne Ayres Wilcox, Leo E. Rose, and Gavin Boyd, eds., Asia and the International System (Cambridge, Mass.: Winthrop, 1972).

108. Justus M. Van der Kroef, Australian Security Policies and Problems (New York: National Strategy Information Center, 1970), p. 21.

109. Ibid.

110. Ashok Kapur, "Indo-Soviet Treaty and the Emerging Asian Balance," Asian Survey 12 (June 1972): 463-74.

111. Ibid.

112. For a detailed discussion, see Robert H. Donaldson, "India: The Soviet Stake in Stability," Asian Survey 12 (June 1972): 483 ff; see also Robert H. Donaldson, Soviet Policy Toward India: Ideology and Strategy (Cambridge, Mass.: Harvard University Press, 1974). For an historic account of the said relationships, see J. A. Naik, Soviet Policy Towards Indian from Stalin to Brezhnev (Delhi: Vikas Publications, 1970).

113. The recent thaw between Peking and New Delhi indicates the possibility that China may wish to befriend India to work jointly against "superpower imperialism" in the wake of the Moscow-Washington detente. See Ashok Kapur, "India and China: Adversaries or Potential Partners ?" World Today 30 (March 1974): 129-34.

114. Franda, 'The Indian Ocean," op. cit., p. 11.

115. The Joint Committee on Foreign Affairs Report cites the reasons for the reappraisal of the traditional Australian attitude of an eastern-oriented base as the major British withdrawal, the Soviet naval and economic activities, the uncertainty of U.S. intentions in the area, the anticipated large increase in mineral exports from western Australia, and the extension of the influences of great powers

in the ocean whose policies and ideologies differ from those of Australia. Australia, Parliament, Joint Committee on Foreign Affairs Report, Parliamentary Paper no. 258, 1971.

116. The statement was made in August 1969. According to T. B. Millar, "The Asian Quadrilateral: An Australian View,"Australian Outlook, 27, no. 2 (August 1973): 134–39, in issuing the statement Freeth apparently meant that "Australia might need the Russians to contain the real threat to the peace in Asia, i.e., China."

117. Denis Warner, "An Assessment of Potential Threats to Australia's Essential Interests Over the Next Ten Years," in T. B. Millar, ed., Britain's Withdrawal from Asia. Its Implications for Australia (Australian National University: Strategic and Defence Studies Center, 1967), p. 21.

118. J. Gentilli, "Australia-Indian or Pacific?" Australian Quarterly 21, no. 1 (March 1949): 72–73.

119. "Australia: Asia Without British Power," Round Table, January 1968, p. 82. The Pacific Security Pact of 1951 (known as ANZUS) among Australia, New Zealand, and the United States and the South East Asia Collective Treaty (SEATO) of later years (1954), provided a sense of reassurance to Australia. For details, see T. B. Millar, Australia's Defence (Victoria: Melbourne University Press, 1969).

120. Australia had forces in Malaya (Malaysia) to help the campaign against Communist insurrections. Again, Australian forces were in Malaysia as part of the five-power forces (Malaysia, Singapore, Great Britain, New Zealand, Australia) used against Indonesian "confrontation." For details see T. B. Millar, "Defence Under Labor, " Current Affairs Bulletin 52, no. 7 (December 1975): 4–18.

121. J. L. Richardson, "Australian Strategic Perspectives," Current History 62 (March 1972): 144.

122. Van der Kroef, op. cit., p. 6; see also H. G. Gelber, The Australian American Alliance: Costs and Benefits (Baltimore: Penguin, 1968). Gelber defined the syndrome in the following way (p. 121): "Americans never forgot the help given to George Washington by the French under young Lafayette. Ever since, a marked feature of the relationship between American public opinion and foreign policy has been the strength of the Lafayette syndrome. It makes good sense for Australians to count upon it."

123. Barnard K. Gordon, "Open Options: Australia's Foreign Policy in the Seventies," Current History 62 (March 1972): 130.

124. Ibid.

125. Bruce Grant, "Toward a New Balance in Asia," Foreign Affairs (July 1969): 174.

126. By an official account in 1969, there were 16 installations and facilities in Australia. Commonwealth Parliamentary Debates, House of Representatives, September 9, 1969, pp. 1010-012, cited in Desmond Ball, "American Bases in Australia: The Strategic Implications," Current Affairs Bulletin 51, no. 10 (March 1975): 4. For details, see Ball, pp. 4-17.

127. For the texts, see U.S., Department of State, "Battle-Berwick Agreement," Treaties and Other International Acts, Series 5377, 14 UST 908. The treaty entered into force on June 28, 1963.

128. John Gorton, former prime minister of Australia, cited in Justus M. Van der Kroef, "Australia's New Search for Collective Security," ORBIS 13 (Summer 1969): 528.

129. Millar, Australia's Defence, op. cit., p. 34.

130. For a discussion of the "shocks" from Nixon's visit to Peking, see Gordon, op. cit.

131. Cited in J. D. Miller, "Australian Foreign Policy: Constraints and Opportunities. I," International Affairs (April 1974): 229. Conflicting interpretations exist on Australian foreign policy under Whitlam. Some believe that the changes had been definitive and unprecedented. See E. G. Whitlam, Australia's Foreign Policy: New Directions, New Definitions (Canberra: Australian Institute of International Affairs, November 1973); and G. S. Barclay, "Problems on Australian Foreign Policy, July-December 1974," Australian Journal of Politics and History 21 (April 1975): 1-10. However, Hedley Bull, in Advance Australia Where?, ed. B. D. Beddie, (Melbourne: Oxford University Press, 1975), writes that the Labour government under Whitlam only changed the means and modalities of Australia's foreign policy.

132. Richardson, op. cit.

133. Grant, op. cit., p. 175.

134. Miller, op. cit.

135. Meet the Press, NBC broadcast, cited by Senator Stuart Symington in U.S., Congress, Senate, Committee on Armed Services, Disapprove Construction Projects on the Island of Diego Garcia, 94th Cong., 1st sess., 1975, p. 3.

136. Engelhardt, op. cit.

137. For a study of the southern hemisphere strategy, see Tom Engelhardt, "Indian Ocean Fleet—The Navy's $10 Billion Gamble," Pacific News Service, 1974.

10

U.S. STRATEGY:
AN EVALUATION

The expanded Diego Garcia facility and regular naval deployments in Indian Ocean waters signify the American desire to widen policy and strategic concerns in the Indian Ocean. In the aftermath of the 1973 Mideast War, the Department of Defense signaled the changed U.S. posture toward the ocean with the announcement of its intention to maintain militarily significant forces in the Indian Ocean for periods of time amounting to 30 to 60 days each quarter.[1]

The periodic deployment of carrier-led task forces in the Indian Ocean reflects the U.S. resolve to be visibly present in the region. The extended visibility also underscores the fact that the United States has the capability and the will to resort to naval deployments in pursuance of its interests. During the height of the oil embargo (November-December 1973), for example, the 80,000-ton carrier Constellation entered the Persian Gulf ostensibly to take part in the largest Indian Ocean exercise over conducted under CENTO auspices. The presence of a U.S. carrier in those waters after a two-decade absence (1948) emphasized Washington's concern with the continued oil embargo. The show of potential force was as clear as the prior official statements of possible armed intervention.

The extended U.S. activity in the ocean contrasts with the original plan to limit projection of U.S. power into the area. The early programs relating to Diego Garcia assumed that a relatively small facility at the isolated, strategically located atoll would serve the needs of U.S. visibility and provide a substitute for base facilities in and around the littoral countries. The planners attached to the Chief of Naval Operations (CNO) saw the possibility of unnecessary and complicated entanglements in the littoral countries' squabbles as a result of America's search for a base in the littoral countries.[2]

The Diego Garcia facility itself was tied to three basic requirements: surveillance, a low profile presence as an indication of the U.S. desire not to let the ocean become a Soviet lake, and a logistics point to back up contingency operations in the area by units from the Western Pacific.[3] The austere facility was seen as sufficient for the projected U.S. naval role in the Indian Ocean.

At the beginning of the congressional debate over the proposed expansion of the Diego Garcia facility, the administration character- ized any talk of a U.S. Indian Ocean policy as presumptuous.[4] How- ever, security objectives for the region were described in the fol- lowing terms:

> First, we wish to provide an effective alternative to
> the growth of the Soviet influence in the region; second,
> we wish to have continued access to vital Middle East-
> ern oil supplies for ourselves and other nations of the
> free world; third, we want to insure the continued free
> movement of U.S. ships and aircraft into and out of
> the area.[5]

Much has happened since that testimony, and the United States has now moved into the ocean decisively, foreclosing the option of lengthy deliberations.

When the Diego Garcia expansion was debated by the Senate under the Mansfield resolution (Senate Resolution 160), Senator Ken- nedy aptly remarked that the issue was not merely an expansion pro- posal involving a few millions of dollars, but that it involved larger questions of principle and policy.[6] "At heart," he said

> this debate is not about whether we should extend the
> runway at Diego Garcia another few thousand feet, or
> dredge the harbor to accommodate larger ships, or
> put up some barracks to house several hundred mili-
> tary personnel. This debate is about the role the
> United States will play in the coming years in the
> Indian Ocean and in the nations that line its shores.
> ... It is about our view of the world of the late 1970s
> and 1980s and America's position in that world.[7]

Deploring the military approach to Indian Ocean policy, Kennedy asked:

> Are we going to recognize a most valuable lesson of
> the last decade; the need to put political objectives and

> interests first; to think through problems before acting;
> and to exhaust diplomacy before once again reaching for
> the instruments of war?[8]

The enormous political and diplomatic risks the United States has
taken in its efforts to acquire the tactical advantages of "greater
maneuverability and flexibility" through an expanded Diego Garcia
facility are seen as a glaring example of Pentagon-dominated U.S.
foreign policy.[9]

Some congressional leaders believed that the Soviet threat in
the Indian Ocean was used as a red herring by the Department of
Defense to justify its expansion proposal, which, in reality, had
been planned since the early 1960s. Misleading statements and mis-
representation of facts—the portrayal of the atoll as being "without
population," the statement that it was secured from the British "without charge," and the exaggerated picture of the Soviet buildup of bases
and facilities in the area—all showed a planned course of action that
justifiably led to congressional charges of "deception and cover-up."[10]
Only the secretary of defense, James R. Schlesinger, seemed to have
been candid enough to admit that the Department of Defense would go
ahead with its Diego Garcia expansion plans even if there were no
Soviets in the Indian Ocean.[11] As we know today, the Department of
Defense persuaded the Department of State not to pursue a Saudi
offer to lessen the alleged Soviet inroads into Somalia lest there be
no immediate justification for the proposed expansion requests.[12]

From the vantage point of Capitol Hill, the cavalier attitude
of the executive toward the congressional request for Indian Ocean
arms limitation talks appeared as an indication of its refusal to pursue a "peaceful, less costly, no risk alternative."[13] The neglect
of the politicodiplomatic importance of its actions seemed to indicate
that the U.S. Navy was totally oblivious to the Alfred T. Mahan observation that "diplomatic conditions affect military actions, and military
considerations diplomatic measures."[14]

Although the relatively modest expansion of the facility keeps
Diego Garcia from becoming a strategic base, per se, navy plans for
further expansion can be safely expected. The possibility that the
U.S. Navy will not stop halfway has already been expressed.[15] With
the increasing success of the navy in asserting its claims in the
Defense Department, a navy claim for further buildup on the pretext
of indispensable necessity would be difficult to refute.[16] An Indian
Ocean fleet, the long-cherished dream of the U.S. Navy, is thus a
distinct possibility. As the Soviets achieve or approach naval parity
with the United States, demands for a further augmented capability
will arise, and a general support for the navy's desire for preemi-

nence in the Indian Ocean would be hard to resist. In fact, a retrenchment of American commitments abroad in such a situation would be
ironic   in the light of the past policy of containment.[17]

The administration implied that, with the Diego Garcia expansion, the perceived imbalance in the Soviet and American presence in
the Indian Ocean would be corrected, and that the resultant rough
equivalence would enable the administration to pursue the naval arms
limitation talks with greater equanimity. In view of domestic factors
that force the Kremlin to appreciate only visible military capability
as the essential reality, such an emphasis on the determined display
of power can be well understood. Indeed, it is argued that the Soviets
have never reciprocated many Western gestures of goodwill, and that
the overtures of the Kennedy administration were rebuffed until the
Cuban missile crisis demonstrated "that the balance of forces was not
in fact favorable for a test of strength."[18]

Congressional critics, however, saw the overt emphasis on
visibility and display of force as compromising possible politicodiplomatic approaches to maximizing American influence and authority in
the region. The overwhelming emphasis on building up military power
in the Indian Ocean, even at the cost of political and diplomatic influence among the nations of the area, is seen as an indication that the
United States still fails to understand that a successful strategy means
the systematic "development and employment of national power,
including but not limited to military power, to secure the goals
established by national policy."[19] It has been suggested that in an
area that resents outside military presence and is greatly stirred by
references to imperialism and colonialism, the United States ought
to have viewed the effectiveness of naval arms only in the context
of the full "panoply of the instruments of foreign policy and not
exaggerate it."[20]

A fresh approach toward the full use of those instruments in
the Indian Ocean area appears all the more essential in the context
of long-term U.S. interests. The problem of protecting national
interests from adverse developments that are bound to appear with
further buildup of U.S. military force in the region continues to
attract congressional attention. The administration is still under
congressional obligation to pursue such a course. Under Section
407 (a) of the International Security Assistance and Arms Export
Control Act of 1976 (Public Law 94-329), the president is urged to
pursue the possibility of agreed limitations on military forces in the
Indian Ocean. The president is required to report to the Congress
on the matter not later than December 1, 1976.* A sharing of

---

*The presidental report submitted on December 1, 1976, as
required by law, reiterated the administration's belief (stated in its

congressional concern for the devastating effects of a spiraling arms race and an acknowledgement, however belated, of the littoral concerns regarding an extended arms rivalry would enable the administration to recover some ground lost as a consequence of emphasis on a naval buildup in and around the ocean.

U.S. interests in the Indian Ocean demand a U.S. presence in those waters. As a superpower, the United States cannot abdicate what it perceives as its responsiblity. With the complications inherent in land bases located in the territory of littoral countries to bar foreign bases in order to avoid entanglements in superpower rivalries, Diego Garcia and the Chagos Archipelago appear as ideal and secure locations for necessary base sites in the strategically important ocean.[21]

The United States does not, however, benefit from an intensified arms rivalry in the Indian Ocean area. In fact, some analysts hold that it is in the U.S. interest to respect the littoral countries' wishes and see that the region does not become the center of great power rivalry. It has been argued that the U.S. interests should aim at strengthening the littoral countries' capability to withstand pressures from the outside.

A naval arms limitation agreement indeed provides an ideal instrument to arrest the growth of a costly and potentially harmful arms race in the Indian Ocean, a race that scarcely could provide benefit to the United States. The administration's contention that without a Diego Garcia expansion such naval arms limitations might prove a boon to the Soviets no longer seems valid. A recent 500-word statement sent by the State Department to Congress holds the view that such an arms limitation initiative for the Indian Ocean is not "in the U.S. interest at this time."[22] The administration even believes that such an initiative would imply acquiescence in the Soviet "irresponsible" behavior in Angola and Somalia.[23] Faced with increasing congressional concern for the issues, the administration very likely will be obliged to reconsider the question. As in the case of the

---

report of April 15, 1976) that circumstances are not appropriate for an American initiative toward any Indian Ocean arms limitations. Refusing to accept the administration's contention, Senator John Culver and Representative Lee Hamilton wrote a joint letter to President Gerald Ford asserting that "Arms control efforts in this region deserve a high priority, regardless of any preconceived judgments of the likelihood of success. Nothing will be achieved if there is no will or effort to succeed." See letter of December 16, 1976 accompanying the Culver-Hamilton press release of December 17, 1976.

strategic arms limitation talks, naval arms limitation talks for the Indian Ocean will probably generate increased interest in forthcoming months.

However, emphasis on a bilateral agreement between Moscow and Washington for an Indian Ocean regime will undoubtedly face problems. An arrangement between the two external powers, made without the participation of the area countries, will naturally raise the question of superpower condescension as well as the specter of superpower hegemony over the region. Such an arrangement would thus lend credence to the charge of superpower hegemony. It follows that any naval arms limitation talks for the Indian Ocean must contemplate the participation of the littoral countries. In addition to the participation of those countries, both the United Kingdom and France must be included, since their presence is still formidable. Thus, for a successful attempt at reducing the pace of the Indian Ocean arms buildup, a multilateral rather than a superpower bilateral approach is required.

The United States can offer a coup de main and regain its lost political and diplomatic grounds in the region by taking the initiative on such talks. Through farsightedness, it can deliver a diplomatic counterpunch by proposing such a comprehensive arrangement for naval arms limitation in the Indian Ocean. In the present international context, especially with the changed Afro-Asian scene and the new multipolar power configuration, the need for a fresh evaluation of U.S. foreign policy appears as the central task of U.S. strategy in the Indian Ocean.

The time seems opportune for such an initiative, for Leonid Brezhnev, the Soviet leader, as recently as June 1976 has specifically talked of Moscow's openness to such an agreement. Brezhnev is reported to have assured the visiting Indian prime minister, Indira Gandhi, of Moscow's willingness to work for the ideal of an Indian Ocean zone of peace. He maintained:

> The Soviet Union is not all that indifferent as to whether the Indian Ocean will be a zone of peace or whether existing foreign military bases will be [expanded]. Our position is clear-cut. We have plainly stated that the Soviet Union neither had nor has any intention to build military bases in the Indian Ocean. We have called upon the United States to do likewise and are awaiting their definite answer. [24]

An American offer for a naval arms limitation agreement will offer a stiff test of the stated Soviet desire.

The U.S. position in the Indian Ocean has remained militarily stronger than that of the Soviet Union, despite the latter's geographic proximity. The addition of the logistics base at Diego Garcia increases U.S. advantages considerably. With a sense of confidence based on its superior strength, the United States could rededicate itself to an Indian Ocean policy that would moderate its emphasis on force, per se. A balanced Indian Ocean policy would restore the equilibrium between reliance on force, on the one hand, and power based on influence, on the other—an equilibrium essential for a successful strategy.

Promotion of a naval arms limitation agreement would doubt-less restore the United States to its position of leadership in the pursuit of peace. While negotiations for a naval arms limitation agreement are in progress, an Indian Ocean posture statement, pro-claimed unilaterally by the United States, would be both profitable and timely. The posture statement might incorporate the following language:

1. There will be no expansion of the airfield on Diego Garcia (in both the width and thickness of the runway) to take regular deploy-ment of B-52s or any such bombers in the future (B-1s). The parking facilities, aprons, aircraft maintenance facilities, and personnel ashore will not be utilized for deployment of SR-7s or U-2s engaged in long-range surveillance.

2. There will be no stationing of ground forces on the atoll. The personnel ashore will be technicians and other related personnel essential for a logistics facility. The base will house fewer than 500 personnel.

3. There will be no storage for the support of combat units of any kind.

4. There will be no major ship repair workshops or facilities except for anchorages for tenders and repair ships.

5. There will be no additional requests for expansion of the Diego Garcia facility in accordance with the promise already made, in public, by the U.S. Navy.

6. There will be no deployment of naval units except for exclusive flag-showing purposes. At no time will such deployment exceed more than one combat flagship, three destroyers, and one aircraft carrier.

7. There will be no basing of any strategic submarines on the Diego Garcia or any other atoll of the Chagos Archipelago, so long as such units can enjoy their present basing rights in Rota, Spain, or any other such base in the Mediterranean.

8. There will be no storing or emplacing of any nuclear weapons on Diego Garcia. *

Such a statement of U.S. intentions will allay the fears of the littoral countries that Diego Garcia is a strategic base. By prohibiting the regular deployment of B-1s, the United States will prove, by action, what has otherwise been implied, that is, that Diego Garcia will be only a logistics base for the support of U.S. naval operations in the ocean in times of need. The purely logistics nature of Diego Garcia, once plausibly established, hopefully will remove lingering apprehensions concerning U.S. intention.

The petroleum, oil, and lubricant (POL) storage of Diego Garcia (700,000 barrels) will act as a visible reminder of the seriousness of U.S. determination to withstand any Soviet attempt to exploit targets of opportunity in the Indian Ocean. The Soviet strategic planners surely understand the significance of POL in military operations, and the fact that a 30-day supply for task force operations is on hand will act as a strong deterrent to the Soviet navy.

NOTES

1. U.S., Department of Defense, press release, November 30, 1973.

2. Interview with Stuart Barber, civilian assistant director, CNO Long-Range Objectives Group (Ret.), March 1976.

3. Ibid.

4. U.S., Congress, House, Subcommittee on the Near East and South Asia, Committee on Foreign Affairs, Proposed Expansion of U.S. Military Facilities in the Indian Ocean, testimony of James Noyes, 93d Cong., 2d sess., 1974, p. 52.

5. Ibid.

6. Congressional Record, 94th Cong., 1st sess., July 28, 1975, 121: S13954-3955.

7. Ibid.

8. Ibid., S13955.

9. Ibid.

10. John Culver, Congressional Record, May 6, 1976, S6625.

---

*In listing these provisions I have relied on discussions with Stuart Barber, one of the planners involved with the earliest planning for the Diego Garcia base.

11. Schlesinger curtly said: "Berbera does not make the differ-
ence. We want it [Diego Garcia base] anyway." Cited in Congressional Record, 94th Cong., 2d sess., November 6, 1975, 122: S19458.

12. For a detailed discussion of the issue, see Laurence Stern,
"Saudi Offer of Aid Reported," Washington Post, May 5, 1976, p. 5;
"U.S. Apparently Favored Building Base over Eviction of Soviet
Troops in Somalia," Wall Street Journal, May 5, 1976, p. 4; and
Robert Smith, "Ex-Envoy Charges U.S. Ignored Offer on Soviet
Somalia Role," New York Times, May 5, 1976, p. 3. For senatorial
chagrin over the issue, see Congressional Record, May 6, 1976,
op. cit., pp. S6625-631.

13. Congressional Record, July 28, 1975, op. cit., S13934.

14. Admiral Alfred T. Mahan's letter to President Theodore
Roosevelt (1911), cited in Raymond G. O'Connor, "Current Concepts
and Philosophy of Warfare," Naval War College Review 20, no. 6
(January 1968): 5. The U.S. Navy historically has opposed any limi-
tation to its freedom of navigation. See Warren Unna, "Diego Garcia,"
New Republic 170, no. 10 (March 9, 1974): 8.

15. Martin Walcott, "Strife on the Ocean Wave," Guardian
(London), March 9, 1974, p. 11.

16. Leslie H. Gelb, military correspondent for the New York
Times, wrote on June 15, 1975, pt. 4, p. 2, that "The Navy increasingly will become the dominant service as the budget pie is sliced
each year, with the Army descending into the last place." See also
columnist Jack Anderson, "Washington Merry Go Round," Washington
Post, April 19, 1976, B-11.

17. See Thomas W. Wolfe, The Soviet Quest for More Globally
Mobile Military Power (Santa Monica, Calif.: Rand, 1967). George
Kennan, the author of the famed "X" article, however, believes that
the policy of containment proved counterproductive inasmuch as it
resulted in the strengthening of the Warsaw bloc to prevent Western
penetration. See George Kennan, Memoirs 1925-1950 (Boston: Little,
Brown, 1967), Ch. 15.

18. Henry A. Kissinger, American Foreign Policy. Three
Essays (New York: Norton, 1969), p. 36. The Soviet penchant for
visible force of arms is also evident from the oft-quoted Stalin remark
(to Pierre Laval in May 1935), "The Pope: How many divisions has he
got?"

19. Ralph L. Giddings, Jr., "Power Strategy and Will," Air
University Review no. 2 (January-February 1971): 20.

20. U.S., Congress, House, Committee on Foreign Affairs,
The Indian Ocean: Political and Strategic Future, testimony of William
P. Bundy, 92d Cong., 1st sess., 1971, p. 20.

21. The sultan of Bahrain has asked the United States to leave the island (the homeport for MIDEASTFOR), as Bahrain does not want to be dragged "into international conflicts." Reported in the Washington Post, March 12, 1976, p. 17. The Thais had also revised their attitude toward the American bases located within their country. BIOT itself has been reduced to the Chagos Archipelago (including Diego Garcia) only. Great Britain had returned the Deschorres, Aldabra, and Farquhar to the Seychelles, which became independent in the latter part of 1976. The Seychelles, in accordance with its professed acceptance of nonalignment, has promised to bar any foreign base on its soil. However, the station at Mahe will remain. See The Asian Student 24, no. 10 (January 31, 1976): 10.

22. Report on Indian Ocean Arms Limitation, cited in Congressional Record, May 6, 1976, op. cit., p. S8826.

23. Ibid.

24. India News, June 18, 1976, p. 3.

11

Within the decade 1968-75, the geopolitically important Indian Ocean fell squarely within the primary strategic concerns of the United States. Although the U. S. Joint Chiefs of Staff recommended a joint U. S. -U. K. base in the Indian Ocean in 1968, the Department of the Navy had its eyes on the world's third largest ocean since the early 1960s, and even before. The long-range planners in the office of the chief of naval operations formulated a future contingency plan for the Indian Ocean as soon as the British incapability for a prolonged presence in the ocean became evident in the aftermath of the Suez fiasco (1956).

Known also as the "strategic island concept," the plan aimed to secure for the United States a preeminent position in the Indian Ocean area through a strong naval presence secured by firm control of the ingresses and egresses of the vital sea-lanes. Establishing bases on certain strategically located, sparsely populated islands was seen as a preferable alternative to securing bases on the populated shores, which tended to generate "problems." The island of Diego Garcia was selected as an ideal site by virtue of its strategic location and geographic characteristics.

The British Indian Ocean Territory was itself an American concept, designed primarily to secure the strategically located islands for future military uses without encumbrances. The British association, moreover, was seen as offering legitimacy to U. S. intrusion into an area that long had been considered a British lake.

The U. S. Congress rejected the navy's initial request for a base on Diego Garcia as unnecessary. In 1971, however, a pared-down proposal for an "austere" communications station on the island was approved. The shift had come in response to the changing political climate of the area. Growing unrest in Ethiopia threatened the security of the navy's major communications facility at Asmara, and the search for a safer alternative led to the isolated and more stable British-owned Diego Garcia.

A chain of fortuitous developments—increasing Soviet activity in the ocean, the Arab-Israeli War of October 1973, the oil embargo that followed the war, and the prospective opening of the Suez Canal—offered the Department of Defense a set of "shifting rationales" for expanding facilities at Diego Garcia. Congressional approval was soon obtained for upgrading the previously approved communications facility into the present status of a multipurpose logistics-cum-communications base.

The United States stands today at the crossroads with respect to its Indian Ocean strategy.

In the course of the foregoing study, the following themes have emerged: The Soviet entry into the Indian Ocean was a natural outcome of its recently acquired "blue water" capability. The Soviet presence in the Indian Ocean is also logical in terms of its political, economic, and strategic interests in the region. Soviet activity in the ocean has expanded with the growth of its overall naval capability and its capability for projecting power.

The Soviet presence and capability in the Indian Ocean have remained considerably less than those of the United States. The U.S. Navy's overemphasis on ship-days as a measure of respective naval capability and presence is faulty, inasmuch as it neglects certain important considerations. A more valid means of measurement would include such factors as port calls, tonnage, force characteristics, and underway replenishment capability. Such factors would show that the United States has maintained its lead over the Soviets in both terms of presence and capability in the ocean. When the combined Western presence (the United States, Great Britain, and France) is considered, the relative Soviet presence and capability appear even lower, and by a substantial margin.

The attempt to overestimate the so-called Soviet threat must be viewed in the light of the belief that congressional appropriations increase in proportion to the projected threat from the Soviets, that is, the more potent the threat, the greater the allocations. In the process of making its case, the Department of Defense tends to ignore the political costs to the United States of differing third-party perceptions of the respective U.S. and USSR capabilities.

The apprehension of the possibility of a Soviet threat to the sea-lanes, particularly a disruption in the flow of vital oil, has been unfounded. The Soviets have neither the capability nor the gumption for such adventure. The possibility of a disruption of oil flow to the West by a cutoff at the oil heads is much greater than that of interception by the Soviets at sea.

Although the Soviet capability and buildups are limited, the Soviet presence in the Indian Ocean has reduced the scope and extent of the U. S. freedom to resort to show of force or gunboat diplomacy. The United States no longer enjoys the naval superiority that ensured its unchallenged intervention in Lebanon (1958) or in the Dominican Republic (1965).

The American naval presence in the Indian Ocean undoubtedly provides a credible and visible deterrent to any future oil embargo. The stated U. S. decision to intervene militarily in the case of a calamitous oil embargo still remains a potent force. In the present context, however, such an intervention would be prohibitively costly in both terms of immediate losses and long-term repercussions.

The Nixon doctrine assigned a considerably increased role for the navy in the development of U. S. Indian Ocean strategy.

The United States has secured a position of influence in the lands that control the ingresses and egresses of the ocean. The recent rapprochement with Egypt ensures U. S. influence over the Suez Canal route to the Indian Ocean. The Cape route, the Straits of Malacca, and the strategic Gulf of Hormuz were earlier brought under increased U. S. influence through closer relations with South Africa, Australia, Indonesia, Iran, and Saudi Arabia.

U. S. Indian Ocean policy has been largely determined by the Department of Defense, a fact that has led to charges of a militarized Indian Ocean policy. Congress itself was kept in the dark concerning the nature, extent, and cost of the creation of BIOT and about the nature nature of developments surrounding Diego Garcia. Even the threats that were cited as justification for the proposed expansion of the communications facility on Diego Garcia were not properly revealed to Congress. The Department of Defense successfully used shifting rationales to circumvent the reservations of some of the congressional members.

The development of U. S. strategy in the Indian Ocean also raises questions concerning the nature of departmental bargaining. The sudden switch of the Department of State from a position of low profile and coolness toward expansion of Diego Garcia to one of support of the Defense Department's request for expansion raises the speculative possibility that Secretary of State Henry Kissinger traded off his reservations for Defense Secretary James Schlesinger's support of strategic arms limitation talks.

Fundamental to a U. S. Indian Ocean strategy for the future are the concerns and interests of peoples in the area. The U. S. buildup involves not only current money costs but also forces and factors of a more general nature that will shape the future. The buildup of an Indian Ocean fleet will escalate the power rivalry and will pave the way for the expenditure of billions of dollars in newer units and millions of dollars in annual operating costs.

Although differences in the private and public responses of foreign nations to the U.S. buildup on Diego Garcia are understandable, U.S. justification of its expansion on the basis of such "private" encouragement appears unhealthy in the aftermath of the Vietnam experience.

U.S. identification with the littoral aspirations for a zone of peace offers substantial advantages for long-term political and diplomatic gains. Such an identification restores the traditional U.S. leadership for peace and peaceful developments of the region. The concept of the zone of peace does not contravene the traditional rights of freedom of the seas and the right of innocent passage. In fact, the concept offers a workable model for future U.S. negotiations relating to other oceans.

Opportunities for reducing the intensity of great-power rivalry are presented in the current situation in the Indian Ocean. By exercising leadership, the United States can seize those opportunities for its advantage. A comprehensive naval arms limitation agreement appears an ideal and essential means for securing U.S. and world interests in the Indian Ocean. The United States has lost some diplomatic and political ground by its failure to reciprocate the expressed Soviet willingness for an Indian Ocean arms limitation agreement. The present is an opportune moment for recovering that ground by taking initiatives leading to such an agreement. Such an agreement offers the United States the best course of action to maintain freedom of the seas, secure global sea-lanes, ensure access to raw materials, and, above all, preclude escalation of an arms race that will cost the world billions of dollars in unnecessary armaments.

While negotiations for an agreement are under way, the United States can gain additional diplomatic and political leverage by unilaterally issuing an Indian Ocean military posture statement. In the absence of such efforts, the Indian Ocean will become the center of intensified great-power rivalries and the scene of ever-increasing deployments of military might, possibly leading to a calamitous military confrontation.

———————————

Postscript: The United States may find an excellent opportunity to mend fences and restore lost ground in the proposed International Conference on the Indian Ocean that the United Nations is planning to hold in Sri Lanka sometime during 1977. The United States may closely identify itself with the conference and may assert the initiative for the conclusion of a comprehensive naval arms limitation agreement.

BOOKS

Adie, W. A. C. Oil, Politics, and Seapower: The Indian Ocean Vortex. New York: Crane, Russak, 1975.

al-Izzi, Khalid Yahya. The Shatt Al-Arab River Dispute. Groninaen: State University, 1971.

Anderson, Chandler Parsons. Freedom of the Seas. Philadelphia: American Academy of Political and Social Science, 1917.

Bacon, Reginald, and Francis E. McMurtrie, Modern Naval Strategy. New York: Chemical Publishing, 1941.

Barker, A. J. Suez: The Seven Day War. New York: Praeger, 1965.

Barnds, William J. India, Pakistan, and the Great Powers. New York: Praeger, for the Council on Foreign Relations, 1974.

Barnet, J. Richard. Roots of War: The Men and Institutions Behind U.S. Foreign Policy. Baltimore: Penguin Books, 1971.

Basham, A. L. The Wonder That Was India. New York: Hawthorn Books, 1963.

Bastable, C. F. Public Finance. London: Macmillan, 1892.

Beddie, B. D., ed. Advance Australia Where? Melbourne: Oxford Oxford University Press, 1975.

Bhagat, G. Americans in India 1784-1860. New York: New York University Press, 1970.

Binkin, Martin, and Jeffrey Record. Where Does the Marine Corps Go from Here? Studies in Defense Policy. Washington, D.C.: Brookings Institution, 1976.

Blechman, Barry M. The Control of Naval Armaments: Prospects and Possibilities. Studies in Defense Policy. Washington, D.C.: Brookings Institution, 1975.

——. The Changing Soviet Navy. Studies in Defense Policy. Washington, D.C.: Brookings Institution, 1973.

——. Edward M. Gramlich, and Robert W. Hartman. Setting National Priorities: The 1976 Budget. Washington, D.C.: Brookings Institution, 1976.

——. Setting National Priorities: The 1975 Budget. Washington, D. C.: Brookings Institution, 1975.

Booth, Ken. The Military Instrument in Soviet Foreign Policy 1917-1972. London: Royal United Services Institute for Defense Studies, 1973.

Bowman, Isaiah. The New World. Problems in Political Geography. New York: World Book, 1922.

Breasted, J. H. History of Egypt. New York: Scribner Sons, 1912.

Brodie, Bernard. Strategy and National Interests: Reflections for the Future. New York: National Strategy Information Center, 1971.

Bunbury, E. H. A History of Ancient Geography. London: John Murray, 1879.

Bury, J. B., S. A. Cook, and F. E. Adcock. The Cambridge Ancient History. Vol. 1. Cambridge: University Press, 1928.

Busch, Briton Cooper. Britain and the Persian Gulf, 1894-1914. Berkeley: University of California Press, 1967.

Cable, James. Gunboat Diplomacy: Political Applications of Limited Naval Force. New York: Praeger, 1971.

Carrington, C. E. The liquidation of the British Empire. London: George C. Harrap, 1961.

Cary, M., and E. H. Warmington. The Ancient Explorers. Baltimore: Penguin Books, 1929.

Casson, Lionel. Travel in the Ancient World. London: Allen & Unwin, 1974.

Centre d'etude du Sud-Est asiatique et de l'Extreme-Orient, ed. The Politics of the Great Powers in the Indian Ocean, Brussels: Free University of Brussels, 1971.

Chapin, William. The Asian Balance of Power: An American View. Adelphi Paper Number Thirty-Five. London: Institute for Strategic Studies, April 1967.

Chestkov, David Gngorevich. The Soviet Union and Developing Countries: Experience and Prospects of Economic Cooperation. Moscow: Novosti Press Agency Publication House, 1972.

Clarke, Arthur Charles. Indian Ocean Adventure. New York: Harper, 1961.

Coffey, Joseph I. Strategic Power and National Security. Pittsburgh: University of Pittsburgh Press, 1971.

Coleman-Norton, Paul R. Studies in Roman Economic and Social History. New York: Books for Libraries Press, 1951.

Corbett, Julian S. Some Principles of Maritime Strategy. New York: Longmans, Green, 1911.

Cotter, Charles H. The Physical Geography of the Oceans. New York: American Elsevier, 1965.

Cottrell, Alvin, and Walter F. Hahn. Indian Ocean Naval Limitations. Regional Issues and Global Implications. New York: National Strategy Information Center, 1976.

Cottrell, Alvin, and R. M. Burrell, eds. The Indian Ocean: Its Political, Economic, and Military Importance. New York: Praeger, 1972.

Cranwell, John Philips. The Destiny of Sea Power and Its Influence on Land Power and Air Power. New York: Norton, 1941.

Crecraft, Earl Willis. Freedom of the Seas. Freeport, N.Y.: Books for Libraries Press, 1969.

Critchlow, Keith. Into the Hidden Environment Oceans: Lifestream of Our Planet. London: George Philip and Son, 1972.

Cromie, William J. Exploring the Secrets of the Sea. Englewood Cliffs, N.J.: Prentice-Hall, 1962.

Crozier, Brian. The Soviet Presence in Somalia. London: Institute for the Study of Conflict, 1975.

Darby, Phillip. British Defense Policy East of Suez 1947-1968. London: Oxford University Press, 1973.

Dietrich, Gunter. Oceanography: The Physical Geography of the Oceans. English edited by Cyril A. Halstead. London: Grant Educational Co., 1959.

Donaldson, Robert H. Soviet Policy Toward India: Ideology and Strategy. Cambridge, Mass.: Harvard University Press, 1974.

Doyle, Adrian Conan. Heaven Has Claws. New York: Random House, 1953.

Earle, Edward Mead. Makers of Modern Strategy. Princeton, N.J.: Princeton University Press, 1943.

Eden, Anthony. Full Circle. Boston: Houghton Mifflin, 1960.

Eilertsen, James T. The Soviet Versus United States Naval Presence in the Indian Ocean. Research Study no. 0870-73, Air University, Air War College. Alabama: Maxwell Air Force Base, 1973.

Eisenhower, Dwight D. The White House Years. New York: Doubleday, 1965.

Eldrige, Frank B. The Background of Eastern Sea Power. London: Phoenix House, 1948.

Emmerson, John K. Arms, Yen and Power: The Japanese Dilemma. Tokyo: Tuttle, 1972.

Erickson, John. Soviet Military Power. Washington, D.C.: United States Strategic Institute, 1973.

Erisman, Alva Lewis. "China: Agriculture in the 1970s." In In China: A Reassessment of the Economy. A Compendium of Papers Submitted to the Joint Economic Committee, U.S. Congress. Washington, D.C.: Government Printing Office, 1975.

Farer, Tom J. War Clouds on the Horn of Africa: A Crisis for Detente. New York: Carnegie Endowment for International Peace, 1976.

FitzGerald, Charles P. The Southern Expansion of the Chinese People. New York: Praeger, 1972.

Fitzgibbon, Russell H., ed. Global Politics. Berkeley: University of California Press, 1944.

Fitzsimons, M. A. The Foreign Policy of the British Labour Government. Notre Dame, Ind.: University of Notre Dame Press, 1953.

Fogarty, Carol H. "China's Economic Relations with the Third World." In In China: A Reassessment of the Economy. A Compendium of Papers to the Joint Economic Committee, U.S. Congress. Washington, D.C.: Government Printing Office, 1975.

Furnivall, J. S. Netherlands India. A Study of Plural Economy. Cambridge: University Press, 1967.

Gleason, John Howes. The Genesis of Russophobia in Great Britain. Cambridge, Mass.: Harvard University Press, 1950.

Goldstein, Walter. The Dilemma of British Defence: The Imbalance Between Commitments and Resources. Columbus: Ohio State University Press, 1966.

Gopal, Madan. India as a World Power: Aspects of Foreign Policy. New Delhi: Sasar Publications, 1974.

Graham, Gerald S. Great Britain in the Indian Ocean: A Study of Maritime Enterprise 1810–1850. Oxford: Oxford University Press, 1967.

Gupta, Vinod. Anderson Papers: A Study of Nixon's Blackmail of India. New Delhi: Indian School Supply Depot, Publication Division, 1972.

Hallo, William W., and William Kelly Simpson. The Ancient Near East. A History. New York: Harcourt Brace Jovanovich, 1971.

Halperin, Morton H. Contemporary Military Strategy. London: Faber & Faber, 1972.

Heckel, Gayle D. Geostrategic Restraint: Changing the Face of War. Provo, Utah: Brigham Young University, 1969.

Herne, Eric. My Dangerous World. London: Robert Hale, 1966.

Herrick, Carl H. The Indian Ocean: The End of an Era. Report no. 3928, March 23, 1970. Air War College, Air University. Alabama: Maxwell Air Force Base, 1970.

Herrick, Robert W. The U.S.S.R.'s "Blue Belt Defense" Concept. Arlington, Va.: Center for Naval Analyses, 1973.

——. Soviet Naval Strategy: Fifty Years of Theory and Practice. Annapolis, Md.: U.S. Naval Institute, 1968.

Hinton, Harold C. Peking–Washington, Chinese Foreign Policy and the United States. Beverly Hills, Calif.: Sage Publications, 1976.

——. "China's Foreign Policy: Recent Developments." Asian Studies: Occasional Paper Series no. 8. Edited by Gene T. Hsiao. Edwardsville, Ill.: Southern Illinois University, 1973.

————. The Bear at the Gate: Chinese Policymaking Under Soviet
    Pressure. AEI-Hoover Policy Study 1, 1971. Washington,
    D.C.: American Enterprise Institute for Public Policy Research,
    1971.
Hirth, F. China and the Roman Orient: Researches into Their Ancient
    and Medieval Relations as Represented in Old Chinese Records.
    Munich: Georg Hirth, 1885.
Hodson, Henry Vincent. Twentieth Century Empire. London: Faber &
    Faber, 1948.
Hommel, Fritz, Dr. The Ancient Hebrew Tradition. New York:
    E. & J. B. Young 1897.
Hourani, George Fadio. Arab Seafaring in the Indian Ocean in Ancient
    and Early Medieval Times. New York: Octagon Books, 1975.
Huck, Arthur. The Security of China: Chinese Approaches to Prob-
    lems of War and Strategy. London: Chatto & Windus for the
    Institute for Strategic Studies, 1970.
Hudson, G. F. Europe and China: A Survey of Their Relation from
    the Earliest Times to 1800. London: E. Arnold, 1931.
Hunter, Robert T. The Soviet Dilemma in the Middle East. Part I.
    Problems of Commitment. London: Institute for Strategic
    Studies, 1969.
Hutchinson, Alaister G. L. The Strategic Significance of the Indian
    Ocean. Professional Study no. 4619, Air War College, Air
    University. Alabama: Maxwell Air Force Base, April 1972.
Jukes, Geoffrey. The Soviet Union in Asia. Berkeley: University
    of California Press, 1973.
Kanet, Roser E., ed. The Soviet Union and the Developing Nations.
    Baltimore: Johns Hopkins University Press, 1974.
Kapur, Harish. The Embattled Triangle, Moscow-Peking-New Delhi.
    New York: Humanities Press, 1973.
————. The Soviet Union and the Emerging Nations: A Case Study of
    Soviet Policy Towards India. London: Joseph for the Gradu-
    ate Institute of International Studies (Geneva), 1972.
Kaushik, Devendra. The Indian Ocean: Towards a Peace Zone.
    Delhi: Vikas Publications, 1972.
Kelly, John Barrett. Britain and the Persian Gulf, 1795-1880.
    Oxford: Clarendon Press, 1968.
Kennan, George F. Memoirs 1925-1950. Boston: Little, Brown,
    1967.
Kent, Sherman. Strategic Intelligence for American World Policy.
    Princeton, N.J.: Princeton University Press, 1966.
Khan, Rashid Ahmad. Scramble for the Indian Ocean. Lahore:
    Progressive Publishers, 1973.
Kilmarx, Robert A., ed. Soviet-United States Naval Balance. Wash-
    ington, D.C.: Center for Strategic and International Studies, 1975.

Kincaid, Charles V. The Energy Crisis and Japan: Future Strategic and Foreign Policy Implications. Washington, D. C.: National War College, Strategic Research Group, 1975.

King, Peter. The Strategy of Total Withholding. Canberra Papers on Strategy and Defence 12. Canberra: Australian National University Press, 1971.

Kintner, William Roscoe. "Peace and Strategy Conflict." In A Foreign Policy Research Institute Book. New York: Praeger, 1967.

Kirkman, William Patrick. Unscrambling an Empire. A Critique of British Colonial Policy 1956-1966. London: Chatto & Windus, 1966.

Kissinger, Henry A. Nuclear Weapons and Foreign Policy. New York: Harper & Brothers, 1957.

——. American Foreign Policy: Three Essays. New York: Norton, 1969.

Klare, Michael T. War Without End: American Planning for the Next Vietnams. New York: Knopf, 1972.

Kulski, Wadysaw Wszebor. The Soviet Union in World Affairs: A Documented Analysis, 1964-1972. Syracuse, N. Y.: Syracuse University Press, 1973.

Kumar, Ravinder. India and the Persian Gulf Region 1858-1907. A Study in British Imperial Policy. Bombay: Asia Publishing House, 1965.

Kun, Joseph. Sino-Soviet Competition in Africa: The Crucial Role of Military Assistance. Munich: Radio Liberty Research, 1976.

Kunhi Krishnan, T. V. The Unfriendly Friends, India and America. Thompson, Conn.: InterCulture Associates, 1974.

Lacouperie De, Terrien. Western Origin of the Early Chinese Civilization. London: Asher & Co., 1894.

Lederer, Ivo J., and Wayne S. Vucinich, eds. The Soviet Union and the Middle East: The Post-World War II Era. Stanford, Calif.: Hoover Institution Press, 1974.

Luttwak, Edward. American Naval Power in the Mediterranean. Part I. The Political Application of Naval Force. Newport, R. I.: Naval War College, 1973.

——. The U.S.-U.S.S.R. Nuclear Weapons Balance. Beverly Hills, Calif.: Sage Publications, 1974.

McCrindle, John Watson. Periplus maris Ersthrael. Amsterdam: Philo Press, 1973.

MccGwire, Michael, Ken Booth, and John McDonnel, eds. Soviet Naval Developments: Context and Capability. Halifax: Center for Foreign Policy Studies, Dalhousie University, 1973.

——. Soviet Naval Policy: Objectives and Constraints. New York: Praeger, 1975.

Mackinder, Halford J. Democratic Ideals and Reality. New York: Henry Holt, 1942.

McLaurin, Ronald D. The Soviet Union and the Middle East. Washington, D. C.: American Institute for Research, Social Environment Research Center, 1974.

Maclean, Donald. British Foreign Policy Since Suez, 1956-1968. London: Hodder and Stoughton, 1970.

Macmillan, Harold. At the End of the Day: 1961-1963. New York: Harper & Row, 1973.

Mahan, A. T. The Problem of Asia and Its Effect Upon International Policies. Boston: Little, Brown, 1900.

————. The Influence of Sea Power Upon History. 1660-1783. Boston: Little, Brown, 1890.

Martin, L. W. The Sea in Modern Strategy. London: Chatto & Windus, 1967.

Mayhew, Christopher. Britain's Role Tomorrow. London: Hutchinson & Co., 1967.

Menon, Kumara Padmanabha Sivasankara. The Indo-Soviet Treaty: Setting and Meaning. Delhi: Vikas Publications, 1971.

Millar, T. B. Soviet Policies in the Indian Ocean Area. Canberra Papers on Strategy and Defence, no. 7. Canberra: Australian National University Press, 1970.

————. Australia's Defence. Victoria: Melbourne University Press, 1969.

————, ed. Britain's Withdrawal from Asia. Its Implications for Australia. Australia: Strategic and Defense Studies Center, Australian National University, 1967.

Miller, J. Innes. The Spice Trade of the Roman Empire, 29 B. C. to A. D. 641. Oxford: Clarendon Press, 1969.

Mookerji, Radha Kumud. A History of Indian Shipping. Allahabad: Kitab Mahal Private, 1962.

Mordechei, Abir. "Red Sea Politics." In Conflicts in Africa. Adelphi Paper no. 93. London: Institute for Strategic Studies, 1972.

Moulton, J. L. Defence in a Changing World. London: Eyre & Spottiswoode, 1964.

————. British Maritime Strategy in the 1970s. London: Royal United Service Institution, 1969.

Naik, J. A. Soviet Policy Towards India from Stalin to Brezhnev. Delhi: Vikas Publications, 1970.

Neil, William. The Cleghorn Papers. London: A & C Black, 1927.

Northedge, F. S. Freedom and Necessity in British Foreign Policy. London: Weidenfeld and Nicolson, 1972.

————. British Foreign Policy: The Process of Readjustment 1945-1961. New York: Praeger, 1962.

Nunnerley, David. President Kennedy and Britain. New York: St. Martin's Press, 1972.

Nutting, Anthony. No End of a Lesson: The Story of Suez. London: Constable, 1967.

Oddvar, B. The Soviet Union in International Shipping. Bergen, Norway: Institute for Shipping Research, 1970.

Paget, Julian. Last Post: Aden 1964–1967. London: Faber & Faber, 1969.

Panikkar, K. M. Asia and Western Dominance. London: Allen & Unwin, 1959.

———. India and the Indian Ocean. London: Allen & Unwin, 1945.

———. Malabar and the Dutch. Bombay: D. B. Taraporevala Sons, 1931.

———. Malabar and the Portuguese. Bombay: D. B. Taraporevala Sons, 1929.

Peaslee, Amos Jenkins. Constitutions of Nations. Vol. 2. The Hague: Martinus Nijhoff, 1966.

Piggot, S. Prehistoric India to 1000 B. C. London: Cassell, 1962.

Polmar, Norman. Soviet Naval Power: Challenge for the 1970s. New York: National Strategy Information Center, 1972.

Poulose, T. T., ed. Indian Ocean Power Rivalry. New Delhi: Young Asia Publications, 1974.

Qanbeck, Alton H., and Barry M. Blechman. Strategic Forces. Issues for the Mid-Seventies. Washington, D. C.: Brookings Institution, 1973.

Ramazani, Rouhollah K. The Persian Gulf: Iran's Role. Charlottesville: University Press of Virginia, 1972.

Rawlinson, H. G. Intercourse Between India and the Western World. Cambridge: University Press, 1916.

Reppa, Robert B. Israel and Iran: Bilateral Relationships and Effect on the Indian Ocean Basin. New York: Praeger, 1974.

Riedl, Harold A., The Indian Ocean Power Vacuum. Report no. 4701, April 1972. Air War College, Air University. Alabama: Maxwell Air Force Base, 1972.

Rohwer, Jurgen. Superpower Confrontation on the Seas: Naval Development and Strategy Since 1945. Beverly Hills, Calif.: Sage Publications, 1975.

Rose, Saul. Britain and South-East Asia. Baltimore: Johns Hopkins University Press, 1962.

Rosecrance, Richard N. Defense of the Realm: British Strategy in the Nuclear Epoch. New York: Columbia University Press, 1968.

Rosser, W. H., and J. F. Imray. "The Seaman's Guide to the Navigation of the Indian Ocean and China Sea, Etc." In Indian Ocean Directory. London: James Imray and Son, 1867.

Saletore, Bhasker Anand. India's Diplomatic Relations with the
    West. Bombay: Popular Book Depot, 1958.
Sastri, S. M. McCrindle's Ancient India as Described by Ptolemy.
    Calcutta: Chuckerverty Chatterjee & Co., 1927.
Schneider, William. Food, Foreign Policy, and Raw Materials
    Cartels. Strategy Paper no. 28. New York: National Strategy
    Information Center, 1976.
Schofield, Brian B. British Sea Power: Naval Policy in the Twentieth
    Century. London: B. T. Batsford, 1967.
––––––. The Royal Navy Today. London: Oxford University Press,
    1960.
Schurmann, Franz H. The Logic of World Power: An Inquiry into
    the Origins, Currents, and Contradictions of World Politics.
    New York: Pantheon Books, 1974.
Schwarz, Urs, and Laszlo Hadik. Strategic Terminology. New
    York: Praeger, 1966.
Scott, Robert. Major Theatre of Conflict: British Policy in East
    Asia. London: Atlantic Trade Study, 1968.
Scott, William F. Soviet Sources of Military Doctrine and Strategy.
    New York: Crane, Russak, 1975.
Shaw, K. E., and George G. Thomson. The Straits of Malacca: In
    Relation to the Problems of the Indian and Pacific Oceans.
    Singapore: University Education Press, 1973.
Shinwell, Emanuel. Conflict Without Malice. London: Odhams Press,
    1955.
Sivard, Ruth Leger. World Military and Social Expenditures 1976.
    Leesburg, Va.: WMSE Publications, 1976.
Smith, Arthur Vincent. The Early History of India. Oxford: Claren-
    don Press, 1924.
Smith, Sidney. Early History of Assyria. London: Chatto & Windus,
    1928.
Smolansky, Oles M. The Soviet Union and the Arab East Under
    Kruschev. Lewisburg, Pa.: Bucknell University Press, 1974.
Snyder, William P. The Politics of British Defence Policy, 1945-
    1962. Columbus: Ohio State University Press, 1964.
Sokolovsky, Vasilii Danilovich. Military Strategy. New York:
    Crane, Russak, 1975.
––––––. Military Strategy: Soviet Doctrine and Concept. New York:
    Praeger, 1963.
––––––. Military Strategy. Englewood Cliffs, N. J.: Prentice-Hall,
    1963.
Spear, Percival. A History of India. Vol. 2. Baltimore: Penguin
    Books, 1965.

Spence, John Edward. The Strategic Significance of Southern Africa.
    London: Royal United Services Institution, 1970.
Spiegel, Steven L., ed. At Issue: Politics in the World Arena.
    New York: St. Martin's Press, 1973.
Srinivas Iyengar, P. T. History of the Tamils from the Earliest
    Times to 600 A.D. Madras: C. Coomarasawmy Naidu & Sons,
    1929.
Stein, Arthur Benjamin. India and the Soviet Union: The Nehru Era.
    Chicago: University of Chicago Press, 1969.
Teggart, Frederick J. Rome and China. A Study of Correlations in
    Historical Events. Berkeley: University of California Press,
    1939.
Thapar, Romila. A History of India. Vol. 1. Baltimore: Penguin
    Books, 1966.
Thomas, Charles M. The Strategic Significance of Africa—Raw
    Materials in United States Planning. Alabama: Maxwell Air
    Force Base, 1962.
Thompson, Edward, and G. T. Garratt. Rise and Fulfillment of
    British Rule in India. New York: AMS Press, 1971.
Thomson, George G. Problems of Strategy in the Pacific and Indian
    Oceans. New York: National Strategy Information Center,
    1970.
Thomson, J. Oliver. History of Ancient Geography. Cambridge:
    University Press, 1948.
Toussaint, Auguste. History of the Indian Ocean. Chicago: Univer-
    sity of Chicago Press, 1966.
Tozer, H. F. A History of Ancient Geography. New York: Biblo
    and Tannen, 1964.
Tucker, Robert W. A New Isolation: Threat or Promise? New York:
    Universe Books, 1972.
Vaidya, K. B. The Naval Defence of India. Bombay: Thacker & Co.,
    1949.
Van der Kroef, Justus M. Australian Security Policies and Problems.
    New York: National Strategy Information Center, 1970.
Verrier, Anthony. An Army for the Sixties. A Study in National
    Policy, Contract and Obligation. London: Secker & Warburg,
    1966.
Vichakar, Jagdish. Afro-Asian Security and Indian Ocean. New
    Delhi: Sterling Publishers, 1974.
Vigor, Peter H. The Soviet View of War, Peace and Neutrality.
    Boston: Routledge & Kegan Paul, 1975.
Villiers, Alan. The Indian Ocean. London: Museum Press, 1952.
Vincent, William. The Commerce and Navigation of the Ancients in
    the Indian Ocean. London: T. Cadell and W. Davies, 1807.

Vital, David. The Making of British Foreign Policy. New York: Praeger, 1968.

Vlekke, Bernard H. M. Nusantara: A History of the East Indian Archipelago. Cambridge, Mass.: Harvard University Press, 1944.

Warmington, E. H. The Commerce Between the Roman Empire and India. London: Curzon Press, 1974.

———. Greek Geography. London: J. M. Dent & Sons, 1934.

Westcott, Allan. Mahan on Naval Warfare. Boston: Little, Brown, 1918.

Wheeler, Mortimer. Rome Beyond the Imperial Frontier. Westport. Conn.: Greenwood Press, 1954.

Whiteaway, R. S. The Rise of Portuguese Power in India, 1497–1550. Westminster: Archibald Constable, 1899.

Wilcox, Wayne Ayres. Nuclear Weapon Options and the Strategic Environment in South Asia: Arms Control Implications for India. Santa Monica, Calif.: Southern California Arms Control and Foreign Policy Seminar, 1972.

———. Leo E. Rose, and Gavin Boyd, eds. Asia and International System. Cambridge, Mass.: Winthrop, 1972.

Williams, Shelton L. The U.S., India and the Bomb. Baltimore: Johns Hopkins University Press, 1969.

Wilson, Arnold. The Persian Gulf. London: Allen & Unwin, 1954.

Wilson, Desmond P., and Nicholas Brown. Warfare at Sea: Threat of the Seventies. Professional Paper 79. Arlington, Va.: Center for Navy Analyses, 1971.

Wint, Guy. The British in Asia. London: Faber & Faber, 1947.

Wolfe, Thomas W. The Soviet Quest for More Globally Mobile Military Power. Santa Monica, Calif.: Rand, 1967.

Woodcock, George. The Greeks in India. London: Faber & Faber, 1966.

Woodhouse, Christopher M. British Foreign Policy Since the Second World War. New York: Praeger, 1960.

Wynfred, Joshua. Soviet Penetration into the Middle East. Strategy Paper no. 4. New York: National Strategy Information Center, 1971.

Yar-Shater, Ehsan. Iran Faces the Seventies. New York: Praeger, 1971.

Zafar, Imam. Ideology and Reality in Soviet Policy in Asia: Indo-Soviet Relations. Delhi: Kalyani Publishers, 1975.

Zeitzschel, Bernt. The Biology of the Indian Ocean. New York: Springer Verlag, 1973.

PERIODICALS

Acheson, Dean. "Our Atlantic Alliance." Vital Speeches of the Day 29 (January 1963): 162–66.

Ackley, Richard T.. "The Fishing Fleet and Soviet Strategy." U.S. Naval Institute Proceedings 101 (July 1975): 31–38.

———. "USSR Is Self Sufficient; U.S. Is Not." Sea Power 17 (August 1974): 24–27.

Allen, H. R. "Defence and Diplomacy." RUSI 114 (December 1969): 68–69.

Andrews, William R. "The Azerbaijan Incident: The Soviet Union in Iran, 1941–46." Military Review 54 (August 1974): 74–85.

Apalin, G. "Peking and the 'Third World.'" International Affairs (Moscow), no. 3 (March 1976): 88–97.

Armstrong, DeWitt C. III. "The British Re-Value Their Strategic Bases." RUSI (November 1959): 423–32.

Aspin, Les. "Comparing Soviet and American Defense Efforts." NATO's Fifteen Nations 22 (June–July 1976): 34–36, 39–41, 44–47.

Atkeson, Edward B. "Hemispheric Denial: Geopolitical Imperatives and Soviet Strategy." Strategic Review 4 (Spring 1976): 26–36.

Atkinson, James D. "Who Will Dominate the Strategic Indian Ocean Area in the 1970s ?" Sea Power 11 (September 1968): 22–26.

Bailey, Martin. "Tanzania and China." African Affairs 74 (January 1975): 39–50.

Baker, Arthur Davidson III. "Soviet Major Combatants." U.S. Naval Institute Proceedings 100 (June 1974): 71–83.

Ball, Desmond. "American Bases in Australia: The Strategic Implications." Current Affairs Bulletin 51, no. 10 (March 1975): 4–17.

Barclay, C. N. "Britain's Role in Southeast Asia." Military Review (June 1969): 69–76.

———. "Britain's Place in the Defence of South East Asia." Navy (November 1968): 382.

Barclay, G. St. "Problems in Australian Foreign Policy, July–December 1974." Australian Journal of Politics and History (April 1975): 11.

Barnds, William J. "Japanese Foreign Policy: Continuity Amidst Change." World Today 30 (April 1974): 151–60.

Barrett, R. "A Balance of Power." U.S. Naval Institute Proceedings (April 1972): 18–24.

Bathurst, Robert B. "The Patterns of Naval Analysis." Naval War College Review 27 (November–December 1974): 16–27.

———. "The Lemming Complex: Ritual Death in the Norwegian Sea."
    Naval War College Review 26 (May-June 1974): 35-42.

Bell, J. Bowyer. "Strategic Implications of the Soviet Presence in
    Somalia." ORBIS 19, no. 2 (Summer 1975): 402-11.

Bhagat, G. "Retrenchment of American Power and Regionalism in
    Asia." Indian Political Science Review 8, no. 2 (July 1974):
    129-50.

Binnendijk, Hans. "The U.S. and Japan: Fine-Tuning a New Relation-
    ship." Pacific Community (Tokyo) 6 (October 1974): 23-37.

Blank, Jonas L. "The Impact of Logistics upon Strategy." Air
    University Review 24, no. 3 (March-April 1973): 2-21.

Booth, Ken. "Foreign Policies at Risk: Some Problems of Managing
    Naval Power." Naval War College Review 29 (Summer 1976):
    3-15.

Brezina, Dennis W. "The Blue Water Strategy." Sea Power 14
    (May 1971): 24-28.

Brown, Neville. "Deterrence from the Sea." Survival 12, no. 6
    (June 1970): 194-98.

Brown, Roger Glenn. "Chinese Politics and American Policy: A
    New Look at the Triangle." Foreign Policy, no. 23 (Summer
    1976): 3-23.

Buck, James H. "The Japanese Self-Defense Force." Naval War
    College Review 26 (January-February 1974): 40-54.

———. "Japanese Defense Policy." Asian Affairs, An American
    Review 1 (January-February 1974): 136-150.

Bull, Hedley. "Security in the Indian Ocean." Modern World. Annual
    Review of International Relations, 1969, pp. 61-64.

Burns, Maxine Isaacs. "Tilting Toward South Africa." Africa Report
    21, no. 2 (March-April 1976): 7-8, 10-11.

Burt, Richard. "Soviet Sea-Based Forces and SALT." Survival 17
    (January-February 1975): 9-13.

Calvert, J. F. "Navies in War and in Peace." U.S. Naval Institute
    Proceedings 100 (June 1974): 47-57.

Candlin, A. H. S. "Contrast in Strategies: USA and USSR." Brassey's
    Annual, 1973, pp. 232-44.

Carrington, Lord. British Defense Secretary. "East of Suez: Peril
    for the West." Government Executive 3, no. 1 (January 1971): 43.

Chang, Parris H. "China's Foreign Policy Strategy: Washington or
    Moscow 'Connection'?" Pacific Community 7 (April 1976):
    406-22.

Chelhardt, Alexander O. "Soviet and U.S. Interests in the Indian
    Ocean." Asian Survey (August 1975): 672-83.

Clark, Donald L. "Soviet Strategy for the Seventies." Air Univer-
    sity Review (January-February 1971): 2-18.

Clark, Ian. "Soviet Conceptions of Asian Security: From Balance 'Between' to Balance Within. " Pacific Community (Tokyo) 7 (January 1976): 162-78.

Cottrell, Alvin J. "Indian Ocean of Tomorrow." Sea Power 25 (March 1971): 10-16.

———. and R. M. Burrell "The Soviet Navy and the Indian Ocean. " Strategic Review 2 (Fall 1974): 25-35.

Crossman, R. H. S. "Western Defence in the 1960s." Journal of the Royal United Service Institution (August 1961): 324-41.

Curzon, Lord. "The True Imperialism. " The Nineteenth Century and After 62 (January 1908): 157, 161.

Darby, Phillip. "Beyond East of Suez." International Affairs 46 (October 1970): 655-69.

Das, D. P. "India and the Indian Ocean: A Study of Past and Future Strategy." China Report 10 (January–April 1974): 55-70.

DeRoy, Swadesh R. "Prospects for Militarism in Japan." Pacific Community (Tokyo) 5 (January 1974):289-302.

DeWeerd, H. A. "Britain's Changing Military Policy." Foreign Affairs 34 (October 1955): 102-16.

Elegant, Robert S. "China, the U.S. & Soviet Expansion." Commentary 61 (February 1976): 39-46.

Emmerson, John K. "After Thirty Years: Japan and America." Pacific Community (Tokyo) 6 (July 1975): 475-86.

Eppstein, John, ed. "Strategy of the Southern Oceans." World Survey, November 1969, pp. 1-9.

Fairhall, David. "Soviet Merchant Marine." Brassey's Annual, 1973, pp. 131-46.

Fisher, Edward C., Jr. "A Look at the Nikolaev." U.S. Naval Institute Proceedings 100 (March 1974): 116-18.

Franda, Marcus F. "America and Pakistan: The View from India." American Universities Field Staff. Fieldstaff Reports. South Asia Ser. vol. 19, no. 3, 1975.

———. "India and the Soviets: 1975." American Universities Field Staff· Fieldstaff Reports. South Asia Ser. vol. 19, no. 5, 1975.

———. "The Indian Ocean: A Delhi Perspective." American Universities Field Staff. Fieldstaff Reports. Southeast Asia Ser. vol. 19, no. 1, 1975.

Frankel, Joseph. "Britain's Changing Role." International Affairs (October 1974).

Frankland, Noble. "Britain's Changing Strategic Position." International Affairs 33 (October 1957): 416-26.

Franks, Oliver. "Britain and the Tide of World Affairs." Listener
    (November 11, 1954): 787-88.
Fraser, Angus M. "Military Capabilities in China." Current History
    69 (September 1972): 70.
Furlong, R. D. M. "Strategic Power in the Indian Ocean." Inter-
    national Defense Review (April 1972): 133-40.
Galtung, Johan. "Japan and Future World Politics." Journal of
    Peace Research, no. 4 (1973): 355-85.
Gayler, Noel. "U.S. Strategy for Staying No. 1 Power in Asia."
    U.S. News & World Report March 25, 1974, pp. 42-44, 46.
Gerosa, Guide. "Will the Indian Ocean Become a Soviet Pond?"
    Atlas 19 (November 1970): 20-21.
Gervase, Sean. "Under the NATO Umbrella." Africa Report 21,
    no. 5 (September-October 1976): 12-16.
Ghebhardt, Alexander O. "Soviet and U.S. Interests in the Indian
    Ocean." Asian Survey 15 (August 1975): 672-83.
Giddings, Ralph L., Jr. "Power, Strategy and Will." Air University
    Review (January-February 1971): 19-26.
Giles, Morgan. "The Case for a British Presence East of Suez."
    Brassey's Annual, 1967, pp. 44-51.
Glaubitz, Joachim. "Anti-hegemony Formulas in Chinese Foreign
    Policy." Asian Survey 16 (March 1976): 205-15.
Gordon, Bernard K. "Open Options: Australia's Foreign Policy in
    the Seventies." Current History 62 (March 1972): 129-32.
Gorshkov, S. G. "Navies in War and Peace." U.S. Naval Institute
    Proceedings 100 (January-November 1974).
Graves, William. "Iran Desert Miracle." National Geographic,
    January 1975, pp. 2-46.
Griffith, William E. "The Great Powers, the Indian Ocean and
    the Persian Gulf." Jerusalem Journal of International Relations
    1 (Winter 1975): 5-19.
Groesbeck, Wesley A. "The Transkei—Key to U.S. Naval Strategy
    in the Indian Ocean." Military Review 56 (June 1976): 18-24.
Gunson, W. T. "Developments in Aircraft and Missiles." Brassey's
    Annual, 1972, pp. 252-69.
Gupta, Bhabani Sen. "Soviet Perceptions of Japan in the Seventies."
    Pacific Community 7 (January 1976): 179-98.
————. "Soviet Foreign Policy Strategic Thinking for the Seventies."
    India Quarterly 31 (October-December 1975): 319-41.
Halet, Hughes. "Thoughts on the New British Defense Policy."
    Brassey's Annual, 1957, pp. 267-74.
Halperin, Morton. "Clever Briefers, Crazy Leaders, and Myopic
    Analysts." Washington Monthly (September 1974): 42-49.
Harries, Owen. "Australia's Foreign Policy Under Whitlam."
    ORBIS 19, no. 3 (Fall 1974): 1090-101.

Harrigan, Anthony. "Seapower in History—India and China." Contemporary Review 228 (March 1976): 132-38.

——. "Security Interests in the Persian Gulf and Western Indian Ocean." Strategic Review (Fall 1973): 13-22.

——. "Pentagon's Civilian Planners Think 'Little' When It Comes to U.S. Fleet." Sea Power 11 (August 1968): 18-22.

Harvey, Ian. "Britain: East and West of Suez." Contemporary Review 216, no. 1253 (June 1970): 281-86.

Head, Simon. "The Monarchs of the Persian Gulf." New York Review of Books, March 21, 1974, pp. 29-36.

Healey, Denis. "British Defence Policy." RUSI, 114 (December 1969): 15-22.

Heine, Irwin M. "Red China: The New Maritime Superpower." Sea Power 18 (February 1975): 14-18.

Heinl, R. D., Jr. "American Defence Policy and Strategy for the 1970s." Brassey's Annual, 1970, pp. 28-38.

Hess, Gary R. "The Iranian Crisis of 1945-46 and the Cold War." Political Science Quarterly 89 (March 1974): 117-46.

Hill, J. R. "The Role of Navies." Brassey's Annual, 1970, pp. 91-107.

Hirasaw, Kazushige. "Japan's Emerging Foreign Policy." Foreign Affairs 54 (October 1975): 155-72.

Hogg, Quintin. "Britain Looks Forward." Foreign Affairs 43 (April 1965): 409-25.

Hopker, Wolfgang. "Soviet Global Strategy: The Great Challenge to the West at Sea." U.S. Naval Institute Proceedings 101 (December 1975): 24-29.

Hottinger, Arnold. "The Reopening of the Suez Canal: The Race for Power in the Indian Ocean." Round Table, no. 256 (October 1974): 393-402.

Howard, Michael. "Britain's Defenses: Comments and Capabilities." Foreign Affairs 39 (October 1960): 81-91.

Hudson, George E. "Soviet Naval Doctrine and Soviet Politics, 1953-1975." World Politics 29 (October 1976): 90-113.

——. "Soviet Naval Doctrine Under Lenin and Stalin." Soviet Studies 28 (January 1976): 42-65.

Hughes, Peter C., and M. R. Edwards. "Nuclear War in Soviet Military Thinking—The Implications for U.S. Security." Journal of Social and Political Affairs 1 (April 1976): 113-29.

Hunt, George P. "Our Four-Star Military Mess." Life, June 18, 1971, pp. 50-70.

Hunt, K. "Future Trends in Global Strategies." NATO's Fifteen Nations 15, no. 6 (December 1970-January 1971).

Hurd, Douglas. "Would the Tories Withdraw?" Round Table (October 1968): 369-78.

Hurewitz, J. C. "The Persian Gulf: British Withdrawal and Western
     Security." Annals of the Academy of Political and Social
     Science 401 (May 1972): 106-15.
Hutchison, Alan. "China in Africa: A Record of Pragmatism and
     Conservatism." Round Table, no. 259 (July 1975): 263-71.
———. "Indian Ocean: The Island Viewpoint." African Report 20,
     no. 1 (January-February 1975): 52-54.
———. "Indian Ocean: Why the West Needs South Africa," Africa
     Report 20, no. 1 (January-February 1975): 20.
Iwashima, Hisao. "Japan's Defense Policy." Strategic Review 3
     (Spring 1975): 17-24.
Jacob, Ian. "Principles of British Military Thought." Foreign
     Affairs 29 (January 1951): 219-28.
Jacobsen, C. G. "Japanese Security in a Changing World: The
     Crucible of the Washington-Moscow-Peking 'Triangle'?"
     Pacific Community (Tokyo) 6 (April 1975): 352-65.
———. "The Emergence of a Soviet Doctrine of Flexible Response?"
     Atlantic Community Quarterly 12 (Summer 1974): 231-38.
Jain, J. P. "The Indian Ocean as a Zone of Peace: An Appraisal of
     China's Attitude." China Report 10 (May-June 1974): 3-9.
Johnson, Frank J. "U.S. and Soviet Navies—A Comparison."
     Washington Report (January 1975): 105.
Jukes, Geoffrey. "The Soviet Union and the Indian Ocean." Survival,
     November 1971, pp. 370-75.
Kapur, Ashok. "India and China: Adversaries or Potential Partners?"
     World Today 30 (March 1974): 129-34.
Kaul, Ravi. "The Indo-Pakistani War and the Changing Balance of
     Power in the Indian Ocean." U.S. Naval Institute Proceedings
     (May 1973): 172-95.
Kelly, J. B. "The British Position in the Persian Gulf." The World
     Today 20 (June 1964): 238-49.
Kennan, George F. "From Containment to . . . Self-Containment:
     A Conversation with George F. Kennan." Encounter 47 (Sep-
     tember 1976): 10-43.
———. "The United States and the Soviet Union, 1917-1976." Foreign
     Affairs 54 (July 1976): 670-90.
———. "Europe's Problems, Europe's Choices." Foreign Policy,
     no. 14 (Spring 1974): 3-16.
Khan, Rahmatullah. "The Food Situation in the Indian Ocean Region
     Against the Global Backdrop." International Studies 14 (Octo-
     ber-December 1975): 549-62.
Klare, Michael T. "Superpower Rivalry at Sea." Foreign Policy
     (Winter 1975): 86-96, 160-67.

Kline, Hibberd V. B. III. "Diego Garcia and the Need for a Continuous American Presence in the Indian Ocean." Marine Corps Gazette 59 (April 1975): 29–34.

Klinghoffer, Arthur Jay. "Sino-Soviet Relations and the Politics of Oil." Asian Survey 16 (June 1976): 540–52.

———. "The Soviet Union and the Arab Oil Embargo of 1973–74." International Relations 5 (May 1976): 1011–23.

Konovalov, Y. "The Tentacles of Bases Strategy." International Affairs (Moscow) (July 1963): 52–57.

Kuroda, Mizuo. "Some Basic Elements of Japan's Foreign Policy." Pacific Community (Tokyo) 5 (April 1974): 380–91.

LaRocque, Gene. "An Island Paradise for the Admirals." Washington Monthly (May 1974): 49–51.

Lavrentyev, Alexander. "Indian Ocean: The Soviet Perspective." Africa Report 20, no. 1 (January–February 1975): 46–49.

Lee, Asher. "Soviet Strategy in the 1970s." Brassey's Annual, 1968, pp. 132–40.

Legum, Colin. "The Soviet Union, China and the West in Southern Africa." Foreign Affairs 54 (July 1976): 745–62.

Levine, Emil H. "Soviet Naval Air Power." National Defense 58 (May–June 1974): 525–27.

Libby, W. F. "Thailand's Kra Canal: Site for the World's First Nuclear Industrial Zone." ORBIS 19 (Spring 1975): 200–08.

Lockwood, William W. "Asian Triangle: China, India, Japan." Foreign Affairs 52 (July 1974): 818–38.

London, Herbert I. "Foreign Affairs and the White Australia Policy." ORBIS 13, no. 2 (Summer 1969): 556–77.

Luce, William. "Britain's Withdrawal from the Middle East and Persian Gulf." RUSI (March 1969): 4–10.

McCain, John S. "The Total Wet War." Congressional Record Vol. 112, Part 8, 89th Cong., 2d Sess., May 4, 1966, pp. 9861–64.

McGeoch, I. L. M. "Clausewitz, Mahan, and Mackinder, Inc." RUSI (November 1961): 528–31.

McGeoch, Ian. "Command of the Sea in the Seventies." Strategic Review (Summer 1973): 53–60.

———. "The Unit of Naval Power." Brassey's Annual, 1973, pp. 96–111.

McGhee, George C. "Naval Watching in the Indian Ocean." Saturday Review, July 26, 1975, pp. 12, 57–58.

McGruther, Kenneth R. "The Role of Perception in Naval Diplomacy." Naval War College Review (September–October 1974): 3–19.

MccGwire, M. K. "The Background to Russian Naval Policy." Brassey's Annual, 1968, pp. 141–58.

MacKinder, Halford J. "The Geographical Pivot of History,"
    Geographical Journal (London) 23, no. 4 (April 1904): 421-44.
MacLeod, Alexander. "Shah of the Indian Ocean?" Pacific Commi-
    nity 7 (April 1976): 423-32.
Manning, Robert. "Diego Garcia: The Pentagon's Trump Card."
    Far Eastern Economic Review (November 7, 1975): 27-29.
Marchant, Leslie R. "The People's Republic of China and the Indian
    Ocean Imbroglio: An Indicator of the Need for a Gestalt Approach
    to the Study of Peking's Foreign Relations." Spectrum 3 (Octo-
    ber 1974): 23-41.
Marcum, John A. "Lessons of Angola." Foreign Affairs 54 (April
    1976): 407-25.
Marks, Thomas A. "Djibouti: France's Strategic Toehold in Africa."
    African Affairs 73 (January 1974): 95-104.
Matthews, Samuel W. "Science Explores the Monsoon Sea." National
    Geographic, October 1967, pp. 554-75.
Meister, Jurg. "Diego Garcia: Outpost in the Indian Ocean." Swiss
    Review of World Affairs 24 (April 1974): 6-7.
Middendorf, J. William II. "American Maritime Strategy and Soviet
    Naval Expansion." Strategic Review (Winter 1976): 16-25.
Millar, T. B. "Defence Under Labour." Current Affairs Bulletin
    52, no. 7 (December 1975): 4-18.
————. "Control of the Indian Ocean." Survival 9 (October 1967):
    323-26.
Misra, K. P. "International Politics in the Indian Ocean." ORBIS
    18, no. 4 (Winter 1975): 1088-108.
————. "Survey of Recent Research: International Politics and the
    Security of the Indian Ocean Area." International Studies 12
    (January-March 1973): 141-60.
————. "Afro-Asian Ocean." Seminar 146 (October 1971): 31-35.
Mitsuru, Yamamoto. "Resources Diplomacy Runs into a Stone Wall."
    Japan Quarterly 22 (October-December 1975): 301-26.
Molesworth, G. N. "Some Problems of Future Security in the Indian
    Ocean." Asiatic Review 42 (January 1946): 26-34.
Moore, J. E. "The Soviets and the Sea." NATO's Fifteen Nations
    20 (June-July 1975): 56-58, 60, 62.
Moorer, Joseph P. "U.S. Naval Strategy of the Future." Strategic
    Review 4, no. 2 (Spring 1976): 72-80.
Moorer, Thomas, and Alvin J. Cottrell. "The World Environment
    and U.S. Military Policy for the 1970s and 1980s." Strategic
    Review 4, no. 2 (Spring 1976): 56-65.
"Morskoi Prazdnik Sovetskogo Naroda" (Naval Holiday of the Soviet
    People). Morskoi Sbornik (July 1966): 3-7.
Moskovoj, I. P. "Soviet Sea-Fisheries 1970-75: A Survey." Navy
    International 81 (June 1976): 6-10.

Moulton, J. L. "British Defence Policy 1967." Brassey's Annual,
    1967, pp. 68-79.

——. "The 1966 White Paper and Debate." Brassey's Annual,
    1966, pp. 1-10.

——. "Brush-Fire Operation—Brunei, December, 1962." Brassey's
    Annual, 1963, pp. 77-84.

Muccia, Daniel R. "Japanese Militarism." U.S. Naval Institute Pro-
    ceedings 100 (February 1974): 90-94.

Mukerjee, Dilip. "Maldives Diversifies Contacts with Big Neighbours."
    Pacific Community (Tokyo) 6 (July 1975): 595-607.

Murthy, P. A. Narasimha. "Japan's Dependence on World Resources
    and Its Resources Policy." International Studies 14 (April-June
    1975): 187-217.

Nakamura, Koji. "Oil: Reassessment in Japan." Far Eastern Eco-
    nomic Review (April 1, 1974): 53-54.

Nath, Marie-Luise. "Soviet and Chinese Policies Toward South-East
    Asia in the Early '70s." Spectrum 3 (October 1974): 11-22.

Naugle, J. O. "The Allied Command Atlantic Submarine Challenge."
    NATO's Fifteen Nations 17, no. 1 (February-March 1972): 68.

——. "The Allied Command Atlantic Submarine Challenge." U.S.
    Naval Institute Proceedings (February-March 1972): 66-74.

Nayar, Baldev Raj. "Treat India Seriously." Foreign Policy, no. 18
    (Spring 1975): 133-54.

Niu, Sien-chong. "New Strategic Outlook of the Indian Subcontinent."
    NATO's Fifteen Nations 19 (October-November 1974): 62-65,
    68-70.

Northedge, F. S. "Britain as a Second-Rank Power." International
    Affairs 46 (January 1970): 37-47.

O'Conner, Raymond G. "Current Concepts and Philosophy of War-
    fare." Naval War College Review 20, no. 6 (January 1968):
    3-15.

——, and Vladimir P. Prokofieff. "The Soviet Navy in the Mediter-
    ranean and Indian Ocean." Virginia Quarterly Review (Autumn
    1973): 481-93.

Odell, Peter R. "Oil and Western European Security." Brassey's
    Annual, 1972, pp. 64-77.

Ohno, Katsumi. "On Some Inherent Characteristics of Japanese
    Diplomacy." Pacific Community (Tokyo) 6 (October 1974):
    55-68.

Okimoto, Daniel I. "Japan's Non-Nuclear Policy: The Problem of
    the NPT." Asian Survey 15 (April 1975): 313-27.

Palmer, J. M. "The Balance of Seapower in the Seventies." NATO's
    Fifteen Nations 14, no. 4 (August-September 1969): 28-32.

Panikkar, K. M. "The Basis of an Indo-British Treaty." Asiatic
    Review 42 (October 1946): 357-59.

————. "The Defence of India and In-British Obligations." International Affairs 22 (January 1946): 85-90.

Paone, R. M. "The Big Three and the Indian Ocean." Sea Power 18 (August 1975): 28-34.

Pardo, Arvid. "Who Will Control the Seabed?" Foreign Affairs (October 1968): 123-37.

Parker, J. A. "Indian Ocean: A New Soviet Lake?" New Guard 15 (March 1975): 7-10.

Pavlovsky, V., and Y. Tomilin. "Indian Ocean: Confrontation or Security?" New Times (Moscow), no. 10 (March 1974): 4-5.

Peiris, Denzil. "The Strategy of Brinkmanship." Far Eastern Economic Review (May 6, 1974): 30-34.

Pelliccia, Antonio. "Clausewitz and Soviet Politico-Military Strategy." NATO's Fifteen Nations 20, no. 6 (December 1975-January 1976): 18-21, 24-26, 28-29, 32.

Pillsbury, Michael. "U.S.-Chinese Military Ties?" Foreign Policy, no. 20 (Fall 1975): 50-64.

Pisarov, V. D. "Soviet-American Cooperation in World-Ocean Studies." USA: Economics, Politics, Ideology, no. 10 (October 1974): 7-19.

Plessis, Jan A. du. "The Soviet Union's Foreign Policy Towards Africa: 1956-1973." Bulletin of the Africa Institute 7, no. 3 (1974): 105-06, 111-15.

Plumer, G. A. "The Strait of Malacca." Brassey's Annual, 1973, pp. 188-205.

Poulose, T. T. "Indian Ocean: Prospects of a Nuclear-Free Peace Zone." Pacific Community (Tokyo) 5 (January 1974): 319-34.

Pretty, R. T. "A Review of the World Naval Missile Situation." Navy International 79 (May 1974): 16-17, 21, 25.

Prina, L. Edgar. "At Last, a Base in the Indian Ocean." Sea Power 14 (January 1971): 26-28.

Ra'anan, Uri. "The Soviet View of Navies in Peacetime." Naval War College Review 29 (Summer 1976): 30-38.

Ranft, Brian. 'Russia Takes to the Sea: Why?" Navy International 79 (July 1974): 5-6.

Rao, R. Rama. "A Strategy for the Indian Ocean." Indian & Foreign Review (March 15, 1974): 16-18.

"The Reconstruction of the Subcontinent: The Future of Western Policy." Round Table 247 (July 1974): 275-81.

Reynolds, C. H. B. "The Maldive Islands." Asian Affairs 62 (February 1975): 37-43.

Rhee, T. C. "Peking and Washington in a New Balance of Power." ORBIS 18 (Spring 1974): 151-78.

Richardson, T. L. "Australian Strategic Perspectives." Current History 62 (March 1972): 143-46.

Rogers, Robert F. "China's Policy Options." Military Review 54 (August 1974): 3-11.

Rollins, Patrick J. "Russia's Fictitious Naval Tradition." U.S.
    Naval Institute Proceedings (January 1973): 65-71.
Rubinstein, Alvin Z. "Moscow and Cairo: Currents of Influence."
    Problems of Communism 23 (July-August 1974): 17-28.
Ruhe, W. J. "Seapower in the Seventies." U.S. Naval Institute
    Proceedings 96, no. 4 (April 1970): 26-31.
Sagar, Easwar. "India and the Two 'Wont's.'" Sea Power 16 (March
    1973): 31-34.
Schofield, B. B. "Problems of NATO 1974. I. Soviet Maritime
    Power." World Survey, no. 62 (February 1974): 1-16.
Schwartz, Harry. "The Moscow-Peking-Washington Triangle." In
    USA-USSR: Agenda for Communication. Annals American
    Academy of Political and Social Science 414 (July 1974): 41-50.
Scott, William F. "Soviet Military Doctrine and Strategy: Realities
    and Misunderstandings." Strategic Review 3 (Summer 1975):
    57-66.
Seth, S. P. "The Indian Ocean and Indo-American Relations."
    Asian Survey 15 (August 1975): 645-55.
Seymour, Robert L. "Japan's Self-Defense: The Naganuma Case and
    Its Implications." Pacific Affairs 47 (Winter 1974-75): 421-36.
Shilling, David. "A Reassessment of Japan's Naval Defense Needs."
    Asian Survey 16 (March 1976): 216-29.
Shonfield, Andrew. "The Duncan Report and Its Critics." Interna-
    tional Affairs 46 (April 1970): 247-68.
Shuichi, Miyoshi. "Oil Shock." Japan Quarterly 21 (April-June 1974):
    20-28.
Siegel, Richard L. "Evaluating the Results of Foreign Policy: Soviet
    and American Efforts in India." Monograph Series in World
    Affairs, 6, no. 4 Denver: University of Denver, 1969.
Simmons, Henry T. "The U.S. Navy—Countering the Soviet Buildup."
    International Defense Review 7 (August 1974): 443-47.
Simon, Sheldon W. "The Japan-China-USSR Triangle." Pacific
    Affairs 47 (Summer 1974): 125-38.
Sinha, R. P. "Japan and the Oil Crisis." World Today 30 (August
    1974): 335-44.
Sjaastad, Anderson C. "The Indian Ocean and the Soviet Navy."
    In extension of remarks of Michael Harrington. Congressional
    Record (March 30, 1972): E3143-E3148.
Slonim, Shlomo. "Suez and the Soviets." U.S. Naval Institute Pro-
    ceedings 101 (April 1975): 37-41.
Smith, Clyde A. "Constraints of Naval Geography on Soviet Naval
    Power." Naval War College Review 27 (September-October
    1974): 46-57.

——. "The Meaning and Significance of the Gorshkov Articles."
    Naval War College Review 26 (March–April 1974): 18–37.
Sofinsky, V. "Somalia on the Path of Progress." International
    Affairs (Moscow) (November 1974): 62–66.
Sokol, Anthony E. "Naval Strategy Today." Brassey's Annual, 1958,
    pp. 33–48.
Sorenson, Jay B. "Nuclear Deterrence and Japan Defense." Asian
    Affairs, An American Review 2 (November–December 1974):
    55–69.
Speed, F. W. "Indian Ocean Rivalry." Army Quarterly and Defence
    Journal 105 (October 1975): 457–62.
Spence, J. F. "South Africa and the Defence of the West." Round
    Table 61, no. 241 (January 1971): 15–23.
Steif, William. "The Russians Are Here (Somalia)." Saturday
    Review (September 6, 1975): 8, 58–59.
Stevens, Christopher. "The Soviet Union and Angola." African
    Affairs 75 (April 1976): 137–57.
Stone, Norman L. 'The Trend in Naval Power: A Crisis of Resolve."
    U.S. Naval Institute Proceedings 101 (July 1975): 25–29.
Subrahmanyam, K. "China's Security Outlook: Past and Future."
    Military Review (August 1975): 63–76.
——, and J. P. Anand. "Indian Ocean as an Area of Peace."
    India Quarterly (October–December 1971): 289–315.
Sugita, Ichiji. "Japan and Her National Defence." Pacific Community
    (Tokyo) 5 (July 1974): 495–515.
Svyatov, G., and A. Kokoshin. "Naval Power in the U.S. Strategic
    Plans." International Affairs (Moscow) (April 1973): 56–62.
Swarztrauber, S. A. "On Hugging a Bear, Take Care." U.S. Naval
    Institute Proceedings 100 (July 1974): 19–22.
Sysoyev, V. S. "Cruise to Ethiopia." Morskoi Sbornik (July 1966):
    18–22.
Szulc, Tad. "Why Are We in Johannesburg?" Esquire (October 1974):
    48, 50, 56, 58, 60.
Taira, Koji. "Japan After the 'Oil Shock': An International Resource
    Pauper." Current History 68 (April 1975): 145–48, 179–80,
    184.
Taft, Robert, Jr. "Meeting the Soviet Naval Challenge." Journal
    of Social and Political Affairs 1 (July 1976): 195–201.
"Tarbrook. Britain's Future Strategic Reserve." Brassey's Annual
    1958, pp. 71–84.
Terfloth, Klaus. "The Future of the Indian Ocean." Aussenpolitik
    (English ed.) 26, no. 4 (1975): 463–69.
Thom, William G. "Trends in Soviet Support for African Liberation."
    Air University Review 25 (July–August 1974): 36–43.

Thursfield, H. G. "Defence Today." Brassey's Annual, 1962, pp. 1-5.

Trezige, Philip H. "The Second Phase in U.S.-Japan Relations." Pacific Community (Tokyo) 6 (April 1975): 340-351.

Trout, B. Thomas. "Naval Strategy and Naval Politics: Peacetime Uses of a Wartime Naval Force." Naval War College Review 27 (July-August 1974): 3-16.

Turner, Stansfield. "Missions of the U.S. Navy." Naval War College Review (March-April 1974): 14-19.

Uchida, Kazutomi. "Japan's National Defence and the Role of the Maritime Self-Defence Force." Pacific Community (Tokyo) 6 (October 1974): 38-54.

Uhlig, Frank, Jr. "Speculating On Soviet Naval Strategy." Brassey's Annual, 1973, pp. 112-30.

———. "The Middle Kingdom Goes to Sea. Red China's Navy is World's Third Largest." Sea Power 26 (March 1973): 19-24.

Unna, Warren. "Diego Garcia." New Republic (March 9, 1974): 7-8.

Van der Kroef, Justus. "The Indian Ocean Problem—Some South-East Asian Perspectives." South East Asian Spectrum 3 (April 1975): 27-38.

Vanneman, Peter, and Martin James. "The Soviet Intervention in Angola: Intentions and Implications." Strategic Review 4 (Summer 1976): 92-103.

Verrier, Anthony. "Strategically Mobile Forces—U.S. Theory and British Practice." RUSI, 106 (November 1961): 479-85.

Vigor, P. H. "Admiral S. G. Gorshkov's Views on Seapower." Journal of the Royal United Services Institute for Defence Studies 119 (March 1974): 53-60.

Virpsha, E. S. "Strategic Importance of South Africa." NATO's Fifteen Nations 12, no. 1 (March 1967): 36-43.

Vysotsky, A., and P. Nastin. "On Freedom of Research in the World Ocean." International Affairs (Moscow) (May 1975): 74-82.

Wall, Patrick. "The Vulnerability of the West in the Southern Hemisphere." Strategic Review 4 (Winter 1976): 44-50.

Watson, Bruce W., and Margurite A. Walton. "Okean—75." U.S. Naval Institute Proceedings 102 (July 1976): 93-97.

Watt, D. C. "The Decision to Withdraw from the Gulf." Political Quarterly (July-September 1968): 310-21.

Wegner, Edward. "Theory of Naval Strategy in the Nuclear Age." U.S. Naval Institute Proceedings 98, no. 831 (May 1972): 192-207.

Weinland, Robert G., Robert W. Herrick, Michael MccGwire, and James M. McConnell. "Admiral Gorshkov's 'Navies in War and Peace.'" Survival 17 (March–April 1975): 54–63.

Weinland, Robert G. "The Changing Mission of the Soviet Union." Survival (May–June 1972): 129–33.

Wettern, Desmond. "Who Rules the Waves?" NATO's Fifteen Nations 20 (October–November 1975): 20–32.

Wilhelm, Alfred D., Jr. "The Nixon Shocks and Japan." Military Review 54 (November 1974): 70–77.

Wooldrige, E. T., Jr. "The Gorshkov Papers: Soviet Naval Doctrine for the Nuclear Age." ORBIS 18, no. 4 (Winter 1975): 1153–175.

Wright, C. Ben. "Mr. 'X' and Containment." Slavic Review 35 (March 1976): 1–36.

Wu, Yuan-li. "The Economic, Political and Strategic Implications of Japan's Search for Oil." Spectrum 3 (January 1975): 27–41.

Young, Henry. "A Holocaust for Happy Valley?" U.S. Naval Institute Proceedings 102 (November 1976): 52–61.

Zumwalt, Elmo R. "20th Century Mahan." U.S. Naval Institute Proceedings 100 (November 1974): 70–73.

OFFICIAL PUBLICATIONS

Australia. Parliament. Joint Committee on Foreign Affairs. Parliamentary Paper, 1971, no. 258. Canberra: Commonwealth Government Printing Office, 1972.

——. Parliament. Mission to States Bordering the Indian Ocean. Canberra: Commonwealth Government Printing Office, 1969.

Ceylon. Ceylon's Memorandum of Indian Ocean Security. Presented by Ceylonese Prime Minister Srimavo Bandaranaike at the Commonwealth Heads of State Conference, Singapore, January 1961.

India. Parliament. Lok Sabha (House of the People). Debates. Ser. 3, vol. 24, December 19, 1963, cols. 5667–775; ser. 4, vol. 2, April 6, 1967, cols. 3207–223; ser. 4, vol. 3, June 22, 1967, cols. 3040–049; ser. 4, vol. 26, March 18–31, 1969, cols. 1–10.

——. Parliament. Rajya Subha (Council of the States). Debates. Vol. 54, Part I, November 18, 1965, cols. 1815–822.

Indonesia. Ministry of Foreign Affairs.. Asian-African Conference, 1st, 1955. Djakarta, 1955.

Iran. Foreign Policy. A Compendium of the Writings and Statements of His Imperial Majesty Shahanshah Aryamehr. Teheran: Ministry of Foreign Affairs, 1975.

Malta. Department of Information. United Nations Conference on the Law of the Sea, 1st Geneva, April 29, 1958. Treaty Series no. 50, 1967.

United Kingdom. Ministry of Defence. Statement Relating to Defence, Cmd 6743 (1946), Cmd 7042 (1947), Cmd 7327 (1948). Statement on Defence. Cmd. 7631, 1949; Cmd. 7895, 1950; Cmd. 8475, 1952; Cmd. 8768, 1953; Cmd. 9075, 1954; Cmd. 9391, 1955; Cmd. 9691, 1956; Cmnd. 1639, 1962; Cmnd. 1936, 1963; Cmnd. 2270, 1964. Defence: Outline of Future Policy. Cmnd. 124, 1957: Report on defence, 1960, Cmnd. 952; 1961, Cmnd. 1288. Statement on defence estimates, 1965, Cmnd. 2592; 1966, Cmnd. 2901, Cmnd. 2902. Supplement on the defence estimates, 1967, Cmnd. 3203. Supplementary statement on defence policy, 1967, Cmnd. 3357, 1967. Statement on the defence estimates, 1968, Cmnd. 3540.

——. Ministry of Defence. Exchanges of Letters of Defence Matters Between the Governments of the United Kingdom and the Union of South Africa, June 1955. Cmnd. 9520.

——. Exchange of Notes Regarding Relations Between the United Kingdom of Great Britain and Northern Ireland and the State of Kuwait. Treaty Series no. 93. Cmnd. 1518, 1961.

——. Parliament. Debates (House of Commons). Ser. 5, vol. 437, May 16, 1947, col. 1965-966; ser. 5, vol. 539, April 4, 1955, col. 897-98; ser. 5, vol. 655, March 8, 1962, col. 618; ser. 5, vol. 659, May 17, 1962, col. 1534-535; ser. 5, vol. 687, January 16, 1964, col. 449-50; ser. 5, vol. 690, February 26, 1964, col. 469-70; ser. 5, vol. 702, December 16, 1964, col. 423-24.

——. Parliament. Debates (House of Lords). Vol. 214, March 10, 1959, col. 858; vol. 238, March 21, 1962, col. 579.

United Nations. General Assembly. Declaration of the Indian Ocean as Zone of Peace (A/AC.159/1/Rev. 1), July 11, 1974.

——. Secretary General. Report on Military Powers in Indian Ocean to Be Reviewed (WS/660). Press release, May 24, 1974.

——. General Assembly. Declaration of the Indian Ocean as a Zone of Peace. Letter dated June 13, 1974 from the Charge d'Affaires ad interim of the Permanent Mission of France to the United Nations addressed to the Secretary General (A/AC. 159/8), June 14, 1974.

——. General Assembly. Declaration of the Indian Ocean as a Zone of Peace. Letter dated May 30, 1974 from the Charge d'Affaires ad interim of the Permanent Mission of Madagascar to the United Nations addressed to the Secretary General (A/AC.159/7), May 30, 1974.

——. General Assembly. <u>Declaration of the Indian Ocean as a Zone of Peace</u>. Letter dated 29 May 1974 from the Acting Permanent Representative of Yemen to the United Nations addressed to the Secretary-General (A/AC.159/6), May 30, 1974.

——. General Assembly. <u>Declaration of the Indian Ocean as a Zone of Peace</u>. Letter dated 24 May 1974 from the Permanent Representative of the United Kingdom of Great Britain and Northern Ireland to the United Nations addressed to the Secretary General (A/AC.159/5), May 24, 1974.

——. General Assembly. <u>Declaration of the Indian Ocean as a Zone of Peace</u>. Letter dated 22 May 1974 from the Permanent Representative of Somalia to the United Nations addressed to the Secretary-General (A/AC.159/4), May 23, 1974.

——. General Assembly. <u>Declaration of the Indian Ocean as a Zone of Peace</u>. Note Verbale dated 22 May 1974 from the Permanent Representative of the United States of America addressed to the Secretary-General (A/AC.159/3), May 22, 1974.

——. General Assembly. <u>Declaration of the Indian Ocean as a Zone of Peace</u>. Letter dated 15 May 1974 from the Permanent Representative of the United Republic of Tanzania to the United Nations addressed to the Secretary General (A/AC.159/2), May 16, 1974.

——. General Assembly. <u>Declaration of the Indian Ocean as a Zone of Peace</u>. (A/AC.159/1), May 3, 1974.

——. General Assembly. <u>Declaration of the Indian Ocean as a Zone of Peace</u>. Statement made by H. S. Amerasinghe (A/AC.159/L.3), April 18, 1973.

——. General Assembly. <u>Implementation of the Declaration of the Indian Ocean as a Zone of Peace</u>, December 11, 1975.

——. General Assembly. <u>Implementation of the Delcaration of the Indian Ocean as Zone of Peace</u>, December 9, 1975.

——. General Assembly. <u>Declaration of the Indian Ocean as a Zone of Peace</u>, December 6, 1975.

——. General Assembly. <u>Declaration of the Indian Ocean as a Zone of Peace</u>, December 15, 1975.

——. General Assembly. <u>Declaration of the Indian Ocean as Zone of Peace</u>, December 16, 1971.

——. General Assembly. <u>Declaration of the Indian Ocean as a Zone of peace</u>. Sri Lanka Working Paper (A/AC.159/L.2), March 12, 1973.

——. General Assembly. <u>Declaration of the Indian Ocean as a Zone of Peace</u>. Report of the Ad Hoc Committee on the Indian Ocean (A/9090/Rev. 1), 1972.

————. General Assembly. Request for the Inclusion of an Additional
Item in the Agenda of the Twenty-Sixth Session (A/8492), October 1, 1971.

————. General Assembly. Declaration of the Indian Ocean as a
Zone of Peace. Supplement no. 29, 1974.

————. General Assembly. Declaration of the Indian Ocean as Zone
of Peace. Supplement no. 29 (A/10029), 1975.

————. General Assembly. Declaration of the Indian Ocean as a
Zone of Peace (A/31/29), 1976.

U.S. Congress. Congressional Record. Daily edition 1971–76.

————. Comparison of U.S. and U.S.S.R. Naval Ship Building.
CRS. March 5, 1976. By Alva Bowen.

————. International Security Assistance and Arms Control Act of
1976. Public Law 94–329.

————. Guard and Reserve Forces' Facilities Authorization Act,
1976, 94th Cong., 1st sess., October 7, 1975.

————. Making Appropriations for Military Construction for the
Department of Defense for the Fiscal Year Ending June 30,
1976. 94th Cong., November 28, 1975.

U.S. Congress. House. Committee on Appropriations. Military
Construction Appropriation Bill, 1976. Report 94–530 to
Accompany H.R. 10029. 94th Cong., 1st sess., 1975.

————. Committee on Appropriations. Department of Defense
Appropriations for 1976. Part I. 93d Cong., 2d sess., 1975.

————. Committee on Armed Services. Military Posture and H.R.
11500 (H.R. 12438) (H.A.S.C. 94–33). 94th Cong., 2d sess.,
1976.

————. Committee on Armed Services. Construction at Diego Garcia. Message from the President of the United States. Pursuant to Sec. 163 (a) (I) of Public Law 93–522 (House Document
No. 94–140). 94th Cong., 1st sess., 1975.

————. Committee on Armed Services. Report of the Special Subcommittee to Inspect Facilities at Berbera, Somalia. H.A.S.C.
94–19. 94th Cong., 1st sess., 1975.

————. Committee on Armed Services. Subcommittee on Military
Installations and Facilities. To Authorize Certain Construction
at Military Installations and for Certain Other Purposes.
(H.A.S.C. 94–11). 94th Cong., 1st sess., 1975.

————. Committee on Armed Services. Full Committee Consideration of H.R. 12565 (H.A.S.C. No. 93–40). 93d Cong., 2d sess.,
1974.

————. Committee on Armed Services. Military Construction Authorization, FY 1975. Report 93–1244 to Accompany H.R. 16136.
93d Cong., 2d sess., 1974.

——. Committee on Armed Services. <u>Military Construction Authorization, FY 1975</u> (H.R. 14126). 93d Cong. 2d sess., 1974.

——. Committee of Conferences. <u>Military Construction Appropriations, FY 1976.</u> Conference Report 94-655 to Accompany H.R. 10029. 94th Cong., 1st sess., 1975.

——. Committee of Conferences. <u>Department of Defense Supplemental Authorization for Appropriations, FY 1974.</u> Conference Report 93-1064 to Accompany H.R. 12565. 93d Cong., 2d sess., 1974.

——. Committee on Foreign Affairs. Subcommittee on the Near East and South Asia. <u>The Persian Gulf, 1974: Money, Politics, Arms, and Power.</u> 93d Cong., 2d sess., 1975.

——. Committee on Foreign Affairs. Subcommittee on the Near East and South Asia. <u>Means of Measuring Naval Power with Special Reference to U.S. and Soviet Activities in the Indian Ocean.</u> 93d Cong., 2d sess., May 12, 1974. By John Collins and John Chwat.

——. Committee on Foreign Affairs. Subcommittee on the Near East and South Asia. <u>Proposed Expansion of U.S. Military Facilities in the Indian Ocean.</u> 93d Cong., 2d sess., 1974.

——. Committee on Foreign Affairs. Subcommittee on the Near East and South Asia. <u>The U.S. Role in Opening the Suez Canal.</u> 93d Cong., 2d sess., 1974.

——. Committee on Foreign Affairs. <u>U.S. Foreign Policy for the 1970s. An Analysis of the President's 1973 Foreign Policy Report and Congressional Action.</u> 93d Cong., 1st sess., 1973.

——. Committee on Foreign Affairs. <u>Data and Analysis Concerning the Possibility of a U.S. Food Embargo as a Response to the Present Arab Oil Boycott.</u> CRS. 93d Cong., 1st sess., 1973.

——. Committee of Foreign Affairs. Subcommittee on the Near East and South Asia. <u>New Perspectives on the Persian Gulf.</u> 93d Cong., 1st sess., 1973.

——. Committee on Foreign Affairs. Subcommittee on Asian and Pacific Affairs. <u>Oil and Asian Rivals: Sino-Soviet Conflict; Japan and the Oil Crisis.</u> 93d Cong., 1st and 2d sess., 1973.

——. Committee on Foreign Affairs. Subcommittee on the Near East and South Asia. <u>U.S. Interests in and Policies Toward South Asia.</u> 93d Cong., 1st sess., 1973.

——. Committee on Foreign Affairs. Subcommittee on the Near East and South Asia. <u>The United States and South Asia.</u> 93d Cong., 1st sess., 1973.

——. Committee on Foreign Affairs. Subcommittee on National Security Policy and Scientific Developments. <u>The Indian Ocean: Political and Strategic Future.</u> 92d Cong., 1st sess., 1971.

——. Committee on International Relations. Subcommittee on Future Foreign Policy Research and Development. United States-Soviet Union-China: The Great Power Triangle. Part I. 94th Cong., 1st sess., 1976.

——. Committee on International Relations. Subcommittee on Future Foreign Policy Research and Development. Shifting Balance of Power in Asia: Implications for Future U.S. Policy. 94th Cong., 2d sess., 1976.

——. Committee on International Relations. Subcommittee on Future Foreign Policy Research and Development. United States-Soviet Union-China: The Great Power Triangle. Part II. 94th Cong., 2d sess., 1976.

——. Committee on International Relations. Special Subcommittee on Investigations. The Persian Gulf, 1975: The Continuing Debate on Arms Sales. 94th Cong., 1st sess., 1975.

——. Committee on International Relations. Subcommittee on Investigations. Diego Garcia, 1975: The Debate over the Base and the Island's Former Inhabitants. 94th Cong., 1st sess., 1975.

——. Committee on International Relations. Subcommittee on Investigations. CRS. Oil Fields as Military Objectives, A Feasibility Study. 94th Cong., 1st sess., 1975.

——. Control of Military Force in the Indian Ocean. Report 94-848 (Union Calendar No. 426) to Accompany H.R. 11963. 94th Cong., 2d sess., 1975.

——. Foreign Relations Authorization Act, FY 1976. Conference Report 94-660 to Accompany S. 1517. 94th Cong., 1st sess., 1975.

——. Military Construction Authorization, FY 1975. Conference Report 93-1545 to Accompany H.R. 16136. 93d Cong., 2d sess., 1974.

——. To Authorize Certain Construction at Military Installations. 93d Cong., December 27, 1974.

——. The United States and South Asia. Report 93-934 to Accompany H.R. 12565. 93d Cong., 2d sess., 1974.

U.S. Congress. Senate. Committee on Appropriations. Military Construction Appropriations Bill, 1976. Report 94-442 (Calendar No. 428) to Accompany H.R. 10029. 94th Cong., 1st sess., 1975.

——. Committee on Appropriations. Visit to the Democratic Republic of Somalia. 94th Cong., 1st sess., July 14, 1975.

——. Committee on Appropriations. Military Construction Appropriations, FY 1975. 93d Cong., 2d sess., 1974.

——. Committee on Appropriations. Military Construction Appropriation Bill, FY 1975. Report 93-1302 (Calendar No. 1236) to

Accompany H.R. 17468. 93d Cong., 2d sess., 1974.

———. Committee on Appropriations. Second Supplemental Appropriations, FY 1974 (H.R. 14013). 2 Parts. 93d Cong., 2d sess., 1974.

———. Committee on Appropriations. Department of Defense Appropriations, FY 1974. 4 Parts. 93d Cong., 1st sess., 1973.

———. Committee on Appropriations. Department of Defense Appropriations, FY 1972. 3 Parts. 92d Cong., 1st sess., 1972.

———. Committee on Appropriations. Department of Defense Appropriations, FY 1973. Part 2. 92d Cong., 2d sess., 1972.

———. Committee on Armed Services. United States/Soviet Military Balance: A Frame of Reference for Congress, 94th Cong., 2d sess., January 1976. By John Collins and John Chwat.

———. Committee on Armed Services. Activities Related to Resettlement of Refugees in Somalia. Report of Senator Dewey F. Bartlett. 94th Cong., 1st sess., September 2, 1975.

———. Committee on Armed Services. Disapprove Construction Projects on the Island of Diego Garcia (S.R. 160). 94th Cong., 1st sess., 1975.

———. Committee on Armed Services. Disapproving Construction Projects on the Island of Diego Garcia. Report 94-00 to Accompany S.R. 160. 94th Cong., 1st sess., 1975.

———. Committee on Armed Services. Military Construction Authorization, Fiscal Year 1976. Report 94-157 (Calendar No. 153) to Accompany S. 1247. 94th Cong., 1st sess., 1975.

———. Committee on Armed Services. Selected Materials on Diego Garcia. 94th Cong., 1st sess., 1975.

———. Committee on Armed Services. Soviet Military Capability in Berbera, Somalia. Report of Senator Bartlett. 94th Cong., 1st sess., July 1975.

———. Committee on Armed Services. Subcommittee on Military Construction. Military Construction Authorization, FY 1975. (S. 3471). 93d Cong., 2d sess., 1974.

———. Committee on Armed Services. Military Construction Authorization, FY 1975. Report 93-1136 (Calendar No. 1084) to Accompany H.R. 16136. 93d Cong., 2d sess., 1974.

———. Committee on Armed Services. Military Procurement Supplemental, FY 1974 (S. 2999). 93d Cong., 2d sess., 1974.

———. Committee on Commerce. Soviet Ocean Activities: A Preliminary Survey. 94th Cong., 1st sess., 1975. CRS. Senate Committee Print.

———. Committee on Foreign Relations. Foreign Affairs Authorization Bill, FY 1976. Report 94-337 (Calendar No. 327) to Accompany S. 1517. 94th Cong., 1st sess., 1975.

——. Committee on Foreign Relations. Subcommittee on Multi-national Corporations. U.S. Oil Companies and the Arab Oil Embargo: The International Allocation of Constricted Supplies. 94th Cong., 1st sess., 1975. Federal Energy Administration.

——. Committee on Foreign Relations. Briefings on Diego Garcia and Patrol Frigate. 93d Cong., 2d sess., 1974.

——. Committee on Foreign Relations. Seabed Arms Control Treaty (Ex. H. 92-1). 93d Cong., 2d sess., 1974.

——. Committee on Foreign Relations. U.S. Commitment to SEATO (S. R. 174). 93d Cong., 2d sess., 1974.

——. Committee on Foreign Relations. Subcommittee on Oceans and International Environment. U.S. Oceans Policy (S.R. 82). 93d Cong., 1st sess., 1973.

——. Committee on Foreign Relations. Subcommittee on Arms Control, International Law and Organization. U.S.-U.S.S.R. Strategic Policies. 93d Cong., 2d sess., 1974.

MISCELLANEOUS

Adelphi Papers. The Implications of Military Technology in the 1970s. London: Institute for Strategic Studies, 1968.

——. Japanese and Indian National Security Strategies in the Asia of the 1970s: The Prospect for Nuclear Proliferation. No. 92. London: Institute for Strategic Studies, 1972.

——. The Middle East and the International System. II. Security and the Energy Crisis. No. 115. London: International Institute for Strategic Studies, 1975.

——. Power at Sea. II. Super-Powers and Navies. No. 123. London: International Institute for Strategic Studies, 1976.

——. Power at Sea. III. Competition and Conflict. No. 124. London: International Institute for Strategic Studies, 1976.

Africa Institute Bulletin. China's Decade in Africa. Vol. 11, no. 8, 1973.

——. Indian Ocean Security. Vol. 13, no. 2, 1975.

All Hands. A Look at the Soviet Navy. No. 704. September 1975.

Center for Strategic and International Studies, Georgetown University. The Gulf: Implications of British Withdrawal. Special Report Series, no. 8, 1969.

Columbia University. India and Japan: The Emerging Balance of Power in Asia and Opportunities for Arms Control. New York: Southern Asian Institute, Columbia University, 1971.

Costello, Mary. Navy Rebuilding. Washington Editorial Research Reports. 1976.

The Defense Monitor. The Indian Ocean: A New Naval Arms Race,
    April 1974. Detente and Military Power, December 1974. U.S.
    Arms to the Persian Gulf: $10 Billion Since 1973, May 1975.
    Washington, D.C.: Center for Defense Information.
——. U.S. Military Commitments: Too Far, Too Wide, Too Thin,
    August 1975.
Disarmament Report. The Indian Ocean as a Zone of Peace. World
    Conference of Religion for Peace. Dr. Homer A. Jack.
    New York, June 30, 1973.
Exxon Company, U.S.A. Public Affairs Department. Energy Out-
    look 1976-1990. Houston, 1975.
Fabian Publications. Fabian Colonial Bureau. Strategic Colonies and
    Their Future: The Problems of Hong Kong, Gibraltar, Malta
    and Cyprus. Research Series no. 100. London, 1945.
Fabian Society. Arabia: When Britain Goes. London, 1967.
Hirst, F. W. "What the Americans Mean by Freedom of the Seas."
    Grotius Society, Problems of the War, Vol. 4. London, 1919.
Hurewitz, J. C. The Persian Gulf. New York: Foreign Policy
    Association, 1974.
Information Centre. For the Indian Ocean as a Zone of Peace/The
    International Conference Against Foreign Military Bases and
    for a Zone of Peace in the Indian Ocean, New Delhi, Novem-
    ber 14-17, 1974. Helsinki: World Peace Council, 1974.
Indian Council of World Affairs. Defence and Security in the Indian
    Ocean Area. New York: Asia Publishing House, 1958.
Institute for Defense Studies and Analyses. A Strategy for India for
    a Credible Posture Against a Nuclear Adversary. New Delhi,
    1973.
Jane's Fighting Ships, 1976-1977. New York: Franklin Watts, 1976.
Labour's Foreign Policy. Report of the 44th Annual Conference of
    the Labour Party. London, 1945.
National Strategy Information Center. The Military Unbalance: Is
    the U.S. Becoming a Second Class Power? New York, 1971.
Novosti Press Agency Publishing House. Soviet Navy. Moscow,
    1971.
National Oceanographic Data Center. Hydrodynamics Branch.
    Indian Ocean Atlas. Washington, D.C.: U.S. Naval Oceano-
    graphic Office, 1967.
Royal United Services Institute for Defence Studies. The Security
    of the Southern Oceans: Southern Africa the Key. Report of
    a Seminar. London, 1972.
U.S. Naval War College. Indian Ocean. Committee 3. Final
    Presentation by Rks Gandhi, Indian Navy, Third
    International Seapower Symposium. Newport, R. I., Octo-
    ber 15-19, 1973.

University of Southampton. Department of Extra-Mural Studies.
    Study Conference on the Indian Ocean in International Politics.
    Southhampton, May 17-19, 1972.
World Armaments and Disarmament. SIPRI Yearbook 1971, 1972,
    1975.

PERSONAL INTERVIEWS

Barber, Stuart. Civilian assistant director, CNO Long Range
    Objectives Group (Ret.). March 1976.
Burke, Arleigh. Admiral, U.S. Navy (Ret.). March 1976.
Churchill, George T. Director, Office of International Security
    Operations, Department of State. March 1976.
Kaul, T. N. Indian Ambassador to the United States. March 1976.
La Rocque, Gene R. Rear Admiral, U.S. Navy (Ret.). June-
    November 1975.
McCain, John C. Admiral, U.S. Navy (Ret.). March 1976.
Ravenal, Earl C., Dr. Former director, Asian Division in
    Systems Analysis, Office of the Secretary of Defense. March
    1976.
Rexrod, Vorley Michael. Professional staff member, Senate Appro-
    priations Committee. March 1976.
Sick, Gary G. Commander. Director for the Persian Gulf and
    Indian Ocean, Office of the Assistant Secretary of Defense
    for International Security Affairs, Department of Defense.
    February-March 1976.
Van Dusen, Michael H. Subcommittee Staff Consultant. Subcom-
    mittee on Investigations of the Committee on International
    Relations. House of Representatives. August 1974.

ABOUT THE AUTHOR

MONORANJAN BEZBORUAH earned a doctoral degree in political science at the University of Mississippi. He also holds an LL. B. from the University of Gauhati, India. Before coming to the United States, Dr. Bezboruah was a lecturer at the University of Gauhati. His research interests and scholarly work focus on international security issues, the global military balance, and South Asian political affairs. Dr. Bezboruah is currently a resident of Washington, D. C.

SOVIET NAVAL INFLUENCE: Domestic and Foreign Dimensions
edited by Michael MccGwire
John McDonnell

THE POLITICS OF THE WESTERN INDIAN OCEAN ISLANDS
edited by John M. Ostheimer

ARMED FORCES OF THE WORLD: A Reference Handbook,
fourth edition
edited by Robert C. Sellers

*FOREIGN POLICY AND U.S. NATIONAL SECURITY: Major
Postelection Issues
edited by William W. Whitson

SOVIET-ASIAN RELATIONS IN THE 1970s AND BEYOND: An
Interperceptional Study
Bhabani Sen Gupta

CURRENT ISSUES IN U.S. DEFENSE POLICY
Center for Defense Information
edited by David T. Johnson
Barry R. Schneider

*Also available in paperback as a PSS Student Edition.